Craft Entrepreneurship

Craft Entrepreneurship

Edited by
Annette Naudin
and Karen Patel

ROWMAN & LITTLEFIELD
Lanham • Boulder • New York • London

Published by Rowman & Littlefield
An imprint of The Rowman & Littlefield Publishing Group, Inc.
4501 Forbes Boulevard, Suite 200, Lanham, Maryland 20706
www.rowman.com

6 Tinworth Street, London SE11 5AL, United Kingdom

British Library Cataloguing in Publication Information Available

ISBN HB: 978-1-7-8661-374-5

Library of Congress Cataloging-in-Publication Data

Names: Naudin, Annette, editor. | Patel, Karen, 1987- editor.
Title: Craft entrepreneurship / edited by Annette Naudin and Karen Patel.
Description: Lanham : Rowman & Littlefield, [2020] | Includes
  bibliographical references and index. | Summary: "This book reveals the
  individual experience of craft entrepreneurship, drawing on case studies
  from around the world, considering questions of identity, policy,
  community, and the digital in crafting a life"—Provided by publisher.
Identifiers: LCCN 2020024793 (print) | LCCN 2020024794 (ebook) | ISBN
  9781786613745 (cloth) | ISBN 9781786613752 (epub) | 9781538147054 (pbk)
Subjects: LCSH: Handicraft industries--Case studies. | Handicraft—Economic
  aspects—Case studies. | Entrepreneurship—Case studies.
Classification: LCC HD9999.H362 C73 2020 (print) | LCC HD9999.H362
  (ebook) | DDC 745.5068—dc23
LC record available at https://lccn.loc.gov/2020024793

Contents

vi *Contents*

Chapter One

Introduction

Craft Entrepreneurship

Annette Naudin and Karen Patel

In the face of climate change and economic uncertainties, craft entrepreneurs are increasingly understood as part of a movement that celebrates locally made, small scale artisanal production.[1] Although the craft sector is not usually associated with entrepreneurship because of the relatively low income it generates, it seems reasonable to explore the entrepreneurial practices of craft makers, given that compared to other cultural industries a high proportion of makers are sole traders.[2] Craft workers have become the subject of interest for scholars exploring the relationship between creative economy and cultural work.[3] Previous work on the craft economy indicates that contemporary craft entrepreneurs are highly resourceful, making the most of digital technologies by embracing platforms such as Etsy and social media sites such as Instagram to build brand awareness and reputation.[4] However, as Susan Luckman and Jane Andrew argue, "the ease of establishing online shopfronts hides the complex work required to start and run a small business, especially one in an increasingly globally competitive space with isolated producers and narrow profit margins."[5] Indeed as Luckman and others have shown,[6] sustaining a craft enterprise is not easy. While some policy interventions encourage craft businesses, there are complex issues at stake in balancing aesthetic considerations with economic needs.

This book brings together historical, policy and individual narratives to inform a broad understanding of craft entrepreneurship. In doing so, we find craft activities to be positioned between or across the arts, heritage, notion of a bohemian lifestyle and micro-entrepreneurship. Part One offers insights into communities in which craft entrepreneurs emerge and develop, situating crafts in relation to wider political and geographical environment as evidenced by Champion, Mikic and Peach's chapters. Entrepreneurial practices have tended to be linked to creative industries policies of the last 20 years but Mikic and

Peach's chapters demonstrate that this link existed well before that cultural policy moment.

Part Two invites the reader to follow individual narratives through the lived experiences of craft entrepreneurs. Some common themes emerge including contradictions between attempts to be commercially sustainable as a business and setting out for a bohemian lifestyle which as Peach states, can result in 'churning out souvenirs for tourists'. From that, we might deduce that entrepreneurship scholars would suggest that this book offers little insights into entrepreneurial practices and to the field of research. Despite a level of resistance to commercialising their craft, as Bennett suggests the chapters in this book refresh and review entrepreneurial practices. By engaging with the contradictions and fragility of sustaining a craft practice, the chapters in this book contribute to different perspectives for entrepreneurship studies. Our aims has been to illustrate the craft entrepreneurs' identity, motivation and sense of creative purpose through their craft, as these collide with the tensions brought about through entrepreneurship. Adopting entrepreneurial approaches tends to come secondary to the love of making and a passion for the craft artefact, causing an uneasiness with notions of entrepreneurship and business acumen.[7]

Navigating a sense of expertise and professionalism as a craft entrepreneur can be a challenge particularly for young people, women and especially women of colour.[8] For some, craft entrepreneurship appears to offer a route to emancipation, presenting entrepreneurial women with the capacity to utilise their personal agency to define their entrepreneurial selves.[9] But the precariousness associated with cultural work in general[10] is just as pervasive in this subsector of the cultural industries. Craft entrepreneurs attempt to mitigate the risks of precarious self-employment, which, in the UK context at least, is mostly experienced by women. According to figures by Crafts Council UK, the majority of craft workers who are self-employed or freelance are women.[11] Women's precarious status as craft entrepreneurs and as experts is exacerbated by traditional binaries of amateur/professional and domestic/industry. Even in the "post-Etsy"[12] age where ostensibly anyone can become a craft entrepreneur, traditional hierarchies persist. Most of the chapters in this book bring to light many of the challenges faced by women in craft at all stages—from nascent (early career) craft entrepreneurs, to women "on the verge" of turning their craft hobby into a business, to well established makers with careers spanning decades.

We have taken a broad definition of "craft," choosing to include a wide variety of practices and products, captured by diverse scholarly contributions. Craft in this book is understood as making 3D objects by hand, using materials such as textiles, ceramics, metal and wood. We recognise that our focus is dominated by cases from the global North, somewhat limiting the scope of this book, but in so doing, we situate the contributions as part of a Western creative industries discourse.[13] In other words, for the purposes of this book, craft entrepreneurs are categorised as part of the creative industries and in many cases, they are impacted by relevant public policies. Following Ana Alacovska and Rosalind Gill's important argument on de-Westernizing creative labour studies, this book does not intend to "take on the status of offering general understandings or principles regarding informality or entre-preneurial subjectivity"[14] but instead to offer some insight into the specific micro-experiences of craft entrepreneurs and the local cultural policies that shape those experiences.

In the context of this book, craft entrepreneurship is not defined by a high growth model. Rather, it encompasses micro-enterprises, portfolio careers, nascent entrepreneurs and freelance work, including those in the process of becoming entrepreneurs,[15] who might be shifting between professional and amateur practice. Craft entrepreneurs discussed in each chapter are likely to have received a level of technical and/or aesthetic training and so have de-veloped a level of craft expertise. As a result, our working definition of craft entrepreneurship is quite broad but two themes have guided our approach. First, our book contributes to debates that explore the relationship between entrepreneurship and cultural work, including a critique of cultural policies that have over-celebrated entrepreneurial modes of work. Second, many of the chapters in this book explore what it means to be a craft maker from the perspective of negotiating the opportunities and challenges of entrepreneurial modes of work through personal experiences.

THE CHAPTERS IN THIS BOOK

By bringing together the structural context and lived experience, we present an overview of contemporary debates in craft entrepreneurship drawing on specific cases in the global North context. The book is organised into two sections: "Craft Entrepreneurship and Cultural Policy" and "Challenges of Craft Entrepreneurship." We begin with Julia Bennett's chapter in which she argues that craft offers the opportunity to review entrepreneurship and the idea of "growth" in business by exploring makers' motivations and practices. Echoing Luckman's work, Bennett suggests that locality and community is a significant factor for craft entrepreneurs, citing examples in the UK such as Birmingham's Jewellery Quarter and Stoke-On-Trent's historical roots with the ceramics industry. While those two areas of the UK have well-documented links with craft, Hristina Mikic's chapter highlights how cultural policymakers have tried to support the growth of craft entrepreneurship in

Serbia. The structure of cultural governance in Serbia means that a number of different government departments deal with different aspects of the craft industry, resulting in a lack of cohesion in cultural policies relating to the craft sector. The impact for policymakers is to note that increasingly, micro-enterprises might be less focused on individual turnover and more motivated by their contribution to the local ecology, alongside wider cultural, social, and environmental priorities. Focusing on a rural environment, Katherine Champion's chapter also draws attention to the local and to new entrepreneurial modes of work as a means of mitigating against some of the challenges of craft entrepreneurship. The examples from Champion's study include the need to develop a portfolio career, the use of online and digital technologies and different spaces for selling and making.

Both Champion and Andrea Peach discuss the tourism sector as a significant market for craft entrepreneurs, reminding us of the geographical specificity of some makers and the degree to which their relationship to place informs their craft enterprises. Peach's chapter provides a historical perspective by discussing the Balnakeil Craft Village in Scotland as a means of exploring the relationship between government policy and the lived experience of craft entrepreneurship. Notions of "the good life," which attracted craft makers to a bohemian lifestyle in Balnakeil appear to be in contrast with the economic goals of policymakers. The pressure to be commercially successful impacts craft practices, resulting in the production of craft souvenirs for tourists, with a "Craftmade" label provided by the Highland Board. Champion and Peach both argue that if craft entrepreneurship in rural Scotland is going to be sustainable, it needs to be based on a sense of community and to draw on innovative entrepreneurial practices. Policy interventions that focus on commercialising crafts tend not to succeed due to their lack of attention to the motivations for craft and artistic practices. As Guillaume Sirois argues in his chapter, the tension between selling craft objects and a resistance to capitalism is not new to the sector, but interestingly, the notion of entrepreneurship is not rejected. In his study of Montreal craft entrepreneurs, the idea of being an entrepreneur is greeted with a positive sense of "adventure," a challenge which can be addressed creatively. Again, Sirois finds that locality is significant for his respondents alongside issues relating to environmental sustainability, also challenging the notion of "growth" which echoes Mark Banks's work on the moral economy of cultural work.[16] Authors in this first section articulate some familiar tensions in cultural work between the creative motivations of cultural workers and a push to embrace entrepreneurial modes of work as part of wider policies linked to the regeneration of an area, or to encourage business growth. We also find craft entrepreneurs offering new models for entrepreneurship, a more socially engaged practice rooted in their locality and encompassing a wide range of values. The possibilities of offering sustainable social enterprise opportunities and addressing challenges of economic and social inclusion are key reasons why craft is increasingly being championed by individuals, communities and governments.[17]

The second half of the book focuses on the lived experiences and challenges of craft entrepreneurship. Lauren England explores the relationship between online identity and intellectual property for nascent makers in the UK. England reflects on the issues that arise for these nascent craft entrepreneurs in their use of social media for self-promotion and as a means through which to network and sell work.[18] The growth in craft micro-enterprise in recent years is in some respects attributed to social media and websites such as Etsy lowering the barriers for craft enterprise. The platform is free and it draws in potential customers, making it relatively easy for new craft entrepreneurs to reach consumers. However, as Karen Patel demonstrates in her chapter, online craft spaces are not as inclusive and accessible as they might appear. Patel discusses the racism in knitting debates that took place on Instagram during 2019, exploring the experiences of a group of women knitters of colour who shared their experiences of racism in craft online. These women invested a great deal of time and energy into relaying their experiences, collating and curating the contributions of other women using Instagram stories and dealing with backlash, abuse and thousands of comments on a daily basis. Patel highlights the additional labour these women undertake—the "diversity work"[19] required to address issues of racism and inequality in craft, which have received relatively little attention in scholarship.

Mary Kay Culpepper and David Gauntlett look at the experiences of women "on the verge" of craft entrepreneurship—the point at which makers decide to turn their hobby into a business. They utilise affordance theory to explore the experiences of those who may not have initially aspired to pursue craft enterprise, highlighting the struggle of creativity and identity formation at the juncture of hobbyism and enterprise. Vishalakshi Roy takes a different approach to explore the same juncture, focusing on the micro-experiences of one maker and her long-term journey to becoming a craft entrepreneur. Roy's chapter investigates identity construction as the maker navigates a series of career changes to harness her passion for knitting and establishing a craft enterprise. Indeed, in existing scholarship little attention has been paid to the longevity of a craft career, and how makers have adapted to changes in the craft economy. In response, Annette Naudin's chapter provides insight into the experiences of four women makers who are relatively well established, with careers spanning up to twenty-five years. Naudin reveals the various challenges these women have faced throughout their careers where, despite having developed a high level of craft expertise, their experiences of craft work and perception of their success is filtered through dominant stereotypes associated with the entrepreneur, and thus their career reflections are tinged by disillusionment. The women in Naudin's study have experienced a range of life challenges, including serious illness and deaths of close family members, which have shaped their careers. The reality of craft entrepreneurship for these women is in sharp contrast to common perceptions of craft micro-enterprises that are presented on Etsy and social media, which portray a sense of the "good life," an idyllic hipster domesticity where women craft entrepreneurs appear to seamlessly manage the demands of home life with running a craft business.[20]

Finally, Jess Ring explores maker spaces and maker culture in Canada, focusing on the activities of feminist makers. She argues that the democratising ethos of maker culture is flawed, and this is due to the two competing and overlapping logics of neoliberal entrepreneurialism and "passionate work," which solidify creative work as a neoliberal enterprise. However, Ring suggests that the feminist makers are adopting such logics for their own ends, particularly harnessing the potential of makerspaces to highlight issues around equalities, care work in craft and foster collective action and solidarity. Indeed this is one of many chapters within the book which allow us to think about future possibilities for craft entrepreneurship. The critique of neoliberal, precarious cultural work is wide-ranging and well known within studies of cultural labour,[21] and this condition is seemingly exacerbated by social media and mobile technology.[22] However, the appeal of craft is the "aura of the analogue"[23] and for some scholars, craft can point the way towards a more inclusive and sustainable cultural economy.[24] There are examples here of the potential for collaboration, mutual aid[25] and resistance, to challenge entrenched structures and regimes of value in the craft sector and the cultural industries more widely.

It is interesting that craft entrepreneurship is an area that is so underresearched, given the range and longevity of craft practice all around the world and the increasing centrality of craft in creative industries policy and discourse. This may be because craft is an area which is now dominated by women, and is a skilled form of cultural production which has been carried out by women in a variety of settings for centuries. Women's work has always been devalued and craft is a prime example of this. It remains that the type of craft produced by women craft entrepreneurs, particularly in textiles, is commonly perceived as "amateur," even in the "post-Etsy" age which demands a level of professionalism and expertise.

It is perhaps not surprising that this is the first collection to address an area of cultural entrepreneurship that happens to be dominated by women. As we have discussed, there is much more to be done to explore craft entrepreneurship in a variety of contexts, and we hope the chapters in this book inspire further work.

NOTES

1. Susan Luckman, "Craft Entrepreneurialism and Sustainable Scale: Resistance and Disavowal of the Creative Industries as Champions of Capitalist Growth," *Cultural Trends* 27, no. 5 (2018): 313–26.

2. BOP Consulting note that in the UK, 88 percent of makers are sole traders. In Josephine Burns, Chris Gibbon, Cristina Rosemberg, and Karen Yair, "Craft in an Age of Change," February 2012, https://www.craftscouncil.org.uk/content/files/Craft_in_an_Age_of_Change.pdf.

3. Susan Luckman, *Craft and the Creative Economy* (London: Springer, 2015); Susan Luckman and Nicola Thomas, "Crafting Economies: Contemporary Cultural Economies of the Handmade," in *Craft Economies*, eds. Susan Luckman and Nicola Thomas (London: Bloomsbury, 2018), 1–14.

4. Susan Luckman and Jane Andrew, "Establishing the Crafting Self in the Contemporary Creative Economy," in *Craft Economies*, eds. Susan Luckman and Nicola Thomas (London: Bloomsbury, 2018), 119–28.

5. Luckman and Andrew, "Establishing the Crafting Self," 119.

6. See Luckman, *Craft and the Creative Economy*; Xin Gu, "Crafts Community: Physical and Virtual," in *Craft Economies*, eds. Susan Luckman and Nicola Thomas (London: Bloomsbury, 2018), 17–27; Luckman and Andrew, "Establishing the Crafting Self."

7. Susan Luckman, "Craft Entrepreneurialism and Sustainable Scale: Resistance and Disavowal of the Creative Industries as Champions of Capitalist Growth," *Cultural Trends* 27, no. 5 (2018): 313–26.

8. Karen Patel, "Diversity Initiatives and Addressing Inequalities in Craft," in *Pathways Into Creative Working Lives*, eds. Stephanie Taylor and Susan Luckman (Basingstoke: Palgrave Macmillan, 2020).

9. Karen Hughes, Jennifer Jennings, Candida Brush, Sara Carter, and Friederike Welter, "Extending Women's Entrepreneurship Research in New Directions," *Entrepreneurship Theory and Practice* 36 no. 3 (2012): 429–42.

10. See Mark Banks, *The Politics of Cultural Work* (Basingstoke: Palgrave Macmillan, 2007); Rosalind Gill, "Cool, Creative and Egalitarian? Exploring Gender in Project-Based New Media Work in Europe," *Information, Communication and Society* 5, no. 1 (2002): 70–89; Angela McRobbie, "Clubs to Companies: Notes on the Decline of Political Culture in Speeded Up Creative Worlds," *Cultural Studies* 16, no. 4 (2002): 516–31.

11. Mark Spilsbury, "Who Makes? An Analysis of People Working in Craft Occupations," Crafts Council UK, February 2018, https://www.craftscouncil.org.uk/downloads/who-makes-an-analysis-of-people-working-in-craft-occupations.

12. Luckman, *Craft and the Creative Economy*.

13. This creative industries discourse relates to policy interventions, which include or were inspired by the New Labour "creative industries" reforms by the UK's Department for Digital, Culture, Media and Sport in the late 1990s. For a comprehensive analysis and critique, see David Hesmondhalgh, Kate Oakley, David Lee, and Melissa

Nisbett, *Culture, Economy and Politics: The Case of New Labour* (Basingstoke: Palgrave Macmillan, 2015).

14. Ana Alacovska and Rosalind Gill, "De-Westernizing Creative Labour Studies: The Informality of Creative Work from an Ex-Centric Perspective," *International Journal of Cultural Studies* 22, no. 2 (2019): 198.

15. Annette Naudin, *Cultural Entrepreneurship: The Cultural Worker's Experience of Entrepreneurship* (London: Routledge, 2017).

16. Mark Banks, "Moral Economy and Cultural Work," *Sociology* 40, no. 3 (2006): 455–72.

17. Luckman and Thomas, "Crafting Economies," 1.

18. Luckman and Andrew, "Establishing the Crafting Self."

19. Sara Ahmed, *On Being Included: Racism and Diversity in Institutional Life* (London: Duke University Press, 2012).

20. Luckman, *Craft and the Creative Economy*.

21. See Alacovska and Gill, "De-Westernizing Creative Labour Studies."

22. See Melissa Gregg, *Work's Intimacy* (New York: Wiley, 2013); Brooke Erin Duffy, *(Not) Getting Paid to Do What You Love: Gender, Social Media, and Aspirational Work* (New Haven, CT: Yale University Press, 2017).

23. Luckman, *Craft and the Creative Economy*.

24. See Carl Grodach, Justin O'Connor, and Chris Gibson. "Manufacturing and Cultural Production: Towards a Progressive Policy Agenda for the Cultural Economy," *City, Culture and Society* 10 (2017): 17–25; Luckman and Thomas, "Crafting Economies."

25. Greig De Peuter and Nicole Cohen, "Emerging Labour Politics in Creative Industries," in *The Routledge Companion to the Culture Industries*, eds. Kate Oakley and Justin O'Connor (London: Routledge, 2015), 305–18.

BIBLIOGRAPHY

Ahmed, Sara. *On Being Included: Racism and Diversity in Institutional Life*. London: Duke University Press, 2012.

Alacovska, Ana, and Rosalind Gill. "De-Westernizing Creative Labour Studies: The Informality of Creative Work from an Ex-Centric Perspective." *International Journal of Cultural Studies* 22 no. 2 (2019): 195–212.

Banks, Mark. "Moral Economy and Cultural Work." *Sociology* 40, no. 3 (2006): 455–72.

———. *The Politics of Cultural Work*. Basingstoke: Palgrave Macmillan, 2007.

Burns, Josephine, Chris Gibbon, Cristina Rosemberg, and Karen Yair. "Craft in an Age of Change," last modified February 2012, https://www.craftscouncil.org.uk/content/files/Craft_in_an_Age_of_Change.pdf.

De Peuter, Greig, and Nicole Cohen. "Emerging Labour Politics in Creative Industries." In *The Routledge Companion to the Culture Industries*, edited by Kate Oakley and Justin O'Connor, 305–18. London: Routledge, 2015.

Duffy, Brooke Erin. *(Not) Getting Paid to Do What You Love: Gender, Social Media, and Aspirational Work.* New Haven, CT: Yale University Press, 2017.

Gill, Rosalind. "Cool, Creative and Egalitarian? Exploring Gender in Project-Based New Media Work in Europe." *Information, Communication and Society* 5 no. 1 (2002): 70–89.

Gregg, Melissa. *Work's Intimacy.* New York: Wiley, 2013.

Grodach, Carl, Justin O'Connor, and Chris Gibson. "Manufacturing and Cultural Production: Towards a Progressive Policy Agenda for the Cultural Economy." *City, Culture and Society* 10 (2017): 17–25.

Gu, Xin. "Crafts Community: Physical and Virtual." In *Craft Economies*, edited by Susan Luckman and Nicola Thomas, 17–27. London: Bloomsbury, 2018.

Hesmondhalgh, David, Kate Oakley, David Lee, and Melissa Nisbett. *Culture, Economy and Politics: The Case of New Labour.* Basingstoke: Palgrave Macmillan, 2015.

Hughes, Karen, Jennifer Jennings, Candida Brush, Sara Carter, and Friederike Welter,. "Extending Women's Entrepreneurship Research in New Directions." *Entrepreneurship Theory and Practice* 36, no. 3 (2012): 429–42.

Luckman, Susan. *Craft and the Creative Economy.* London: Springer, 2015.

———. "Craft Entrepreneurialism and Sustainable Scale: Resistance and Disavowal of the Creative Industries as Champions of Capitalist Growth." *Cultural Trends* 27, no. 5 (2018): 313–26.

Luckman, Susan, and Jane Andrew. "Establishing the Crafting Self in the Contemporary Creative Economy." In *Craft Economies*, edited by Susan Luckman and Nicola Thomas, 119–28. London: Bloomsbury, 2018.

Luckman, Susan, and Nicola Thomas. "Crafting Economies: Contemporary Cultural Economies of the Handmade." In *Craft Economies*, edited by Susan Luckman and Nicola Thomas, 1–14. London: Bloomsbury, 2018.

McRobbie, Angela. "Clubs to Companies: Notes on the Decline of Political Culture in Speeded Up Creative Worlds." *Cultural Studies* 16, no. 4 (2002): 516–31.

Naudin, Annette. *Cultural Entrepreneurship: The Cultural Worker's Experience of Entrepreneurship.* London: Routledge, 2017.

Patel, Karen. "Diversity Initiatives and Addressing Inequalities in Craft." In *Pathways into Creative Working Lives*, edited by Stephanie Taylor and Susan Luckman. Basingstoke: Palgrave Macmillan, 2020.

Spilsbury, Mark. "Who Makes? An Analysis of People Working in Craft Occupations." Crafts Council UK, February 2018, https://www.craftscouncil.org.uk/down loads/who-makes-an-analysis-of-people-working-in-craft-occupations.

Part I

Craft Entrepreneurship
and Cultural Policy

Chapter Two

Towards a New Entrepreneurship

Julia Bennett

To what extent is "entrepreneurship" applicable to craft businesses? In this chapter I explore how entrepreneurship expresses itself in craft businesses, describing the practices, needs, and challenges of professional craft. I ask what the notion of entrepreneurship has to offer craft, how it has relevance for the craft sector, and what needs to be put in place by policymakers to enable craft to engage effectively with its agenda of growth. In examining the nature of craft business I will consider if there are distinguishing characteristics that suggest craft offers a new vision for entrepreneurship.[1]

The term "craft" is often used to denote skill, engagement and attention to a process that is frequently rooted in material reality. Whether we're talking about food, creative writing or physical making, it offers us an expression of what it is to be human. In this chapter I focus in particular on those craft businesses in the UK that rely on a creative making process that is usually, but not always, through the intelligence of the hand; one that involves technical skill and design capability, along with a deep understanding of materials. Craft disciplines range from furniture to jewellery to stand-alone unique pieces of work that may include the use of more unusual materials or the fusion of technologies across industries, such as wearable technology or high value manufacturing.

Yair[2] views craft as "the most entrepreneurial of all the creative industries sectors," citing the 88 percent of makers who set up their own businesses. So what do we mean by "entrepreneurship" in this context of craft businesses? Theories of entrepreneurship are often based on the idea of the single entrepreneur who relies on essential components for setting up in business, such as access to capital and how resources are leveraged, building on ideas Schumpeter[3] set out in his early work.

Chell and Karataş-Özkan, in contrast, remind us of Bourdieu's framing which situates the action within a much broader context: "entrepreneurship and small business is couched in social, political and economic relationships that exert multiple influences on the behaviours of individuals, firms and industries and the wider sociopolitical economy."[4] More recently, theories of "cultural" entrepreneurship have evolved, "conventionally conceptualized as an innovative activity that generates cultural value and/ or wealth via the creation of novel cultural products, services, or forms."[5] Lounsbury and Glynn describe a more scholarly idea of cultural entrepreneurship that "accounts for a wider variety of socioeconomic processes and outcomes, including entrepreneurial efforts in high technology, in large, traditional bureaucracies, and in efforts aimed at generating social change." But they seek to distinguish their own approach, asserting that "the pervasiveness of culture and focalizing cultural meaning-making provide novel insights about general mechanisms and processes that shape the sources and consequences of entrepreneurship across space and time." In exploring evidence about the characteristics of craft businesses, I argue that this concept of "meaning-making" has resonance for craft entrepreneurship. In seeking to place their business ambitions within a broader and more responsible social context, makers reveal motivations and add value outside the narrower definitions of entrepreneurship and economy. Entrepreneurship in the craft sector thus helps us to rethink entrepreneurship more widely.

THE CHARACTERISTICS OF CRAFT BUSINESSES

In order to explore entrepreneurship in relation to craft, we need to consider its characteristics as an industrial sector and how such businesses operate. Taken as a sector, UK craft generates £3.4 billion[6] and employs around 150,000 people. Craft skills and knowledge have been shown not only to have a strong economic impact, but they also have significant potential to drive further growth and innovation in other sectors beyond craft.[7]

UK craft now has an increasingly international presence: the total value of craft exports grew by 31 percent in seven years, 2010–2017, from £3,698m in 2010 to £4.848 billion in 2017.[8] Representing 1.4 percent of the total value of UK exports of goods in 2017, craft makes the highest level of contribution of any creative industry category to overall UK exports. (It should be noted that the value of craft exports is influenced by the export of gemstones and precious metals through the jewellery trade which amount to around 12 percent of craft exports).

The sector spans businesses that are set up by makers in familiar disciplines including jewellery, textiles, wood and ceramics, as well as those who work across the creative industries in, for example, film or theatre, and those who apply their skills in the wider creative economy in sectors such as bioscience, health care and aerospace.[9] People employed in craft occupations are more likely to be male—around four-fifths are male (compared to just over half of employment across all occupations), but more likely to be female if they are self-employed and working part time.[10] They are also more likely to be self-employed (40 percent compared to 15 percent of all jobs) and likely to earn less than the national average wage.

BUSINESS CHALLENGES

Portfolio Workers and Sole Traders

Many of those working in craft occupations are applying craft knowledge and processes in education services or consultancy, operating as portfolio workers.

> Literature from the past two decades demonstrates that craft practice is no longer exclusively focused on the making of objects, but also on the development of knowledge-based services. Examples of such use of skills included makers working in architectural, interior and industrial design, in fashion, retail and advertising, and in film and television. Makers were found to complement the work of other professionals with their understanding of the dynamic between people, materials and objects, as well as with their specialist knowledge—and ability to stretch the capabilities of—materials and technical processes.[11]

This aptitude is reflected across the creative industries:[12] a Creative Industries Federation survey found that "creative freelancers are often innovative and entrepreneurial, with many juggling a string of different contracts and work streams in portfolio careers."[13] Increasingly, this trend is reflected in the wider economy, in which the number of people choosing self-employment is increasing.[14] National policy initiatives, such as tax credits, have been introduced in an attempt to improve conditions for self-employed workers, yet the Federation report notes that "the policy efforts of recent years have too often been piecemeal and based on outdated business stereotypes."[15]

Declining Opportunities in Creative Education

In spite of this trend, those seeking a future career as a professional maker face a number of challenges in establishing themselves. In the face of a decline in the quality of primary age arts education,[16] under-recruitment of Art & Design teachers[17] and a stark decline in the potential talent supply chain,[18] pupils are fortunate when they can pursue creative subjects in secondary school. If they follow their interest, students may then confront inconsistencies in professional practice development in higher education. Early findings from a collaborative PhD between King's College London and the Crafts Council point to a range of approaches in higher education institutions; England notes in her Crafts Council blog[19] that some are "staking a claim to the development of entrepreneurial skill sets and business acumen, while others do not (explicitly) engage with entrepreneurship at all."

Setting Up in Business

What happens to makers once they are qualified? Historically, there has been a lack of accurate data on the destinations of creative graduates, particularly for those in early career self-employment and portfolio careers[20] and destinations surveys have been ill-equipped to capture the experiences of portfolio workers and entrepreneurs.[21] For those who have graduated or pursued an alternative route into craft practice (through, for example, further education, an apprenticeship or self-education), anecdotal evidence suggests craft sole traders and micro-businesses face obstacles in sustaining their livelihoods and making a meaningful contribution to the economy. Any sole trader or micro-business has to ensure not only that they design, make and take products successfully to market, but are also skilled in all the other associated marketing, accounting and general business planning activities. Even taking on support is not easy: Young[22] identified in a report for the UK government how the challenges of taking on a first employee form a barrier that may be undermining potential for growth. Anecdotal evidence suggests that a multitasking mindset is a strength for many makers, yet the pressures it creates may also reduce any appetite to participate in formal government apprenticeship schemes through which employees could be recruited. Successful beneficiaries of the scheme tend to be located in shared studio spaces, in which an apprentice can be shared between businesses.

Once established in practice, it is important for a craft business to ensure that skills are honed and that knowledge of new techniques and material capabilities is regularly refreshed, either in the maker's own discipline or in seeking to extend their practice. Yet this career investment also needs to be funded and accommodated alongside the range of other activities outlined, as time spent on training is time away from the product. The option of claiming tax reliefs for those self-funding work-related training can usually only be accessed where the costs are incurred to update an individual's existing skills, rather than to invest in training to develop new skills, such as in working in a different material or discipline to extend practice.

Specific communities may also face particular challenges. As Patel highlights,[23] black women receive more online abuse than anyone else. Black and minority ethnic women may face challenges in using social media including lack of confidence, risks of feeling exposed online and skills needs.

Access to Investment

Other supply side challenges include access to business loans and investment. The Creative Industries Council, a UK government and industry body, found that in creative businesses "there was a significant reliance on informal sources of funding from friends and family with 27% of businesses using this source as opposed to 9% of businesses generally." In addition, "67% believed that financiers found their sector hard to understand and only 15% felt that they had always been able to access the funding they needed. 62% agreed that their growth had been restricted by a lack of funding."[24] Respondents to a Crafts Council survey of makers' business development needs (unpublished) also identified finance as one of the top priorities, alongside enterprise, intellectual property rights and export skills.

Opportunities to Collaborate

The process of designing and developing a product for market often relies on collaboration with those working in other disciplines or sectors. Structured opportunities to collaborate would accelerate the benefits to the economy of fusion between craft and other skillsets, yet such opportunities are rare. Makers such as Oluwaseyi Sosanya, a craft practitioner from an engineering and materials science background (featured in KPMG's report for the Crafts Council),[25] combined his skills to create a 3D loom to develop woven materials that he is seeking to apply in sectors such as health, architecture, aerospace and clothing. KPMG suggest that for makers who struggle to overcome barriers to finance and access to industry support, "new and improved products resulting from such collaboration would be expected to generate additional revenues, and hence GVA [gross value added] and employment."[26] They note that, "craft skills and knowledge have a strong economic impact and significant potential to drive further growth and innovation in other sectors, as this report demonstrates."[27]

Infrastructure Support

With studio space at a premium, infrastructure issues are an increasing challenge. Makers, who have often in the past found suitable premises in former industrial spaces, are being priced out by urban development and the demand for more domestic housing. The mayor of London announced in 2019 the creation of a new independent trust to bring together public, philanthropic and social investment funds to support affordable creative workspace. Together with creative enterprise zones (a 2018 mayoral initiative to increase affordable spaces for artists and entrepreneurs and boost job and training opportunities for local people), the measures are intended to mitigate the impact of rent rises. But the issue is not one that is confined solely to the capital or to urban areas. Tax subsidies would be welcome, for example, to offset the cost of studio rental or conversion, but such initiatives have not yet extended across the creative industries to the craft sector.[28]

The Creative Industries Federation (CIF), the umbrella body for the broader sector, makes a number of recommendations to strengthen the infrastructure to support the creative industries and to improve their capacity to realise their potential.[29] Underpinning these recommendations is the fact that the creative industries are the fastest growing part of the UK economy, contributing "£101.5 billion in gross value added (GVA)—greater than automotive, aerospace, life sciences and oil and gas sectors combined."[30] For businesses facing these challenges, focused infrastructure investment is central to their development, as is a more sophisticated understanding of their motivation for survival and growth against such odds.

CRAFT VALUES AND NEW APPROACHES TO MEASURING THE ECONOMY

Preparatory survey work undertaken to generate data for the above CIF report included the question, "What does 'growth' mean to creative enterprises?" The report notes that governments have traditionally measured enterprise growth by turnover (net sales generated by a business and headcount—the number of individuals carried on a firm's payroll), yet, "These traditional metrics of turnover and profit were important to businesses, but so were other factors, including reputation, profile and social impact. Headcount was not a primary measure of growth for most creative enterprises."[31] For some, "recognition and reach of their creative brand, product and/or service was a key growth measure."[32]

It is this desire to self-define, characteristic of both craft and some elements of the wider creative industries, that suggests an alternative model of entrepreneurship in which the success factors for a business are located in a wider, more socially responsible understanding of impact than the purely financial. The education, training and infrastructure challenges outlined earlier represent a daunting list of obstacles, yet makers continue to start up new craft businesses. Sustainability and business longevity may be pursued as alternative goals that offer a more rewarding experience and lifestyle and a more personal meaning, thus legitimising them as an integral part of a broader healthy economy. James Kennedy, of Kennedy City Bicycles, says: "I get to meet my customers, discuss the design of their bicycle, build it, take them on test rides, teach them how to maintain and service it. I feel really privileged to do that for so many people." Going further, Kennedy says, "People criticise us for being an 'idea that doesn't scale', but I bloody love being an idea that doesn't scale!"[33]

The factors by which businesses are traditionally encouraged to evaluate their success are called into question by economist Diane Coyle who suggests that gross domestic product, or GDP, is the one statistic that almost everyone knows is used to measure economic growth but which may be a poor measure of prosperity. Coyle asks if how we measure the state of the economy is actually doing us any good. "We're not measuring what we see, we're seeing what we measure."[34]

Coyle's redefinition of how we are measuring businesses' value creation echoes what Belfiore describes as "a significant strand of work in this area [that] has been concerned with the ways in which 'economic value' (usually in the guise of 'economic impact,' or contribution to the economic growth agenda) seems to have too often overshadowed other forms of value—cultural, social, aesthetic—in policy discussion."[35] She notes that "cultural economists have been themselves at the forefront of resistance to the excessive predominance of economistic notions of value within cultural policy debates."

The RSA Inclusive Growth Commission sought to grasp this nettle and to define a vision for a new type of economy. Its notion of "inclusive growth" is driven by local generation and ownership of wealth, but also the importance of supporting existing local businesses to grow. The commission's report illustrates what an inclusive economy can look like in practice, based on eight global examples and experiences. It describes how "towns and cities across the UK and the world have in recent years shown real enthusiasm for inclusive growth, against a backdrop of economic uncertainty and persistent inequality."[36]

Burch and McInroy, however, reject the notion of inclusive growth alleging a narrow maintenance of inbuilt social and economic injustices. They go further, asserting that,

An Inclusive Economy offers a genuine progressive conceptual frame in which greater consideration is given to social benefits that flow from, and feed into,

economic activity. With alignment to new forms of economic democracy, new
municipalism and Local Wealth Building, we are seeing the rise of a genuine
new progressive practice to local economic development.[37]

Burch and McInroy argue that an inclusive economy actively seeks to ensure
that wealth is not extracted but rooted locally. This approach to generating
value is a feature of craft businesses that are frequently committed to and embedded within their local community. As Luckman and Thomas argue, craft
has a recognised role in place-making. "Celebrating place-specific associations has become a prominent feature of the current craft zeitgeist, with the
desire to support local economies and makers part of a response to economic
and environmental challenge."[38]

Craft businesses can be seen to situate their work within notions of locality
and community to which they add both cultural and economic value, a context that embraces the sustainable as well as the scalable business. In particular, where craft businesses cluster together, often at a smaller geographical
level and unit size than other sectors within the creative industries, they foster
a sense of identity, encourage mutual support and attract other independent
businesses and organizations seeking a form of branding by association.

One such example is Birmingham Jewellery Quarter, home to one of
Europe's largest concentrations of around seven hundred manufacturing
jewellers and metalworkers. Businesses range from sole traders through to
larger scalable businesses, all supported by the Jewellery Quarter Business
Improvement District (BID),[39] first established in 2012. The opportunity to
learn everyday making skills, for example, ring making or pouch making,
sits alongside sustainable and scaled up micro-businesses, representing a
continuum of craft from participation to professional entrepreneurialism in a
symbiotic relationship that generates value. The local supply chain supporting the quarter includes architecture, legal, marketing and design services
as well as raw materials suppliers such as John Keatley (Metals) Ltd., non-
ferrous metal stockists since 1896.

Make It Stoke-on-Trent & Staffordshire, an investment engine funded by
the county and city councils within the Local Enterprise Partnership boundaries, provides business, financing, property and marketing support for inward
investment. It has a strong focus on the ceramics industry, building on the
sector's historical roots in the city but focusing on the three hundred companies currently supporting seven thousand employees "producing everything
from cups and saucers to composite materials for dental and orthopaedic
applications."[40] Lucideon analysis and consultancy contributes to the development of advanced materials technology providing services to clients
in sectors including healthcare, construction, ceramics, aerospace, defence,

engineering and energy. The Stoke ceramics industry is another example of where business diversity and co-location contribute to its strengths.

Jackson proposes a new prosperity based on a smaller scale economy such as craft-based business, that

> transcends material concerns. Of course the good life has undeniable material dimensions. It is perverse to talk about things going well when there is inadequate food and shelter. But it is also plain to see that the simple equation of prosperity with abundance is false even when it comes to these simple material requirements. Even when it comes to questions of sustenance, more is not always better. Quality is not the same as quantity.[41]

Arguing against the trap of ever-increasing productivity, Jackson cites the example of craft,

> It is the accuracy and detail inherent in crafted goods that endows them with lasting value. It is the attention paid by the carpenter, the tailor and the designer that makes this detail possible. Likewise it is the time spent practicing, rehearsing and performing that gives art its enduring appeal. What—aside from meaningless noise—is to be gained by asking the New York Philharmonic to reduce their rehearsal time and play Beethoven's 9th Symphony faster and faster each year?[42]

Jackson's analysis reflects many craft businesses' engagement with the economy (as it does the growing number of self-employed, freelancers and micro-businesses across the economy). It draws on long-standing traditions and values in the craft sector and, at the same time, asserts a different kind of entrepreneurialism within the wider debates about the characteristics of a healthy economy.

Those wider debates help bear witness to the importance of redefining how we measure economic wealth to include wider environmental concerns. The question of what constitutes a healthy economy is a contested proposition in climate change rhetoric as society seeks to tackle the mounting task of reducing emissions to prevent further degradation of carbon sinks. Raworth uses the Doughnut Economics model to challenge the traditional closed loop of the circular flow of income.[43] Raworth applies Rockström's environmental model (so-called planetary and social boundaries)[44] to define the resource boundaries within which the global economy should more properly operate by taking into account wider environment impact. Raworth moves beyond the traditional approach of monitoring goods and services that can be monetised to include those ecosystems and services that add value outside that economy (back to Diane Coyle's earlier point). Jackson proposes a vision of enterprise that accommodates and builds on the kind of characteristics embodied by many craft businesses, working, "with the grain of community and the long-term social good, rather than against it."[45] This is consistent with Banks's analysis that the idea of growth, in itself, is becoming increasingly problematic as a measure for understanding the creative economy at all.[46] Banks concludes that "under conditions of real economic stagnation and incipient environmental crisis, growth needs to be made limited, but also more fully socialised in a dual sense; made more evenly and equitably redistributed in terms of benefits and rewards, as well as re-conceived in terms that afford greater priority to non-economic values and human prosperity indicators."[47] Building on Oakley and Ward's notion of a vision of "sustainable prosperity,"[48] our objective should thus be to move towards financial systems that support both more productive *and* sustainable enterprise.

Reijonen[49] examines what those wider business objectives might be, looking at the motivations that drive craft microbusinesses in Finland, where 93 percent of businesses employ fewer than ten people. As a consequence of such a high proportion of microbusinesses, policymakers are interested in supporting growth among such entrepreneurs in order to support the economy. Yet, Reijonen observes, "The group of small business owners who have run their business for some years and display willingness to develop their business performance moderately have, however, attracted only a little attention."[50]

Reijonen reviews the literature, noting that the emphasis on financial performance and the assumption of growth is implicitly connected to a successful firm. Reijonen notes how sometimes a business's focus on increasing turnover is, nonetheless, a conscious decision, based on an assessment of the consequences for the entrepreneur's wider goals, rather than solely on aspirations of increasing personal wealth. Reijonen's conclusions are that business motivation amongst those studied was less towards growth, and more to quality of life, job satisfaction and satisfied clientele (once, of course, they could make a reasonable living). In the face of weak infrastructural investment and contested economic models, craft businesses are thus asserting their own economic success criteria and making their own meaning, based on a self-defined entrepreneurialism.

CONCLUSION

In this chapter I've explored the obstacles and constraints facing professional makers when setting up in business, as well as the motivations that drive them to do so. Pitched against them are a set of economic measures that judge their success by criteria they often reject. Yet makers continue to seek careers in craft and to define their own entrepreneurship, reflecting in their ambitions notions of "meaning-making" identified in cultural entrepreneurship theory.

As researchers, policymakers, and advocates, we need to grasp the model of entrepreneurship offered by craft businesses and through their experience advance our understanding of its expression. As I've demonstrated, those seeking to make a living from making often face significant challenges, not only in accessing finance and suitable accommodation, but also in earning an income without relying on portfolio work. Yet craft businesses can make a rich contribution to their local business ecology, to their community, and to the identity of the place in which they invest. Their motivation in entering the market, the manner in which craft businesses nurture future generations of makers and their contribution to a locally invested supply chain all point towards the need to promote more strongly an understanding of the long-term value and sustainability of such enterprises and thereby to tackle the narrow emphasis on growth in national research and public investment priorities.[51]

Successful craft businesses offer us a vision of a future economy that takes into account wider social and environmental needs. As we seek solutions to ever-bigger global challenges, we should be investing with much greater urgency in understanding models of entrepreneurship that seek to embrace more sustainable social values.

NOTES

1. In this chapter I focus primarily on craft businesses in the UK, in line with the remit of the Crafts Council. The charity is a national development agency that supports all types of craft and making, from everyday making to high end professional craft.

2. Karen Yair, *Craft and Enterprise* (London: Crafts Council, 2012).

3. John Schumpeter, *The Theory of Economic Development: An Inquiry into Profits, Capital, Credit, Interest, and the Business Cycle* (New Brunswick, NJ: Transaction Publishers, 1934).

4. Elizabeth Chell and Mine Karataş-Özkan, *Handbook of Research on Small Business and Entrepreneurship* (Cheltenham: Edward Elgar Publishing, 2014), 5.

5. Michael Lounsbury and Mary Ann Glynn, *Cultural Entrepreneurship: A New Agenda for the Study of Entrepreneurial Processes and Possibilities* (Cambridge, UK: Cambridge University Press, 2019), 10.

6. Trends Business Research, *Measuring the Craft Economy* (London: Crafts Council, 2014).

7. KPMG and Knowledge Transfer Network and University of Brighton, *Innovation through Craft: Opportunities for Growth* (London: Crafts Council, 2016).

8. Department for Digital, Culture, Media and Sport Sectors Economic Estimates, *Trade, Table 33: Exports and Imports of Goods by Sub-Sector* (London: DCMS, 2017).

9. KPMG, *Innovation through Craft*; Karen Yair, *Crafting Capital: New Technologies, New Economies* (London: Crafts Council, 2011).

10. Mark Spilsbury, *Who Makes? An Analysis of People Working in Craft Occupations* (London: Crafts Council, 2018).

11. Burns Owen Partnership, *Craft in an Age of Change* (London: Crafts Council, Creative Scotland, Arts Council of Wales and Craft Northern Ireland, 2012).

12. Craft is one of twelve identified creative industries sectors (Department for Culture, Media & Sport, 1998).

13. Eliza Easton and Evy Cauldwell-French, *Creative Freelancers* (London: Creative Industries Federation, 2017).

14. Duncan O'Leary, *Going It Alone* (London: Demos, 2014); HM Government, *Julie Deane's Review of Self-Employment* (London: HMSO, 2016).

15. RSA, *The Entrepreneurial Audit* (London: The RSA, 2017).

16. Ben Cooper, *Primary Colours: The Decline of Arts Education in Primary Schools and How It Can Be Reversed* (London: Fabian Society, 2018), 10.

17. Department for Education, *Initial Teacher Training (ITT) Census: 2018 to 2019*, Main tables (London: DfE, 2018), Table 1c.

18. Design and Technology GCSE entrants were down 57 percent between 2010 and 2018 (Crafts Council, 2016; Joint Council for Qualifications, 2018).

19. Lauren England. *A Pipeline Problem: Exploring Policy Disconnect in Craft Higher Education.* London: King's College London with Crafts Council, 2017.

20. Linda Ball, Will Hunt, and Emma Pollard, *Crafting Futures: A Study of the Early Careers of Crafts Graduates from UK Higher Education Institutions* (London: Institute for Employment Studies/University of the Arts/Crafts Council, 2010).

21. A Higher Education Statistics Agency review acknowledged this and the 2018 Graduate Outcomes recognises that the transition period into work for today's graduates is longer, and thus may make it easier for graduates to record their self-employed status, an important factor in understanding the characteristics of craft businesses.

22. David Young, *Growing Your Business: A Report on Growing Micro Businesses* (London: Business, Innovation and Skills, 2013).

23. Karen Patel, *Supporting Diversity in Craft Practice through Digital Technology Skills Development* (London: Crafts Council, 2019).

24. Easton and Cauldwell-French, *Creative Freelancers.*

25. KPMG, *Innovation through Craft.*

26. Ibid., 4.

27. Ibid., 4.

28. Tax reliefs updated in 2015 now extend to film, animation, television, video games, theatre, orchestras and exhibitions in museums and galleries. See Corporation Tax: creative industry tax reliefs https://www.gov.uk/guidance/corporation-tax -creative-industry-tax-reliefs (accessed March 13, 2019).

29. Easton and Cauldwell-French, *Creative Freelancers.*

30. Ibid., 6.

31. Ibid., 14.

32. Ibid., 3.

33. Charlotte Schreiber and Kate Treggiden, *Makers of East London* (London: Hoxton Mini Press, 2015) 190.

34. David Runciman, *Talking Politics Guide to . . . Economic Well-Being. Talking Politics Podcast*, https://www.talkingpoliticspodcast.com/blog/2018/132-talking-politics-guide-to-economic-well-being, December 22, 2018.

35. Eleonora Belfiore, "Whose Cultural Value? Representation, Power and Creative Industries," *International Journal of Cultural Policy*, 2018, 1–15, doi:10.1080/10286632.2018.1495713.

36. Atif Shafique, Becca Antink, Alexa Clay, and Ed Cox, *Inclusive Growth in Action: Snapshots of a New Economy* (London: The RSA, 2019).

37. David Burch and Neil McInroy, *We Need an Inclusive Economy Not Inclusive Growth*, (London: CLES, 2018), 2.

38. Susan Luckman and Nicola Thomas, eds., *Craft Economies* (London: Bloomsbury Academic, 2018), 8.

39. A Business Improvement District (BID) is a geographically defined area within which the local business community pool their resources to invest in projects and services that improve the business environment and the experiences of visitors, workers and other users. Jewellery Quarter BID, https://jewelleryquarter.net/jqbid/, accessed on June 3, 2019.

40. Make It Stoke-on-Trent & Staffordshire, https://www.makeitstokestaffs.co.uk/industry-sectors/manufacturing/ceramics, accessed on June 3, 2019.

41. Tim Jackson, *Beyond Consumer Capitalism—Foundations for a Sustainable Prosperity* (Guildford: Centre for the Understanding of Sustainable Prosperity, 2016), 12.

42. Ibid., 17.

43. Kate Raworth, *Doughnut Economics: Seven Ways to Think Like a 21st-Century Economist* (New York: Random House, 2017).

44. Johan Rockström, *Planetary Boundaries: Exploring the Safe Operating Space for Humanity* (Masterclass, Stockholm Resilience Centre, Sweden, October 26, 2009).

45. Jackson, *Beyond Consumer Capitalism*, 14.

46. Mark Banks, "Creative Economies of Tomorrow? Limits to Growth and the Uncertain Future," *Cultural Trends* 27, no 5 (2018): 367–80, doi: 10.1080/09548963.2018.1534720.

47. Ibid., 367.

48. Kate Oakley and Jonathan Ward, "The Art of the Good Life: Culture and Sustainable Prosperity," *Cultural Trends* 27, no. (2018): 4–17.

49. Helen Reijonen, "Understanding the Small Business Owner: What They Really Aim at and How This Relates to Firm Performance: A Case Study in North Karelia, Eastern Finland," *Management Research News* 31, no. 8 (2008): 616–29.

50. Ibid., 627.

51. See, for example, the UK Government's Industrial Strategy (HM Government 2017) and the Arts and Humanities Research Council, The Creative Industries Clusters Programme.

BIBLIOGRAPHY

Arts and Humanities Research Council. *The Creative Industries Clusters Programme.* https://ahrc.ukri.org/innovation/creative-economy-research/the-creative-industries-clusters-programme/, accessed November 18, 2019.

Ball, Linda, Will Hunt, and Emma Pollard. *Crafting Futures: A Study of the Early Careers of Crafts Graduates from UK Higher Education Institutions.* London: Institute for Employment Studies/University of the Arts/Crafts Council, 2010.

Banks, Mark. "Creative Economies of Tomorrow? Limits to Growth and the Uncertain Future." *Cultural Trends* 27, no. 5 (2018): 367–80, doi: 10.1080/09548963.2018.1534720.

Belfiore, Eleonora. "Whose Cultural Value? Representation, Power and Creative Industries." *International Journal of Cultural Policy* (2018), doi:10.1080/102866 32.2018.1495713.

Burch, David, and Neil McInroy. *We Need an Inclusive Economy Not Inclusive Growth.* London: CLES, 2018.

Burns Owen Partnership. *Craft in an Age of Change.* London, Crafts Council, Creative Scotland, Arts Council of Wales and Craft Northern Ireland, 2012.

Business Development Research Consultants. *Access to Finance.* London: Creative Industries Council, 2018.

Chell, Elizabeth, and Mine Karataş-Özkan. *Handbook of Research on Small Business and Entrepreneurship.* Cheltenham: Edward Elgar Publishing, 2014.

Cooper, Ben. *Primary Colours: The Decline of Arts Education in Primary Schools and How It Can Be Reversed.* London: Fabian Society, 2018.

Department for Culture, Media & Sport. *Creative Industries Mapping Documents.* London: DCMS, 1998.

Department for Digital, Culture, Media and Sport. *Sectors Economic Estimates Trade, Table 33: Exports and Imports of Goods by Sub-Sector.* London: DCMS, 2017. https://www.gov.uk/government/statistics/dcms-sectors-economic -estimates-2017-trade.

Department for Education. *Initial Teacher Training (ITT) Census: 2018 to 2019.* Main tables, London: DfE, 2018.

Drucker, Peter. "Entrepreneurship in Business Enterprise." *Journal of Business Policy* 1 (1970).

Easton, Eliza, and Evy Cauldwell-French. *Creative Freelancers.* London: Creative Industries Federation, 2017.

England, Lauren. *A Pipeline Problem: Exploring Policy Disconnect in Craft Higher Education.* London: King's College London with Crafts Council, 2017.

Eisenmann, Thomas. "Entrepreneurship: A Working Definition." *Harvard Business Review,* 2013, https://hbr.org/2013/01/what-is-entrepreneurship, accessed March 4, 2019.

HM Government. *Julie Deane's Review of Self-Employment.* London: HMSO, 2016.

HM Government. *Building Our Industrial Strategy: Green Paper.* London: HMSO, 2017.

Jackson, Tim. *Beyond Consumer Capitalism—Foundations for a Sustainable Prosperity.* Guildford: Centre for the Understanding of Sustainable Prosperity, 2016.

Joint Council for Qualifications (JCQ). Annual Results Tables, 2018.

KPMG and Knowledge Transfer Network and University of Brighton. *Innovation through Craft: Opportunities for Growth.* London: Crafts Council, 2016.

Lounsbury, Michael, and Mary Ann Glynn. *Cultural Entrepreneurship: A New Agenda for the Study of Entrepreneurial Processes and Possibilities.* Cambridge: Cambridge University Press, 2019.

Luckman, Susan, and Nicola Thomas, eds. *Craft Economies.* London: Bloomsbury Academic, 2018.

Oakley, Kate, and Jonathan Ward. "The Art of the Good Life: Culture and Sustainable Prosperity." *Cultural Trends* 27, no. 1 (2018): 4–17.

O'Leary, Duncan. *Going It Alone.* London: Demos, 2014.

Patel, Karen. *Supporting Diversity in Craft Practice through Digital Technology Skills Development.* London: Crafts Council, 2019.

Raworth, Kate. *Doughnut Economics: Seven Ways to Think Like a 21st-Century Economist.* New York: Random House, 2017.

Reijonen, Helen. "Understanding the Small Business Owner: What They Really Aim at and How This Relates to Firm Performance: A Case Study in North Karelia, Eastern Finland." *Management Research News* 31, no. 8 (2008).

Rockström, Johan. *Planetary Boundaries: Exploring the Safe Operating Space for Humanity.* Masterclass, Stockholm Resilience Centre, Sweden, October 26, 2009.

RSA. *The Entrepreneurial Audit.* London: The RSA, 2017.

Runciman, David, *Talking Politics Guide to . . . Economic Well-Being. Talking Politics Podcast,* https://www.talkingpoliticspodcast.com/blog/2018/132-talking-politics-guide-to-economic-well-being, December 22, 2018.

Schreiber, Charlotte, and Kate Treggiden. *Makers of East London.* London: Hoxton Mini Press. 2015.

Schumpeter, John. *The Theory of Economic Development: An Inquiry into Profits, Capital, Credit, Interest, and the Business Cycle.* Transaction Publishers, 1934.

Shafique, Atif, Becca Antink, Alexa Clay, and Ed Cox. *Inclusive Growth in Action: Snapshots of a New Economy.* London: The RSA, 2019.

Spilsbury, Mark. *Who Makes? An Analysis of People Working in Craft Occupations.* London: Crafts Council, 2018.

Trends Business Research. *Measuring the Craft Economy.* London: Crafts Council, 2014.

———. *Studying Craft 16.* London: Crafts Council, 2016.

Yair, Karen. *Craft & Enterprise.* London: Crafts Council, 2012.

———. *Crafting Capital: New Technologies, New Economies.* London: Crafts Council, 2011.

Young, David. *Growing Your Business: A Report on Growing Micro Businesses.* London: Business, Innovation and Skills, 2013.

Chapter Three

Craft Entrepreneurship and Public Policies in Serbia

Hristina Mikic

Throughout its history craft entrepreneurship has had different values and societal importance, yet it has been "always related to the unique expression of a particular culture or community through local craftsmanship and materials."[1] The creative economy boom over the past decade has brought a new diversity of craft entrepreneurship. In 2016, the craft market was estimated at 180 billion US dollars, representing approximately 39 percent of the global trade in creative goods.[2] This kind of entrepreneurship has been discussed within the cultural entrepreneurship field,[3] in the context of the creative economy[4] or as a part of the cultural industries.[5] Pret and Cogan documented a variety of perspectives from which craft entrepreneurship can be investigated: behavior, context, motivation, development, resources, diversity and classification.[6] In recent years, increasing attention has been paid to exploring craft entrepreneurship within public policies.[7] Documenting economic behavior, business models and characteristics of craft entrepreneurship in different regional and policy contexts can demonstrate the different roles of craft entrepreneurship in socioeconomic development.

This chapter provides an insight into craft entrepreneurship practices and policy interventions in Serbia, considering the historical context and the complex governance of crafts in the current moment. The main questions it addresses are: What are the structures, geographical distribution, gender distribution and the typical business models of craft entrepreneurs in this region? What are the impacts of existing policy measures on craft entrepreneurship?

The chapter is organized as follows: the introduction, which is followed by a historic overview of craft entrepreneurship in Serbia. In the third section the methodology of research and data collection are explained. The fourth section provides the main findings of research and discussion of results, and this is followed by the conclusion and proposals for improving public policy measures, as well further research.

HISTORY OF CRAFT
ENTREPRENEURSHIP IN SERBIA

The first craft production was developed in Serbia during the Middle Ages in monasteries and medieval cities. With the arrival of the Turks, craft production changed under the influence of Turkish culture. It was primarily developed in the military-trade centers of Serbia that were under Turkish rule.[8] The organization of craft entrepreneurship into guilds also dates back to the Turkish period. Guild associations were formed in order to protect the common interests of craftspeople, and determined standards of promotion, working rules, product prices, minimum quality standards for craft products and career advancement, but also protected the monopoly position of craftspeople. In the middle of the nineteenth century, crafts from the Austria-Hungarian Empire came to Serbia. These were mostly new crafts that the population started to deal with. Crafts were mainly conducted in cities, and products were intended for the city population. Combining elements of the Turkish with elements of the Austrian craft system, the first regulatory framework for crafts development in Serbia was established only after gaining independence from Turkey in 1847.[9] Prior to the adoption of these legal rules, there were 7,913 craftspeople, while the oldest guild was the terziary guild established in 1817.[10]

Craft products produced in the countryside were mostly exchanged for other products that were needed by the rural population, and very rarely sold. For city craftspeople, the main market was the urban population and surrounding towns. Fairs were one of the most important forms of selling craft products. They lasted from three to five days and there was an annual list of fairs in Serbia, in order to better organize this form of sales. City craftspeople's work was regulated by legal rules, and the most important provision was that they were allowed to sell domestic craft products, while the sale of foreign craft products suffered certain restrictions.

Until the beginning of the twentieth century, craft production was gender-differentiated and exclusively performed by men. Women's craft entrepreneurship existed only in the form of home-based practice in the villages. Women's craft included the production of linen, silk and woven cloth, and in addition to this, they were engaged in embroidery, crocheting and knitting.[11] In 1898, there were about 109,000 households in Serbia who had looms and performed weaving.[12] The first women's organized craft production was the launch of workshops in Vranje and Pirot which were established at the end of the nineteenth century, while the real Textile School (dedicated to the education of weavers) was established in Leskovac in 1891.[13]

The development of industrial production, the free import of craft products from Austria, the growth of living standards and the change in consumer habits had an impact on the extinction of certain crafts, for which there was no longer a need, or the production was too expensive. In the implementation of the economic policy, ministries and other state bodies took care of the craft. Privileges were given to those industries that contributed to and developed crafts, under the condition that raw and other materials were procured from domestic craftspeople.[14] Crafts had a very important role in the social and economic life of Serbia and they were proudly presented as an important dimension of Serbian culture, creativity and artisan skills at the Vienna and Paris World's Fairs at the end of nineteenth century. Nevertheless, the period until the end of the Second World War was marked as a turbulent period for crafts.

After the war, the communist authorities nationalized all economic resources, and private property was abolished. Individual craft workshops stopped working, while craft cooperatives became state-owned enterprises. As the system of state-owned enterprises proved to be ineffective, a self-management system was introduced from the mid-1950s. In the first phase, it was of mixed character—management of enterprises was entrusted to workers and state authorities. In later phases under the pressure of workers, it was turned into a complete self-management system, where management of the economy was left to the workers. Through the self-management decision, the workers adopted business plans and shared their revenues. Craft production was carried out through a model of associating craftspeople into working communities. Craft workers as members of working communities did not have disposable income, and the funds were social. One of the most illustrative examples of craft production at that time was the launching of the Sirogojno craft cooperative. This women's cooperative was launched with an exhibition in early 1960s. The cooperative began working with about twenty weavers and after a decade, there were two thousand weavers.[15] The aim of the cooperative was the economic empowerment of women, but also their emancipation and improvement of living conditions for the village. "Women worked from home while taking care of sheep, or doing other jobs,"[16] and the whole village was divided into quarters which represented production units. The chiefs of production visited the houses, delivered materials to women, and established the norms and the deadline for completing the product. Sirogojno women mostly made sweaters known today as "Sirogojno sweaters," and their customers were tourists and foreigners. Markov documented that almost 60 percent of production was exported abroad, and the largest buyers were in Western Europe and Asia.[17] The whole movement that promoted knitted items from this region was called "Sirogojno Fashion." It was characterized by "transposing the cultural heritage of this region into fashion items, high quality production, longevity and authenticity."[18] Later, the cooperative was transformed into a social enterprise, and in the late 1990s it was privatized. Today it works under the name of Sirgojno Company. Such cases also existed in Leskovac, Vranje, Pirot, but in the territory of Vojvodina, as well.

Social ownership proved ineffective, and the restriction of private initiatives hampered economic development. In self-managing companies, management through workers' councils became complicated. Tensions between workers and sociopolitical communities led to a self-management crisis. Misplanning, problems with income distribution and inconsistency in investment decisions were criticized.[19] Thus, economic reforms were inevitable. These were implemented in the mid-1980s where the constitution was changed, and private property became legitimate. Laws regulating private entrepreneurship, regulation of traditional and artistic crafts and cottage industries, were adopted. These changes marked the beginning of the transformation of the socialist economy. Its main characteristic was the strengthening of the role of private capital in the economy, as well as the privatization of social and state-owned enterprises. Many craft cooperatives received new owners. Some of them continued their work, and some were closed. The people who worked in these cooperatives after losing their jobs established their own craft workshops.

In the early 1990s, Yugoslavia was exposed to UN sanctions, and the economic crisis deepened. At the same time, the authoritative regime of Slobodan Milošević was strengthened, as well as the dissatisfaction of the people with the existing political, economic and social situation in the country. During this period, the disintegration of Yugoslavia and civil wars occurred in Bosnia and Herzegovina and Croatia. The difficult situation in the country led to protests by the democratic opposition and citizens against the authorities in the mid-1990s with the aim of overthrowing the existing regime. The massive displacement of the population in Kosovo and the escalation of violence against civilians led to the NATO bombing of Yugoslavia in 1999. It ended with an armistice, and the Milosevic regime was overthrown on October 5, 2000. On that day, democratic opposition and dissatisfied citizens overthrew Slobodan Milosevic due to the electoral theft that took place during the Presidential elections on September 24, 2000. These happenings are known as the "5th October democratic changes."

Since the year 2000, a new era of development of craft entrepreneurship has begun. Four ministries have been responsible for crafts: the Ministry of

Economy; the Ministry of Culture and Media; the Ministry of Trade, Tourism and Telecommunications and the Ministry of Agriculture (and later rural development, as well). The Ministry of Economy is in charge of certification of crafts and keeping records on the number of certified workshops for artistic and traditional crafts and cottage industry. These registers have been kept since 1997. In order for a workshop to be found in this register, it is necessary to pass the field control of the expert commission of the Ministry of Economy (that the production is conducted in the manner and in line with procedures that are characteristic for that kind of crafts, that there are funds for the work that enable the performance of the crafts and so on). The certificate issued by the Ministry of Economy is valid for ten years. In addition, the ministry deals with legal regulations in the field of craft production.

The Ministry of Culture and Media is in charge of the protection of the intangible heritage, where crafts, as bearers of this type of heritage, occupy a significant place. The strategy and measures for the protection of intangible heritage are determined by the National Committee for Intangible Heritage. It also takes care of the nomination of elements for registration on UNESCO's representative list of intangible heritage, as well as proposals to be placed on the list of endangered intangible heritage. Support to crafts is not provided directly, but indirectly—by regional museums and associations working on the promotion of these crafts. Therefore, the Ministry of Culture supports this area through different forms of heritage protection activities, documentation and promotion. The most important measure in this field is the open call for intangible cultural heritage projects, which is organized every year. The second body responsible for intangible heritage and crafts protection is the Center for Intangible Heritage. It was established after the ratification of the UNESCO Convention for the Safeguarding of the Intangible Cultural Heritage (2003) as a body functioning within the Ethnographic Museum in charge of registration of the intangible heritage elements on the national list, protecting, promoting and valorizing the intangible cultural heritage. Its functioning encounters many problems—unresolved legal status, lack of funds and people for efficient work, poor communication and a lack of cooperation with the Ministry of Culture.

The Ministry of Trade and Telecommunications treats crafts as a specific trade activity and grants subsidies for improving production, procurement of equipment and co-financing work of craftspeople and cooperatives. In 2009, initiatives for opening of craft shops across the country started. Several craft shops were opened in Belgrade, Novi Sad, and Bela Palanka, but they were closed after a few years due to unsustainable costs of their work. The Ministry of Agriculture deals with crafts in terms of the development of rural tourism and the diversification of rural economy. Subsidies are granted to agricultural and rural households in the form of subsidies for the purchase of equipment and raw materials for craft production, if the craft has the function of improving the economic life of the countryside. In addition to direct assistance, the ministry is also in charge of legal regulations and standards relating to the production of traditional food.

Each of these ministries carries out independent projects, without involving other bodies, with the argument that such projects are implemented within their own portfolio. The lack of coordination, vanity and overlapping jurisdictions are negative consequences of the existing multisectoral government approach.[20] It is evident that there is a lack of awareness in government bodies about the multidimensional nature of craft entrepreneurship, and that it also contributes to the transfer of cultural values and the promotion and protection of the diversity of cultural expressions, but also has implications for the local economy, tourism, rural development and employment. Another characteristic of public policies is the support of traditional craft entrepreneurship through existing measures. On the other hand, artistic crafts and contemporary creativity carried out through craft entrepreneurship are not sufficiently recognised through public policy measures.

The importance of craft entrepreneurship is especially visible at the local level. Bennett emphasises that clusterization of craft business "at a smaller geographical level and unit size than other sectors within the creative industries foster[s] a sense of identity, encourage[s] mutual support and attract[s] other independent businesses and organizations seeking a form of branding by association."[21] Craft entrepreneurship employs a significant number of people and many families especially in rural areas in Serbia, where crafts are an important source of household income. In urban areas, there is a similar situation and there are plenty of artists who have found opportunities for their employment by starting some kind of artistic workshop. Urban craft entrepreneurship is predominantly related to gastronomy, ceramics, and the production of unique silk and textile items.

However, despite the local importance of craft entrepreneurship, it is still on the margins of public policies. This is because the craft economy's significance is judged on the basis of its size and contribution to the economic growth of Serbia. This creates a climate where craft entrepreneurship has attracted little attention in comparison to provincial carriers of economic and cultural life, such as large enterprises and public cultural institutions.[22] The recognition of new values of crafts entrepreneurship in the Serbian creative economy, as well as its role in the protection and promotion of diversity of cultural expression, is crucial for its wider inclusion into public policies.

METHODOLOGY AND DATA COLLECTION

This research is based on the desk research of the Ministry of Economy certified crafts database. It contains records on fifty types of traditional crafts, fourteen artistic crafts, and ten types of cottage industry. In the database, there are a total of 667 craftspeople who have certificates. Of that number, nineteen of them stopped working, while 109 did not renew the certificates after their expiration. The Register of Certified Crafts was processed according to the analysis criteria, and for additional business data, the Entrepreneurs Register of the Business Registers Agency was used. Desk analysis was complemented with the results of a pilot survey on creative entrepreneurs in Pirot (188 respondents) and Kikinda (120 respondents) conducted in 2016–2018. This was carried out by examining the entrepreneurial capacities of local creative industries and craftspeople. In this research we used the term "entrepreneurial capacity" to describe family traditions in craft entrepreneurship and their impact on the creation of new entrepreneurial ventures, ability of craft entrepreneurs to use business opportunities and their ability for collaborative work as well as the capacity to implement their own business idea.

In addition to those sociometric methods, several methods for anthropological discipline were employed, including personal interviews with thirty creative entrepreneurs and focus group discussions with creative entrepreneurs in Pirot (2015–2016) and Kikinda (2017–2018). These interviews and group discussions were conducted within several different projects: "Straightening institutional capacity for development of creative industries in Serbia" (2015–2016), "Creative entrepreneurship and intangible heritage of Kikinda" (2017) and "Communities connecting heritage" (2017–2018). We also carried out content analysis of twenty craft entrepreneur case studies[23] and public interviews as well as desk research of public policies measure implemented by the Ministry of Economy; Ministry of Culture and Media; Ministry of Trade, Tourism and Telecommunications and Ministry of Agriculture and Rural Development.

Our research has several limitations. First, the survey covers only craft entrepreneurs that have been certified by the Ministry of Economy, and certainly there is a large number of those who have not undergone the certification process. The estimate is that this sample represents about 40 percent of the total number of people involved in craft entrepreneurship. However, many of the entrepreneurs who are not included in the analysis consider craft as an additional job or hobby, and besides craft production, they carry out other unrelated jobs. This information was found in the Ministry of Trade crafts database that was created within the Project "Support to the Protection and Promotion of Old Crafts in the Republic of Serbia," where 1,406 craftspeople and twenty-six associations dealing with this business were registered.

This database could not be used because its last update was in 2009. Thus, its data and comparisons regarding the number of craftspeople are more illustrative. Another limitation of research is the credibility of a register of certified crafts. Namely, during the research, we found that some of the registered companies are no longer engaged in craft production, but that they still have certificates. Therefore, we estimate that in the database there are certainly those who have certificates, but no longer deal with craft entrepreneurship. The third limitation is that data from empirical studies in Pirot and Kikinda refer to creative entrepreneurship in rural areas of Serbia, and that urban entrepreneurs are covered only by interviews and case studies, so that the detail of data on urban and rural entrepreneurs is different. However, as this is the first study of crafts in Serbia, it provides a useful starting point for further comprehensive research in this area.

BUSINESS PROFILES OF
CRAFT ENTREPRENEURSHIP IN SERBIA

As described throughout this chapter, crafts in Serbia are categorized as traditional crafts, artistic crafts and cottage industry. Traditional crafts include the production and completion of objects that preserve and maintain traditional folk art, including construction trades that serve to restore monuments of traditional architecture.[24] For this type of craft, it is characteristic that traditional techniques, materials and procedures are used. They are mostly made manually or using simple devices.[25] Artistic crafts encompass the design of materials where the making primarily depends on the personal taste and skill of the producer. The objects are made according to the idea and design of the craftsperson, where their personal creativity and skill are reflected in the product.[26] Cottage industry involves the activities of making objects by manual labor, characterized by folk art.[27]

In the structure of certified crafts, traditional crafts cover the highest percentage (40.8 percent), followed by artistic crafts (31 percent), cottage industry (15.7 percent) and mixed crafts—the combination of all three types of crafts (12.5 percent). According to the type of activity (see figure 3.1), the most popular is textiles (39 percent), as well as jewellery and fashion accessories (23 percent).

Geographical distribution of crafts shows that over 55 percent of craft entrepreneurs are registered in cities, most of them in Belgrade (23 percent) and Novi Sad (7.1 percent). These mainly include workshops of art and traditional crafts. In other territories, workshops for cottage industry and traditional crafts dominate (see Figure 3.2). In relation to the type of activities, the most

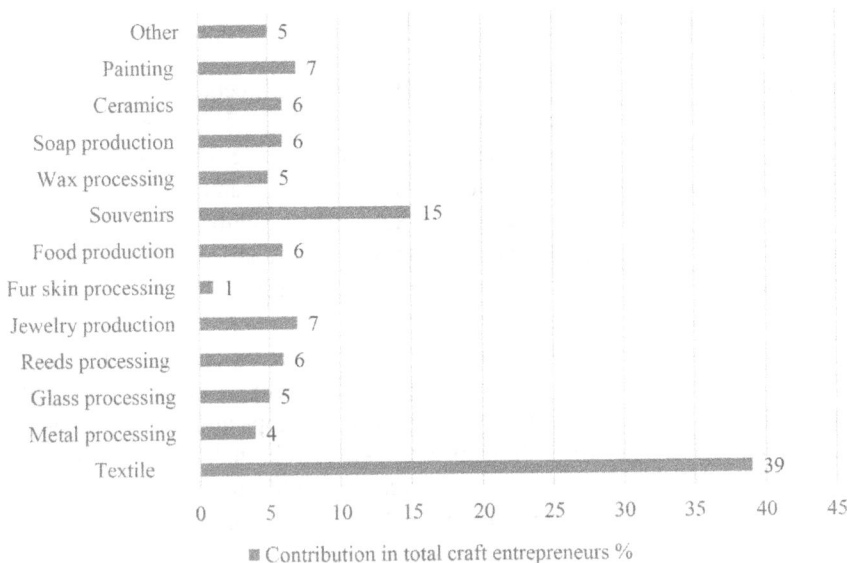

Figure 3.1.   Craft structure by type of activity, 2019.

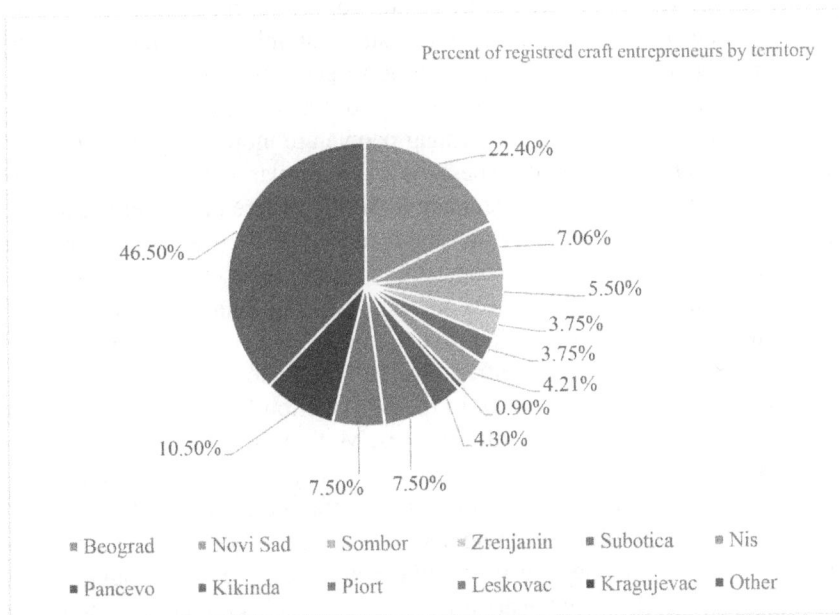

Figure 3.2.   Geographical distribution of crafts, 2019.

common are needlework, knitting, crocheting, hand-knitted carpets, carpeting and weaving.

According to gender, participation of women (49 percent) and men (51 percent) engaged in craft entrepreneurship is almost equal. However, the gender differentiation by type of craft is noticeable. Most of the traditional crafts are performed by men (about 93 percent), while women prefer artistic crafts and cottage industry (about 84 percent). By age, a large number of producers are forty-five to sixty years old (77 percent). It is also characteristic that young entrepreneurs are more oriented towards artistic crafts, whereas older entrepreneurs are more involved in traditional crafts.

Such tendencies are in line with the usual processes of transferring craft knowledge. While access to knowledge in the field of artistic, especially modern crafts, is facilitated by the internet, workshops and YouTube tutorials, so far the transfer of traditional craft skills is limited. Research in Pirot and Kikinda suggested that craft skills and knowledge are mostly transmitted within the family via nonformal channels. Family members between fifty to seventy-five years of age predominantly practice traditional crafts, and younger people who decided to continue their family tradition see them as role models. There are limited activities to transfer craft skills and knowledge to people outside of the family.

As for other younger craft entrepreneurs, they do not usually decide to start their own ventures in this area due to the unfavorable business climate in Serbia which includes high taxes, a bureaucratic state administration and uncertainty in the market. Evidence from the interviews show that if certain crafts are valued as old-fashioned and unprofitable, and craftspeople are seen as representatives of lower social classes, young people are more likely to negatively perceive craft entrepreneurship. These views are similar to the general attitudes of young people about entrepreneurship in Serbia, where they rarely decide to start their own business as they are dissatisfied with the way their education system prepares them for entrepreneurship and poor business conditions.[28]

There are significant differences among crafts in urban and rural areas. In urban areas, the market for craft entrepreneurship is a major part of tourism, media and other creative activities. This is dominated by young entrepreneurs, the majority of which work in food production (handmade chocolates, pasta, candy, etc.), or artistic craft products. Motives to start an entrepreneurial venture mostly come from love for a particular creative skill, which they hope they can make an income from. In rural areas, crafts are mostly at risk of extinction. For example, Jovanovic documented the existence of about 3,600 crafts in Pirot until the Second World War,[29] and recent research suggests that few have continued.[30] Women are primarily engaged in craft entrepreneurship as a part of their economic empowerment, as suggested by this interviewee:

I started to take up crafts after leaving my job because of the poor working conditions. Artistic crafts production has always been my hobby. I made them for my friends as a gift, and the first orders came through them. I realized that I could earn extra income from this job and that it would improve my economic independence, so I turned to crafts as my main occupation. (A female respondent, forty-seven years old)

Through crafts, women see themselves as custodians of tradition and patrons of cultural heritage, and most often these activities take place within rural tourism activities.[31]

Business models for craft entrepreneurship tend to be characterised by civil association or co-working practices. Labour associations develop project activities in the local community such as craft training, demonstration of crafts, participation in cultural programs and so on. Funds are obtained from local governments. When they gain a certain level of visibility of their work and improve the quality of their products, they are included in the tourist offer of the municipality. Independently or in cooperation with a tourist organization, they participate in fairs of the surrounding cities and take part in the promotion of the municipality. In this way, tourist organizations become focal points for selling craft products.

The research carried out suggests that women are more inclined to collaborate and work with other women. In this way, they feel more secure and motivated to work. It is common that many female crafts require collective work (e.g., weaving, traditional food production), so collaborative working practice not only allows women to work together, but also to work faster and more efficiently. In the initial stages, craft entrepreneurship is performed alongside another job. In rural areas, this is mostly agriculture or household chores. In urban environments, these are mainly administrative, financial or teaching jobs.

It is interesting that in associations, there are always women who are more skilled and experienced in doing craft jobs and have a more prominent affinity towards craft entrepreneurship. Such women leave the association at a certain stage and start an independent entrepreneurial venture, as illustrated by one respondent:

In our civil society association the members were women of different educational backgrounds and crafts knowledge. Most of us shared a love for cultural heritage and through crafts we saw a way to preserve cultural heritage and tradition from oblivion. That was the basic idea that brought us together. I helped other members learn to knit and weave and to find inspiration in cultural heritage. We organized workshops in our civil organization. I learned this skill from my mother, and she learned from her aunt. I often used to knit and weave

as a hobby, and then I started making items for sale. I attended several entrepreneurship workshops and they helped me figure out how to turn my hobby
into an entrepreneurial venture. I came up with the idea to apply for funds from
the National Employment Service and thus obtain the initial funds to register
an entrepreneurial business. I left the association and started my entrepreneurial
venture. (A female respondent, forty-four years old)

The reasons that led them to this decision are: a personal feeling that they
cannot develop further through the association, the inability to take advantage
of all of the business opportunities provided and disagreements with other
members in the further development of the organization. Most of the women
we interviewed in Pirot and Kikinda, who are now self-employed in craft entrepreneurship, were once members of an association. They positively value
the time spent in associations, but perceive it as a transitional phase in the
development of their entrepreneurial ideas:

At the beginning we felt very nice in the association. Our 10 women registered
a civil organization and started designing programs. We were mainly interested
in protecting cultural heritage through crafts. We socialized, acquired new
skills together, and supported one another in the realization of ideas. Together,
we participated in crafts fairs and bazaars. However, it seems to me that it has
been clear to all of us that working in a civil association is just one transitional
phase, and that when we acquire enough courage and be[come] confident in our
entrepreneurial ideas, we will start working on our own. That's what happened
in the end. We were increasingly focused on our private affairs and less and
less devoted to working together in a civil organization. (A female respondent,
thirty-eight years old)

Some of the women felt that that associations are too slow and bureaucratic
to respond to the market opportunities that appear to them. In addition, they
believed that solidarity among members exists at the beginning, but that
collective culture does not develop sufficiently at a later stage, and there is
always an atmosphere that a number of members invest more in the association than they benefit from it.

I left the association three years ago. I could not sufficiently influence the decisions of the association, and different interests began to emerge among the
members. One group of us wanted the association to work more on improving
our skills and economic empowerment, while another group advocated only the
promotional activities of the association. Out of a total of 70 enrolled members,
only 10 of us actively participated in the work of the association—designing
projects, obtaining funding for our work, organizing programs, etc. At one
point, I realized that I was giving more to the association than benefiting from
the activities realized. It was a key moment for me to make the decision to step

down from the association and start working on my own. (A female respondent, forty-two old years)

In the case of male entrepreneurs, they rarely decide to jointly participate in craft entrepreneurship. Even where this is inevitable, for example in larger craft projects, the association exists only for the realization of a specific project, but not as a lasting business model, nor a way to get to new jobs.

Craft workshops approximately last for about fifteen years. Twenty percent of craft entrepreneurs have been operating for less than five years, while about 10 percent have been doing craft entrepreneurship for more than thirty years. The growth rate of newly certified craftspeople in the period of 2000–2018 was around 9.7 percent per year. During 2000–2010, there was the highest number of certified traditional crafts (around 87 percent). This trend changed in 2010–2018, when the primacy was the certification of artistic crafts. Newer craft entrepreneurs gained knowledge of craft production through the internet and YouTube tutorials, rather than formal forms of education or contact with heritage and museum institutions.

PROBLEMS, BARRIERS, AND SUPPORTING MEASURES FOR CRAFT ENTREPRENEURSHIP

The major problems encountered by craft entrepreneurs are sustainable financing, high taxes, noncompliant measures of various laws governing craft production, a decrease in demand due to lifestyle changes and decrease in the number of younger craftspeople. Pilot studies have shown that entrepreneurs make about 90 percent of their income in the marketplace. Sales of craft products are the main source of income, and in fewer cases, training, corporate team building and other activities are carried out. Therefore, the development of the market for craft entrepreneurship is decisive for its survival. Adverse business circumstances often arise due to their undefined status, which is under the jurisdiction of several ministries, and the multidimensionality of craft entrepreneurship is not recognised. In addition, many entrepreneurs must negotiate innovating craft production while preserving its traditional values, addressing the challenges that arise when a product/service is at maturity phase and its demand is reduced,.

In Serbia, craft entrepreneurship development relies on scarce sectoral policies. Figure 3.3 presents public policy measures in the field of craft entrepreneurship. There is no cooperation between the ministries or the harmonization of program activities. It is noticeable that no state documents explicitly consider measures to support craft entrepreneurship in a comprehensive way.

Table 3.3. Public Policies Measures Focused on Craft Entrepreneurship, 2019.

Measure	Measure description	Jurisdiction	Effects of the measure
Economic measures			
Craft Grants	Supporting the craft production by purchasing new equipment and material	Ministry of Trade, Telecommunication and Tourism	Enhancing the craft production
Grants for protection and promotion of intangible heritage	Supporting the promotion of intangible heritage and ensuring the diversity of traditional cultural expressions	Ministry of Culture and Information, AP Vojvodina	Enhancing the diversity of traditional cultural expression
Grants for diversification of rural economy	Supporting diversification of rural economy through grants for craft production	Ministry of agriculture and rural development	Enhancing the diversification of economy activities of agricultural households
Grant for local handicrafts association and NGOs	Supporting rehabilitation of handicrafts through grants for NGOs and associations	Secretariat for Economy, Employment and Gender Equality	Development and rehabilitation of local handicrafts
Supporting promotion of crafts entrepreneurships through festivals and bazaars	Supporting promotion and cooperation of craft entrepreneurs	Ministry of Trade, Telecommunication and Tourism, Government of Vojvodina, Belgrade City, municipalities	Promoting crafts entrepreneurships at local markets
VAT exemption for craft products/services	Enhancing sustainable sales through VAT exemption of crafts product and services	Ministry of Finance	Better sales of craft product and services
Organizational measures			
National Committee for Intangible Heritage	Contributing to the national policy of protection intangible heritage, suggesting measures for protection and promotion of national intangible heritage, nomination of elements for registration on UNESCO's representative list of intangible heritage, identifying endangered intangible heritage	Ministry of Culture and Information	Better protection and promotion of intangible heritage in Serbia
Center for Intangible Heritage	Administrative and professional support in protection and promotion of intangible heritage	Ethnographic Museum	Better coordination of various stakeholders involved in protection and promotion of intangible heritage
Support to networking and cooperation of craft entrepreneurs	Establishing collaborative platforms in craft entrepreneurship and stimulating cooperation and entrepreneurial spirit	Ministry of Economy, Secretariat for the Economy and Tourism of AP Vojvodina	Establishing the Cluster of Old Crafts "Re-craft", Nis Craft Cluster, Women's Craft Association of South Serbia...
Regulatory measures			
Regulation on classification of professions that are considered as an old and artistic crafts and cottage industry	Protection of quality standards in craft production	Ministry of economy	Better quality standards for craft entrepreneurships

One of the reasons for this situation can be found in the general hostile attitude of the state and elite groups towards ethnological heritage.[32]

Economic measures: The most important measure is subsidizing craft production. This exists at all levels of the government (local, provincial, national). However, by analysing open calls for entrepreneurs and civil society organizations and cooperatives we found that a part of allocated grants is very small—from fifteen to thirty grants annually, while in some cases there are selective categories that can apply for subsidies (e.g., registered farms that deal with craft as a secondary activity). Interviews with entrepreneurs have shown that they often do not apply to these competitions because they do not have clear criteria for granting subsidies. Obtaining documentation is required, which can take months. Grants are awarded for the purchase of materials and equipment, and the funding of promotion, marketing, access to the market or other activities is limited. The grant amount is very low (from 300 Euros to 1,500 Euros). In a domain of tax policy, the respondents pointed to nontransparent income taxation. This includes lump sum taxation without clear criteria, and even on the same territory entrepreneurs can be burdened with different tax levies. This creates a lot of uncertainty, because they never know how much tax they will pay at the end of the year.

Regulatory measures: These measures are of legal character and establish rules, practices and standards necessary for the protection and promotion of craft entrepreneurship. They are currently the weakest aspect of public policies in the field of craft entrepreneurship. The only document that regulates this area is the "Regulation on classification of an traditional, artistic crafts and cottage industry."[33] Other craft production issues are not regulated. Craft entrepreneurs pointed out that many legal provisions are in line with this regulation and that their status is undefined. They mostly complain about the application of general laws that they cannot respect in their work, or high costs.

Organizational measures: Craft entrepreneurs are not united, and their negotiation power is low. There were several attempts to unite craftspeople in clusters (e.g., Re-craft, Nis Craft Cluster, Craft Association of South Serbia), but they did not bring significant results. The protection of craftspeoples' interests through the Crafts Section in the Chamber of Commerce of Serbia does not make a great difference, as there are very few members. In addition, there is a lack of comprehensive promotion of crafts and their evaluation in a contemporary context, which could contribute to the sustainability of the market for craft products. The majority of craft entrepreneurs (87 percent) in Pirot and Kikinda reported that manifestations and bazaars are the most important events for selling craft products and accessing new buyers. The demonstration of craft production and techniques at these events can help people to better understand values of handmade products. Craft entrepreneurs recognized local tourism organizations as a main stakeholder in the promotion of craft entrepreneurship, while museums and other institutions are sporadically dealing with this topic.

CONCLUSION

The focus of this chapter was to provide an insight into craft entrepreneurship in Serbia and the efficacy of policy measures in supporting the development of crafts. Data on craft entrepreneurs is based on the Ministry of Economy certified crafts' database, evidence from empirical studies in Pirot and Kikinda and desk research. Our research shows that the majority of craft entrepreneurship exists in the field of traditional craft. Over 55 percent of craft entrepreneurs are located in cities, most of them in Belgrade and Novi Sad. Over 39 percent of craftspeople work with textiles. Gender differentiation of crafts is noticeable. Most of the traditional crafts are produced by men (about 93 percent), while women prefer artistic crafts and cottage industry (about 84 percent). By age, the largest proportion are forty-five to sixty years old (77 percent). As for young entrepreneurs, they do not usually decide to start their own ventures in this area due to the unfavourable business climate in Serbia. Craft workshops approximately last for about fifteen years. The growth rate of newly certified craftspeople in the period of 2000–2018 was around 9.7 percent per year. Our research suggests that crafts entrepreneurship contributes to the economic empowering of people, especially women.

The major problems facing craft entrepreneurs include sustainable financing, high taxes, noncompliant measures of various laws governing craft production, a decrease in demand due to lifestyle changes and a decrease in the number of young people interested in craft. Our analysis shows that craft entrepreneurship development relies on scarce sectoral policies and their measures, where "policies focusing on a single objective . . . [carry a] risk of falling short."[34] Thus, public policies that integrate craft entrepreneurship have to be holistic, based on evidence and driven by results. Policy interventions should be grounded on strong evidence and more craft research needs to be produced covering a broader range of cultural and economic issues. The effective way to ensure intersectoral cooperation is to formulate a strategy for the development of craft entrepreneurship at the national level. Specific attention should be paid to measures for empowering craft entrepreneurship and its interrelation with the creative industries (e.g., fashion design, tourism, film industry). In this regard, creating a public-private partnership model for developing craft entrepreneurship is necessary. Also, a favorable ecosystem for craft entrepreneurship needs to be created, for example, through a change of regulatory framework for craftsmanship, tax incentives, trade issue, social security and so on. Policy measures should ensure a sustainable market for craft products, not only grants for the survival of craft production, and contribute to a social recognition of crafts.

NOTES

1. USAID, *Global Market Assessment for Handicrafts* (USAID, 2006), 1.
2. Hristina Mikić, *Kreativno preduzetništvo: teorija i praksa* (Beograd: Grupa za kreativnu ekonomiju), 2017.
3. See Victoria Johnson, "What Is Organizational Imprinting? Cultural Entrepreneurship in the Founding of the Paris Opera," *American Journal of Sociology* 113, no. 1 (2017): 97–127, 2017; Vanessa Ratten and Joao Ferreira, "Future Research Direction for Cultural Entrepreneurship and Regional Innovation," *International Journal of Entrepreneurship and Innovation* 21, no. 3 (2017): 163–69.
4. Susan Luckman, *Craft and the Creative Economy* (New York: Palgrave Macmillan, 2015).
5. Paul Hirsch, "Cultural Industries Revisited," *Organization Science* 11, no. 3 (2000): 356–61; Hristina Mikić, *Measuring Economic Contribution of Cultural Industries: Review and Assessment of Methodological Approaches* (Montreal: UNESCO-Institute for Statistics), 2012; UNIDO, *Creative Industries and Micro and Small Scale Enterprise Development* (Vienna: UNIDO), 2010.
6. Tobias Pret and Aviel Cogan, "Artisan Entrepreneurship: A Systematic Literature Review and Research Agenda," *International Journal of Entrepreneurial Behavior and Research* 25, no. 4 (2019): 592–614.
7. Priyatej Kotipalli, "Making Sense of Craft Using Cultural Economics," in *A Cultural Economic Analysis of Craft*, eds. Anna Mignosa and Priyatej Kotipalli (Cham: Palgrave Macmillan, 2019), 39–50; Anna Mignosa and Priyatej Kotipalli, eds., *A Cultural Economic Analysis of Craft* (Cham: Palgrave Macmillan, 2019).
8. Nikola Vučo, *Raspadanje esnafa u Srbiji I* (Beograd: Naučna knjiga, 1954).
9. Ibid.
10. Ibid., 17.
11. Ljubiša Protić, *Razvitak industrije i promet dobara u Srbiji za vreme prve vlade Kneza Miloša* (Beograd: RAD, 1953), 39.
12. Radomir Đunisavljević, *Osnivanje industrijskih preduzeća i razvoj industrija u Srbiji do 1918. godine* (Beograd: Beogradski izdavačko-grafički zavod, 1988), 20.
13. Ibid., 56–57.
14. Hristina Mikić and Estela Radonjić-Živkov, *Privreda Paraćina: od mlina do savremene industrije* (Paraćin: Zavičajni muzej Paraćin & Institut za kreativno preduzetništvo i inovacije, 2018).
15. Svetlana Markov, "Ženska radna snaga i razvoj sela," *Zbornik matice srpske za društvene nauke* br. 90 (1991): 139–47.
16. Ibid., 143.
17. Ibid., 145.
18. For more information, see Ibid., 145.
19. Branko Horvat, *Privredni sistem i ekonomska politika* (Beograd: Institut ekonomskih nauka, 1970).
20. Miša Đurkovic, "Odnos kulturne politike prema narodnoj kulturi u Srbiji," *Sociološki pregled* 45 (9–12), no. 4 (2011): 565.

21. Julia Bennett, "Craft—The New Entrepreneurship?" in *Craft Entrepreneurship*, eds. Annette Naudin and Karen Patel (London: Rowman & Littlefield International, 2020).

22. Ibid., 246.

23. Mikić, *Kreativno preduzetništvo*.

24. Ministry of Economy, "Regulation on Classification of Professions That Are Considered as an Old and Artistic Crafts and Cottage Industry," *Official Gazette* no. 56 (2012).

25. Dragana Stojković, *Stari zanati—Nematerijalno kulturno nasleđe Lužnice u borbi za opstanak* (Babušnica: Opština Babušnica, 2015), 16.

26. Ministry of Economy, "Regulation on Classification of Professions."

27. Ibid.

28. LIBEK, *Istraživanje: Preduzetnička kultura kod mladih* (Beograd: LIBEK, 2015), https://libek.org.rs/uploads/files/1430826083.O7D72SKzVROwm9KG.pdf.

29. Borisav Jovanović, *Old Crafts in Pirot and Neighborhood* (Pirot: National Library, 2012).

30. Marina Cvetković, "Zanati u Pirotu i okolini," *Zbornik Etnografskoj muzeja* 74, no. 1 (2010): 173–234.

31. Hristina Mikić, "Rural Sustainable Innovation and Creative Industries: Case Study of Rural Tourism Households in Pirot, Serbia," in *Management of Sustainable Innovation*, eds. Vanessa Ratten, Marcela Ramirez-Pasillas, and Hans Lundberg (London: Routledge, 2019).

32. Đurkovic, "Odnos kulturne politike prema narodnoj kulturi u Srbiji," 572.

33. Ministry of Economy, "Regulation on Classification of Professions."

34. Anna Mignosa, "Policies for Crafts: Rationale and Tools," in *A Cultural Economic Analysis of Craft*, eds. Anna Mignosa and Priyatej Kotipalli (Cham: Palgrave Macmillan, 2019), 59.

BIBLIOGRAPHY

Bennett, Julia. "Craft—The New Entrepreneurship?" In *Craft Entrepreneurship*, edited by Annette Naudin and Karen Patel. London: Rowman & Littlefield International, 2020.

Cvetković, Marina. "Zanati u Pirotu i okolini." *Zbornik Etnografskoj muzeja* 74, no. 1 (2010): 173–234.

Đunisavljević, Radomir. *Osnivanje industrijskih preduzeća i razvoj industrija u Srbiji do 1918. godine*. Beograd: Beogradski idavačko-grafički zavod, 1988.

Đurkovic, Miša. "Odnos kulturne politike prema narodnoj kulturi u Srbiji." *Sociološki pregled* 45 (9–12), no. 4 (2011): 561–74.

Giuliano, Lucia. "Design and Crafts: The Practitioners' View." In *A Cultural Economic Analysis of Craft*, edited by Mignosa Anna and Kotipalli Priyatej, 245–56. London: Palgrave Macmillan, 2019.

Hirsch, Paul. "Cultural Industries Revisited." *Organization Science* 11, no. 3 (2000): 356–61, 2000.

Horvat, Branko. *Privredni sistem i ekonomska politika.* Beograd: Institut ekonomskih nauka, 1970.

Johnson, Victoria. "What Is Organizational Imprinting? Cultural Entrepreneurship in the Founding of the Paris Opera." *American Journal of Sociology* 113, no. 1 (2017): 97–127.

Jovanović, Borisav. *Old Crafts in Pirot and Neighborhood.* Pirot: National Library, 2012.

Kotipalli, Priyatej. "Making Sense of Craft Using Cultural Economics." In *A Cultural Economic Analysis of Craft*, edited by Mignosa Anna and Priyatej Kotipalli, 39–50. London: Palgrave Macmillan, 2019.

LIBEK. *Istraživanje: Preduzetnička kultura kod mladih.* Beograd: LIBEK, 2015. accessed May 1, 2019, https://libek.org.rs/uploads/files/1430826083.O7D72SKz VROwm9KG.pdf.

Luckman, Susan. *Craft and the Creative Economy.* New York: Palgrave Macmillan, 2015.

Markov, Svetlana. "Ženska radna snaga i razvoj sela." *Zbornik matice srpske za društvene nauke* br. 90 (1991): 139–47.

Mignosa, Anna. "Policies for Crafts: Rationale and Tools." In *A Cultural Economic Analysis of Craft*, edited by Mignosa Anna and Priyatej Kotipalli, 51–60. Cham: Palgrave Macmillan, 2019.

Mignosa, Anna, and Priyatej Kotipalli, eds. *A Cultural Economic Analysis of Craft.* Cham: Palgrave Macmillan, 2019.

Mikić, Hristina. "Economic Freedom and Entrepreneurship in Culture." *Kultura* no. 160 (2018): 234–51.

——. *Kreativno preduzetništvo: teorija i praksa.* Beograd: Grupa za kreativnu eko-nomiju, 2017.

——. *Measuring Economic Contribution of Cultural Industries: Review and Assess-ment of Methodological Approaches.* Montreal: UNESCO-Institute for Statistics, 2012.

——. "Razvoj kreativnih industrija u Srbiji: mogućnosti i ograničenja." *Ekonomski vidici* 2–3 (2016): 101–16.

——. "Rural Sustainable Innovation and Creative Industries: Case Study of Rural Tourism Households in Pirot, Serbia." In *Management of Sustainable Innovation*, edited by Vanessa Ratten, Marcela Ramirez-Pasillas, and Hans Lundberg. London: Routledge, 2019.

Mikić, Hristina, and Estela Radonjić-Živkov. *Privreda Paraćina: od mlina do savremene industrije.* Paraćin: Zavičajni muzej Paraćin & Institut za kreativno preduzetništvo i inovacije, 2018.

Ministry of Economy. "Regulation on Classification of Professions That Are Considered as an Old and Artistic Crafts and Cottage Industry." *Official Gazette* no. 56/2012.

Pret, Tobias, and Aviel Cogan. "Artisan Entrepreneurship: A Systematic Literature Review and Research Agenda." *International Journal of Entrepreneurial Behavior and Research* 25, no. 4 (2019): 592–614.

Protić, Ljubiša. *Razvitak industrije i promet dobara u Srbiji za vreme prve vlade Kneza Miloša*. Beograd: RAD, 1953.

Ratten, Vanessa and Joao Ferreira. "Future Research Direction for Cultural Entrepreneurship and Regional Innovation," *International Journal of Entrepreneurship and Innovation* 21, no. 3 (2017): 163–69.

Stojković, Dragana. *Stari zanati—Nematerijalno kulturno nasleđe Lužnice u borbi za opstanak*, Babušnica: Opština Babušnica, 2015.

UNIDO. *Creative Industries and Micro and Small Scale Enterprise Development*. Vienna: UNIDO, 2010.

USAID. *Global Market Assessment for Handicrafts*. USAID, 2006.

Vučo, Nikola. *Raspadanje esnafa u Srbiji I*. Beograd: Naučna knjiga, 1954.

Chapter Four

Smoothing Out the Peaks and Troughs

Examining the Sustainability Strategies of Island-Based Craft Entrepreneurs

Katherine Champion[1]

This chapter takes as its focus an exploration of the everyday experiences of craft workers in island geographies and how they adapt and manage their activities in distinct, informal and, arguably, entrepreneurial ways. As argued by Annette Naudin, in part two of this book, exploration of the everyday practices of craft workers allows for a more nuanced examination that takes account of some of the contradictions and complexities associated with a conceptualisation of craft entrepreneurship. The chapter draws on a research project aimed at developing a better understanding of contemporary cultural work within geographical contexts considered to be rural and remote. In particular, it contributes to knowledge regarding the factors that support sustainable careers in cultural work in such locations. Focusing on craft entrepreneurs active in the Northern Isles of Scotland, this chapter examines some of the specific challenges and complexities they faced and explores the techniques they have adopted in an effort to reduce their precarious status.

This chapter first introduces the context of non-urban craft enterprise before outlining the methods used in the project. It then explores some of the views of interviewees regarding the challenges they faced linked to the nature of work in the craft sector and to the particular island context within which they were operating. It goes on to examine some of the resourceful techniques and strategies which craft entrepreneurs have employed in order to mitigate such issues. Finally, it reflects on whether such practices might contribute to a distinctive conception of craft entrepreneurship in non-urban locations with unique modes of developing, organising and sustaining craft enterprise beyond the city.

Studies of cultural and creative production have tended to focus on larger cities, either iconic global centres of production or reinvented postindustrial powerhouses. There has been a tendency to overlook and even denigrate the non-urban creative economy, with the lived experience of craft work in rural and remote settings often dissonant with the dominant policy and advocacy discourses associated with the creative economy.[2] Despite this, the effects of a buoyant creative and craft sector in rural areas have been articulated in a range of reports.[3] Identified benefits include enhancing cultural tourism, supporting retail and experience economies, fostering skills development, contributing to community resilience, building cultural capital, diversifying land-based economies, place-making, providing new uses for local waste materials and more.[4] There is also a growing body of academic work which looks beyond "inner-city agglomeration and bohemia"[5] and tries to redress urban bias.[6] Nonetheless, given the heterogeneous nature of "local" creative production, it has been argued that the "smaller-scale creative world of rural, regional and remote cultural work and the affordances of rural as distinct from urban spaces remain largely off the map of creative industries thinking."[7]

The craft sector has historically had a lower profile within the UK creative industries policy agenda than other subsectors of the cultural and creative industries, despite recent re-imaging with the sector's appealing associations with small-scale and micro, artisanal, handmade and with agendas of emancipation, environmental sustainability and locally rooted ethical production and consumption.[8] There are established challenges in the measurement of the craft sector linked to the nature of the work, with more than three-quarters of craft workers undertaking portfolio careers and with high proportions of self-employment.[9] Despite research commissioned by the Crafts Council[10] seeking to more fully account for the economic contribution of crafts—by expanding the estimates to a wider definition that includes microbusinesses and "embedded" workers—the DCMS have acknowledged that their calculations significantly underestimate the scale of the sector in the UK and even suggested that craft be removed as a subsector from the listings of the UK creative industries in 2013.[11] Furthering the challenges of defining and measuring the sector, traditional portrayals of craft work have frequently been pejorative with associations of amateur or hobbyist production. In part, this is linked to the gendered associations with "women's work" and the commonly domestic setting of such production which has historically particularly affected perceptions of textiles and fibre-focused crafts.[12] Despite a critique of this and feminist recuperations of traditional craft techniques,[13] there remains a long-standing obfuscation of the role of craft to the economy and, as I will argue, also to the sustainability and survival of livelihoods and places.

METHOD

The research adopts a case study approach and focuses on the Northern Isles of Scotland, an archipelago consisting of two main island groups: Shetland and Orkney, with a total of twenty-six inhabited islands. The collective population of each island group is similar with Shetland's recorded population of 22,990 and Orkney's 22,190 in 2018.[14] Traditionally the island economies have been reliant on agriculture (Orkney) and fishing and oil (Shetland) and, more recently, tourism constitutes an important income for the islands. Both island groups have a rich history of craft work including the internationally recognized traditions of Orkney chair making and Fair Isle knitting and lace making in Shetland.[15] In both islands, a renaissance in craft production and the craft zeitgeist[16] could be seen to be driving high engagement with the work of the interviewees and was associated with a recent rise in visitors linked to craft tourism, for example, travelling on tours specifically catering this market or visiting craft events, exhibitions, shops, museums, and workshops. The Highlands and Islands of Scotland do, however, face particular innovation challenges, including dispersed working communities and the attendant lack of infrastructure of the region which has been seen as limiting opportunities across the creative economy.[17]

As part of the research project, a total of twelve craft entrepreneurs were interviewed from across the Northern Isles over a period of nine months from July 2017, with five interviews in Shetland and seven in Orkney. In terms of the gender balance of the interviewees, eleven were female and one was male. In line with some of the other contributors to this edited book, the term craft entrepreneurs is applied to the self-employed craft workers who participated in the study. While it is not necessarily a term they would self-apply due to the highly gendered conceptions and stereotypes of the lone, risk-taking entrepreneur,[18] I will argue in this chapter that the resourceful strategies the craft workers were engaged in, possess key tenets of entrepreneurialism. They were drawn from a range of craft activities, including knitting and textiles design, jewellery making, print making and furniture making. Initial participants were drawn from existing contacts in the region developed from past research and knowledge exchange projects undertaken in the Highlands and Islands of Scotland.[19] Following this, sampling was driven by further recommendations from interviewees and colleagues as well as snowballing from one interview to the next. The location of the interviews varied, with some participants interviewed in their place of work (including studio spaces, shops, and arts and cultural organisations) and others in cafes. One interview was conducted via Skype. In Shetland most of the interviews took place in and around Lerwick, and in Orkney mostly in and around Stromness and Kirkwall, with two in Dounby and one on Stronsay. All but one of the interviews took place on the mainlands of Shetland and Orkney, so, while a couple of the participants had experience of living or working on the more dispersed islands of the archipelago, most spoke to experiences of living on the mainlands of the islands.

THE CONSTRAINTS OF
ISLAND-BASED CRAFT WORK

This section outlines a number of the key issues experienced by the craft workers in this study. These included the high costs of island life and lack of attendant infrastructure and creative workspace alongside factors fairly universal to the craft sector—albeit exacerbated by the complex geography—such as how craft work is valued and catering for a tourist market. A common issue dominating the interviews was the precariousness of the income derived from craft work and a common need for the craft workers to supplement this with more financially sustainable activities.

These precarious patterns of work are far from limited to non-urban locations, but in an island location they were exacerbated by the significant peaks and troughs noted by the craft workers and largely driven by seasonality and tourist flows. Many of the interviewees had locally focused markets and therefore there were limitations to the number of customers they could reach at any time. Moreover, if these customers were tourists, they were further constrained by seasonality which was felt acutely by the island-based interviewees. In addition to the impact on the reliability of transport in travelling off the islands in bad weather through the winter months, many of the interviewees were particularly reliant on the tourist market, including the big influx of cruise liner visitors who visited during the summer months. The islands have recently been experiencing a boom related to cruise-ship visitors with, for example, Orkney seeing a 160 percent increase in such visitors in the five-year period from 2011 to 95,750 in 2016.[20]

The peripheral location of the Northern Isles also had implications for the craft entrepreneurs who wanted to develop external markets. Issues included the challenges of investing in equipment (there was not the option to hire expensive kit), self-training (due to a lack of access to education and training provision), and working from home (because of a lack of affordable and accessible workspaces). For those who had to travel (e.g., those attending trade fairs to generate orders for craft or textiles work), the high costs and time associated with living on an island were a major issue:

I think travel is the biggest one for me. Mainly because at certain times of the year the weather's not great so you've got to be on the ball but also Flybe were causing a lot of problems as were Loganair so flights weren't as reliable and rather than going down and back in a day or overnight then you had to take a day either side to make sure that you definitely got there and you know I travel up and down quite a lot for different events. (textiles designer, Orkney)

Similarly interviewees outlined the high additional costs for carriage of raw materials and equipment as well as shipping finished products to customers. For example, a Shetland-based designer and illustrator noted that it cost £90 to have a vinyl cutter delivered to her as compared to £20 on the mainland. This additional cost either had to be added to the price of products or had to be absorbed by the individual practitioner. A furniture maker who imported wood predominantly from the central belt of Scotland explained, "shipping the wood up here adds a lot of money on to the [sale] price." For the customers purchasing his furniture from outside Orkney, this meant that he then had to add further shipping costs as he described: "it costs them £100/£200/£300 more than the price so it makes it quite expensive" (furniture maker, Orkney).

Nearly all of the interviewees articulated challenges in finding appropriate and affordable creative workspaces on the islands. If they had managed to access space, it was often not flexible in meeting the requirements of their creative work, for example, in allowing them to grow or reduce the size of their business easily. As a textiles designer in Orkney explained, "I moved into Kirkwall and I only had a small workroom there but there was just me at that stage," and went on to describe how she moved into a shop which had "a very small back room which was more a stock room" and how her intern "had to do a lot of work in the back cupboard of the shop." Looking back she admitted, "I don't know how we survived that stage." Without purpose-built creative space, some interviewees missed opportunities to scale up or host events, but there was a continuous need to balance the risks of investing in workspace with the needs of the business.

There were also common issues with how creative work was valued, partly related to serving local markets. The issue of undervaluing creative work is not peculiar to the islands, but the craft sector in the Northern Isles is heavily dominated by microbusinesses. There has also been a long-standing obscuring of the role that craft plays in contributing to economic production linked to the levels of informal labour, the highly gendered undertaking of such work and its often domestic setting.[21] Within the craft sector, the preponderance of so-called hobbyists coupled with the tourist market was, in some cases, seen as further driving down the pricing structures and the value that could be leveraged for creative products. As Susan Luckman notes, a strong amateur craft scene particularly in rural areas has contributed to the stereotyping of the sector and made it difficult for "professional" practitioners to have their skill and artistic contributions recognised.[22] This was very resonant within the interviews, especially among the textiles-based craft practitioners, where what could be charged for a product rarely correlated with the time and skills needed to produce it:

> I don't really sell very much but if I'm asked to knit a jumper I'm trying to think how many hours it's going to take me and even when I multiply the hours, if I put a living wage on it nobody would ever [buy it] . . . so it's not even the minimum wage. (textiles designer 2, Shetland)

Most of the interviewees struggled to survive solely on income derived from their main creative practice and undertook "protean" work with "a portfolio of multiple simultaneous or overlapping employment arrangements."[23] In line with the sense of "scavenging for opportunities" found in Annette Naudin's study, the interviewees recounted having to supplement their activities with other work, in some cases this was linked to their practice but often outside of it, including cleaning and shop work:

> I am employed in two part-time cleaning jobs to help pay the bills. I selected this type of employment due to its flexibility and the lack of stress. I am then able to focus on my craft practice for at least five hours per day. (printmaker and illustrator, Shetland)

The pressure of the challenges outlined in the previous section heightened a sense of risk among practitioners. As Susan Luckman[24] warns in her work on craft micro-enterprises, increasing individualisation of responsibility for creating employment opportunities has led to risk commonly being borne by individual workers rather than by the state. When this is further extended to the exacerbated levels of risk experienced by those practitioners based in challenging geographies, it has worrying implications for the sustainability of their livelihoods, but also indicates that very resourceful strategies would be necessary in order to ameliorate them. Further to this, the interviews suggest a significant role for place in shaping the organisation of work practices. As Luckman previously argued in her seminal work on rural cultural workers,[25] the affective relationship between place and creative practice has often been ignored in policy and academia. As she suggests,[26] geographic, climactic, historical and cultural affordances and characteristics shape the nature of the work within places. Annette Naudin also emphasises the significance of place and argues that the embedded nature of cultural work drives a particular type of entrepreneurialism and enterprise among such workers, enabling them "to shape and organise their work, despite structural confines."[27]

SURVIVAL TECHNIQUES: THE STRATEGIES ADOPTED BY CRAFT WORKERS TO MAKE A LIVING

This section describes some of the tactics employed by the interviewees in mitigating the issues they faced making a living via their craft practice within an island context. It then goes on to begin reflecting on how the nature and characteristics of the strategies adopted could be interpreted as a distinct mode of craft entrepreneurialism.

NEGOTIATING COMPLEX PORTFOLIO WORKING

Several interviewees had reached a degree of balance in their portfolio of work with gaps in income from their craft work addressed by work linked to their practice, including employment in arts and tourism agencies, craft shops, a textiles business and educational institutions. To supplement her craft work, one textiles designer worked part time within a related retail business (a wool shop) and this offered her sustainability as she noted that she "wouldn't make enough money off my own stuff" and "so having a steady job here that is still connected to what I am interested in is very important" (textiles designer 1, Shetland). Although she wished she had more time for her own work, she reported that the lines between her day job and her own creative work were "blurred." For example, the shop allowed her to network within the textiles sector and among visitors with an interest in craft. She described how she felt like she was "networking more than a lot of other people might realise" which offset some of the isolation of being self-employed which could "be quite lonely." As found among the craftswomen interviewed by Annette Naudin elsewhere in this book, there was also considerable diversification and reinvention, with craft practitioners offering teaching, training and workshops as a more reliable source of income than solely selling their creative products. As a craft maker who offered workshops to visitors describes: "They're coming to buy, but they're mostly coming to buy yarn and—because they're makers so . . . I can easier sell a workshop to make something . . . rather than I can sell the actual item" (jeweller and lacemaker, Shetland). This responsiveness to the limitations of the local market and to a willingness to experiment with opportunities seen to offer greater sustainability, demonstrates a high degree of agility and flexibility which could be interpreted as entrepreneurial.

Among many of the interviewees, who were predominantly women, there was also consideration of balancing childcare responsibilities at different stages of their life and career. A trend of "down-shifting" into creative enterprise upon having children has been identified,[28] and this was the case for a number of the female craft workers who had seen ways they could make a modest income through craft work whilst also managing caring responsibilities. One textiles practitioner and shop owner in Orkney (2) described initially making "pin money" through dressmaking and alterations when her children were small, while another saw the potential in her craft practice to be become something that she "could create and sell" which "coincided with . . . starting a family too," so she "combined the two and became self-employed" (jeweller and lacemaker, Shetland). Carol Ekinsmyth describes "the spatio-temporal restrictions" that lead mumpreneurs "to structure, organise and embed their businesses within family-friendly time-space routines,"[29] and there was certainly evidence of this among the interviewees. However, the extreme precariousness experienced by respondents of managing layered barriers of insecure, low-paid work, challenging geographies and caring responsibilities were sometimes too difficult to bear and led one of them to note, "I always have on eye on the Shetland Times looking for a job to be honest" (jeweller and lacemaker, Shetland). This echoes the precarious and uneasy balancing found among the craftswomen interviewed in Annette Naudin's chapter, and the sacrifices they made on all fronts—at home, in relation to their craft practice and in job security—to negotiate a craft career.

MITIGATING DISTANCE WITH ONLINE

Another strategy adopted by the craft entrepreneurs to mitigate the issues of island-based working was the use of online platforms to reach new customers, widen markets and build profile. As an Orkney-based furniture maker outlined:

> It's such a help for small craft businesses as well you know you make a design and you put it on your social media and people at the other side of the world see it right away. I started 20 years ago, my boss didn't even have a website it's just so much easier I think for crafts makers these days to get out there and get noticed whereas when I started 20 years ago you were solely reliant on mainly on locals and tourists you know visiting the workshop in the summertime and try and get enough orders to keep you going to the next tourist season. It's not like that anymore. (furniture maker, Orkney)

Capitalising on the "international marketing and distribution pathways enabled by the 'long tail' of internet distribution" has been identified as a trend within the contemporary handmade economy.[30] Online platforms can serve to reduce the distance to consumers, arguably globalising the micro-creative economy and thereby creating new intersections between the local and global.[31] Online connectivity has been further argued to form the basic conditions of survival for rural creative workers.[32]

The craft entrepreneurs were, on the whole, heavily engaged in social media and online platforms for raising the profile of their work, reaching new markets and collaborating. Online blogs, Instagram, Ravelry, Esty and Facebook were commonly used, and the respondents noted that "social media . . . [has] made a big difference to the knitting world" (textiles designer 1, Shetland). Another explained, "on my blog I am getting about 10,000 views a month . . . I don't think I could do any of that without social media" (textiles designer 2, Shetland). The interviewees most heavily engaged in social media, and crafted online images of the personal backstory of their creative practice and the unique geography they were operating from in order to help build an audience for their work. For those adept at using such platforms, there had been significant success and their dexterous use of social media allowed them to innovate their practice. For example, one interviewee explained how she trialled new designs on Instagram to get immediate feedback, saying, "We've just started launching new colours and new products and you get to see people's reaction to those through social media" (textiles designer, Orkney).

A couple of interviewees identified issues with knowing how best to develop their social media presence and, in particular, tensions with the disconnect between a strong social media profile and translating this into sales generation. An additional issue was raised related to the deeply material nature of craft practice, with a textiles designer from Shetland saying, "Something tactile like wool then you really need people to feel the product" (textile designer, Shetland). While the internet can decentre distribution, previous research[33] has found that due to the materiality of craft practice it can be difficult for makers to sell online except to tourists who have already visited studios, workshops, and galleries in person.

Temporal Hubs: Working Seasonally and Capitalising on the Visitor Population

While online platforms fulfilled a number of important roles for many of the craft respondents, temporary events provided an important mechanism for business generation and networking. Both islands have a plethora of festivals and events, some of which are very high profile such as Wool Week, Up-Helly-Aa held in Shetland, or the International St Magnus Festival in Orkney. In Shetland interviewees were keen to mention Wool Week, a ten-year-old, nine-day series of events and workshops, which takes place across the islands every September bringing a global profile of visitors. For a textiles designer it brought high-profile visitors from the craft world to network with: "there are quite a lot of people who are big hand-knit designers so networking-wise you meet a lot of people and form relationships with people who are quite important" (textiles designer 1, Shetland). As the same interviewee went on to explain, before the introduction of this annual event, September would have been "a period that would traditionally have been your quietest time of year, (but) is now our busiest time of year."

While the influx of cruise-ship visitors has not been universally welcomed by island businesses, a number of the interviewees had very much tailored an offer to these tourists and were seeing significant gains:

> We . . . actually set up a stand at the harbour (to sell textiles goods) when some of the ships were in . . . we were astounded and I started to realise that you know we travelled to find markets but there's an international market on our doorstep you know, 3 or 4 times a week from March till September . . . we also realised from that market was that the initial purchases that were made, we were then having return purchases via the website. (textile designer and shop owner 2, Orkney)

Here the repeat and ongoing online purchases also contributed to business sustainability outside of the main visitor season. Other interviewees noted how they planned their activities around the seasonal lulls and busy spells that they were able to predict:

> You do have the quiet winter months that you can build up your stock. Well, except from when you're doing wholesale because that's not the same, but just in terms of running the shop, you do have January, February, March . . . to work on stock, and it gradually picks up. So it's not like opening a door on it and it's bang, it's happening! It's emm—and then you get, around about Easter time you get a busy couple of weeks and then you get a rest again after it. (textiles designer and shop owner 2, Orkney)

INVESTING IN PHYSICAL SPACES

In response to problems accessing creative workspaces, many of the craft entrepreneurs worked from home and some had invested considerably in developing workshops and studios within their own homes. Often this was linked to their families having extra space on their farms and rural dwellings on which they could capitalise on this. For example, in the case of an Orkney-based furniture maker, by initially converting a garage and then a derelict building on the family farm into a workshop. Similarly, a textiles designer and shop owner in Orkney (1) described converting family premises into a workshop and later into a shop and exhibition space.

In a number of cases, to address shortcomings in the availability of creative workspace, some interviewees had invested considerable time and energy in developing retail outlets, craft centres and studios offering various commercial and supporting opportunities to their fellow craft workers. There was a significant bearing of economic risk in developing and delivering a collective creative workspace as well as taking on the administrative and "non-creative" work associated with it. The interviewees who had engaged in such activities experienced some frustrations in not getting the opportunity anymore to spend as much time carrying out their practice. The owner of a craft hub in Orkney reflected on feeling "trapped," torn between delivering the cooking and baking in the café while wanting to be "in [her] craft room."

The branching out into the provision of creative space is not something necessarily peculiar to a non-urban setting. Instrumentalism of cultural policy means that cultural entrepreneurs are often involved in ensuring the sustainability of arts and community-based organisations and projects with social, cultural and economic development remits. There was, however, a particularly acute sense among the island-based craft entrepreneurs of the need to invest in the sustainability and survival of their communities. As the same interviewee described, "when you come from a very small place then you have a lot of other commitments to the community and you do find yourself sometimes being spread a bit thin because the community needs to survive with your input as well." As Annette Naudin outlines when defining the cultural entrepreneur, despite often being committed and ambitious, the end goal for such individuals is rarely commercial success.[34] There was certainly evidence among the practitioners of a strong sense of community and relationship to place which has associations with tenets of social entrepreneurship.

CONCLUSION

The findings reported in this chapter highlight some material differences in the challenges faced by the craft workers that result from their island context. Commonalities around the precarious nature of work could be drawn with the wider sector, but were temporally and geographically accentuated with the seasonal aspects of work in the archipelagos, the role of tourism and the high costs of island life. As a corollary of these conditions, the craft entrepreneurs employed quite specific entrepreneurial techniques which were responsive to their embedded, context-driven circumstances. This included a complex balancing of multiple employment, community, family and creative roles, both paid and unpaid. Where this balancing act seemed to work most successfully and strategically in the eyes of the interviewees, these additional roles were linked to their creative practice. Online presences and events-based activities offered further opportunities seized by interviewees to offset seasonal lulls and mitigate issues with distance. In relation to her mumpreneurs, Carol Ekinsmyth[35] talks about how "socio-spatial confines" can "encourage a level of creativity that can bring about new, innovative business practices and forms," and there was clear evidence that the constraints of island life had led to creative responses among the craft practitioners.

The accounts of the interviewees also, however, illuminated how practitioners absorbed very high levels of risk within this balancing act. High levels of individual risk-taking were undertaken not solely with their own livelihoods in mind, but also with a commitment to the sustainability of the places where they lived and their communities. This suggests a tension with some of the dominant focus on individualism and mobility associated with conceptualisations of entrepreneurialism in the creative economy and a more close linkage to tenets of social entrepreneurialism. There was also a significant blurring of boundaries around home and work which was not limited to those with childcare responsibilities—although here it was arguably heightened. Resonant with the work of Susan Luckman, the high levels of homeworking contributed to "additionally collapsing the already porous relationship between work and other aspects of life."[36]

Islands are often denied centrality and characterised as peripheral, but as this chapter has shown, lessons can be generated about how island-based craft workers adapt, mitigate and manage their work in distinct and often informal ways. These lessons are relevant to conceptualisations of the entrepreneurialism of cultural workers in island and rural locations and also their mainland and urban counterparts. Similarly the craft sector is also often overlooked by policy and academia and, at first glance, seems dissonant with mainstream understandings of entrepreneurship. In bringing to light some of the "hidden"[37] activities of craft practitioners through their everyday lived experiences, it is posited that distinct collaborative, relational and strongly place-based characteristics constituted a specific island-based craft entrepreneurialism. This was very fragile and precarious, however, suggesting more needs to be done to consider alternative supportive frameworks for such practitioners. As one interviewee argued:

> We need a more innovative way, a cost-effective way of supporting those very special creative processes and . . . innovative ways of providing the support that will sustain those businesses but not grow them to change . . . their essence. (craft practitioner and craft centre owner, Orkney)

NOTES

1. I would like to thank and express my gratitude to all those who generously gave up their valuable time for interviews to contribute to this project and the research funders, The Royal Society of Edinburgh, without whom this research would not have been possible.

2. Lynn-Sayers McHattie, Katherine Champion, and Michael Johnson, "Crafting the Local: The Lived Experience of Craft Production in the Northern Isles of Scotland," *Cultural Trends Special Issue Situating the Local in Global Cultural Policy* 28, no. 4 (2019): 305–16.

3. BOP Consulting, *Rural Creative Industries: Findings from the UK* (London: BOP Consulting, 2009); Sami Mahroum et al. *Rural Innovation* (London: NESTA, 2007), https://media.nesta.org.uk/documents/rural_innovation.pdf; TBR, *Measuring the Craft Economy: Defining and Measuring Craft: Report 3* (London: The Crafts Council, 2014), https://www.craftscouncil.org.uk/content/files/Measuring_the_craft _economy-v4.pdf.

4. BOP Consulting, *Rural Creative Industries*; Ann Markusen, "An Arts-Based State Rural Development Policy, Special Issue on State Rural Development Policy," *Journal of Regional Analysis and Policy* 37, no. 1 (2007): 7–10, http://www.jrap-journal.org /pastvolumes/2000/v37/F37-1-markusen.pdf; Sami Mahroum et al. "The Contribution of the Creative Economy to the Resilience of Rural Communities: Exploring Cultural and Digital Capital," *Sociologia Ruralis* 56, no. 2 (2015): 197–219; TBR, *Measuring the Craft Economy*.

5. Chris Gibson, "Introduction—Creative Geographies: Tales from the 'Margins'," in *Creativity in Peripheral Places*, ed. Chris Gibson (Abingdon: Routledge, 2013).

6. Including, but not limited to, David Bell and Mark Jayne, "The Creative Countryside: Policy and Practice in the UK Rural Cultural Economy," *Journal of Rural Studies* 26 (2010): 209–18; Kathryn A. Burnett and Lynda Harling Stalker, "'Shut Up for Five Years': Locating Narratives of Cultural Workers in Scotland's Islands," *Sociologia Ruralis* 58, no. 2 (2018): 237–469; Nicola Thomas, David Harvey, and Harriet Hawkins, "Crafting the Region: Creative Industries and Practices of Regional Space," *Regional Studies* 47, no. 1 (2015): 75–88; Susan Luckman, *Locating Cultural Work: The Politics and Poetics of Rural, Regional and Remote Creativity* (London: Palgrave Macmillan, 2012); Markusen, "An Arts-Based State Rural Development Policy" 7–10; Roberts and Townsend, "The Contribution of the Creative Economy," 197–219.

7. Luckman, *Locating Cultural Work*, 23.

8. Doreen Jakob and Nicola J. Thomas, "Firing Up Craft Capital: The Renaissance of Craft and Craft Policy in the United Kingdom," *International Journal of Cultural Policy* 23, no. 4 (2015): 495–511.

9. TBR, *Measuring the Craft Economy*.

10. TBR, *Measuring the Craft Economy*.

11. DCMS, *Classifying and Measuring the Creative Industries: Consultation on Proposed Changes* (London: DCMS, 2013).

12. Stephanie Taylor and Karen Littlejohn, *Contemporary Identities of Creativity and Creative Work* (Abingdon: Routledge, 2016): 113.

13. Lucy Lippard, "Making Something from Nothing (Toward a Definition of Women's 'Hobby Art')," 1978, *The Craft Reader*, ed. Glenn Adamson (Oxford: Berg, 2010): 483–90; Susan Luckman, "The Aura of the Analogue in a Digital Age: Women's Crafts, Creative Markets and Home-Based Labour after Etsy," *Cultural Studies Review* 19, no. 1 (2013): 249–70; Rozsika Parker, *The Subversive Stitch: Embroidery and the Making of the Feminine* (London: Women's Press, 1984).

14. National Records of Scotland, *Council Area Profiles*, 2019, accessed October 11, 2019, https://www.nrscotland.gov.uk/statistics-and-data/statistics/stats-at-a-glance/council-area-profiles.

15. EKOS, *Creative Industries in Shetland Today—Summary Report for Shetland Creative Industries Unit*, February 2008, EKOS, accessed October 11, 2019, https://c.shetlandarts.org/assets/files/5843/creative-industries-in-shetland-today-final-summary-report.pdf; Francois Matarasso, *Stories and Fables: Reflections on Culture Development in Orkney*, January 2012, accessed October 11, 2019, from https://parliamentofdreams.com/2012/01/23/stories-and-fables-culture-in-orkney/; Orkney Islands Council, *Orkney's Creative Future*, 2017, Orkney Arts Forum, accessed October 11, 2019, from https://www.orkney.gov.uk/Files/Community-Life-and-Leisure/Arts/OAF/Orkney_Arts_Development_Strategy_Print.pdf; Kirsty Scott and Maggie Marr, *Shetland Textiles Sector: A Review*, June 2012, Shetland Islands Council and Highlands and Islands Enterprise, accessed October 11, 2019, from https://www.shetland.gov.uk/economic_development/documents/ShetlandTextileReviewFinalReport.pdf.

16. As explored by Jakob and Thomas, "Firing Up Craft Capital," 495–511; Susan Luckman, *Craft and the Creative Economy* (New York: Palgrave Macmillan, 2015); Susan Luckman and Nicola Thomas, eds., *Craft Economies* (London: Bloomsbury, 2018), among others.

17. HIE, *Creative Industries Strategy 2014–2019 Highlands and Islands Enterprise*, 2013, accessed October 11, 2019, http://timeline.hie.co.uk/media/1361/creative-industries-creativeplusindustriesplusstrategy.pdf.

18. Annette Naudin, *Cultural Entrepreneurship: The Cultural Worker's Experience of Entrepreneurship* (New York: Routledge, 2018), 9.

19. Lynn-Sayers McHattie, Katherine Champion, and Cara Broadley, "Craft, Textiles and Cultural Assets: Design Innovation in the Northern Isles of Scotland," *Island Studies Journal Special Issue Textiles and Clothing* 13, no. 2 (2018): 39–54; Cara Broadley, Katherine Champion, and Lynn-Sayers McHattie, "Materiality Matters: Exploring the Use of Design Tools in Innovation Workshops with the Craft and Creative Sector in the Northern Isles of Scotland," *The Design Journal* 20 (2017); McHattie, Champion, and Johnson, "Crafting the Local."

20. Ekosgen, *Orkney Volume Tourism Management Study: Report for Orkney Islands Council and Highlands and Islands Enterprise*, 2017, accessed October 11, 2019, page 5, http://www.orkney.gov.uk/Files/Committees-and-agendas/Develop

ment%20and%20Infrastructure/DI2017/12-09-2017/I12_Appl_Volume_Tourism _Management_Study.pdf.

21. Luckman, *Craft and the Creative Economy*; McHattie, Champion, and Johnson, "Crafting the Local," 305–16.

22. Luckman, *Craft and the Creative Economy*, 51.

23. Ruth Bridgstock, "Australian Artists, Starving and Well Nourished: What Can We Learn from the Prototypical Protean Career?" *Australian Journal of Career Development* 14 no. 3 (2005): 42.

24. Luckman, *Craft and the Creative Economy*, 136.

25. Luckman, *Locating Cultural Work*, 5.

26. Luckman, *Locating Cultural Work*, 4.

27. Naudin, *Cultural Entrepreneurship*, 39.

28. Luckman, *Craft and the Creative Economy*, 106.

29. Carol Ekinsmyth, "Mothers' Business, Work/Life and the Politics of 'Mumpreneurship'," *Gender, Place and Culture* 21, no. 10 (2014): 1234.

30. Luckman, *Craft and the Creative Economy*, 1.

31. Luckman, *Craft and the Creative Economy*.

32. Alistair R. Anderson, Claire Wallace, and Leanne Townsend, "Great Expectations or a Small Country Living?" *Sociologica Ruralis* 56 (2016): 450–68.

33. Luckman, *Locating Cultural Work*, 158–59.

34. Naudin, *Cultural Entrepreneurship*.

35. Ekinsmyth, "Mothers' Business, Work/Life," 1242.

36. Susan Luckman, "Women's Micro-Entrepreneurial Homeworking," *Australian Feminist Studies* 30, no. 84 (2015): 147.

37. Naudin, *Cultural Entrepreneurship*, 166.

BIBLIOGRAPHY

Anderson, Alistair, R., Claire Wallace, and Leanne Townsend. "Great Expectations or a Small Country Living?" *Sociologica Ruralis* 56 (2016): 450–68, https://doi .org/10.1111/soru.12104.

Bell, David, and Mark Jayne. "The Creative Countryside: Policy and Practice in the UK Rural Cultural Economy," *Journal of Rural Studies* 26 (2010): 209–218, DOI: https://doi.org/10.1016/j.jrurstud.2010.01.001.

BOP Consulting. *Rural Creative Industries: Findings from the UK* (London: BOP Consulting, 2009).

Bridgstock, Ruth. "Australian Artists, Starving and Well Nourished: What Can We Learn from the Prototypical Protean Career?" *Australian Journal of Career Development* 14, no. 3 (2005): 40–48, DOI: https://doi.org/10.1177/103841620501400307.

Broadley Cara, Katherine Champion, and Lynn-Sayers McHattie. "Materiality Matters: Exploring the Use of Design Tools in Innovation Workshops with the Craft and Creative Sector in the Northern Isles of Scotland." *The Design Journal*, 20 (2017).

Burnett, Kathryn A., and Lynda Harling Stalker. "'Shut Up for Five Years': Locating Narratives of Cultural Workers in Scotland's Islands," *Sociologia Ruralis* 58, no. 2 (2018): 237–469, DOI: https://doi.org/10.1111/soru.12137.

DCMS. *Classifying and Measuring the Creative Industries: Consultation on Proposed Changes.* London, DCMS, 2013.

Ekinsmyth, Carol. "Challenging the Boundaries of Entrepreneurship: The Spatialities and Practices of UK 'Mumpreneurs'," *Geoforum* 42 no. 1 (2011): 104–14, 10.1016/j.geoforum.2010.10.005.

———. "Mothers' Business, Work/Life and the Politics of 'Mumpreneurship'," *Gender, Place and Culture* 21, no. 10 (2014): 1230–48, DOI: 10.1080/0966369X.2013.817975.

EKOS. "Creative Industries in Shetland Today—Summary Report for Shetland Creative Industries Unit," February 2008, EKOS, accessed October 11, 2019, https://c.shetlandarts.org/assets/files/5843/creative-industries-in-shetland-today -final-summary-report.pdf.

Ekosgen. "Orkney Volume Tourism Management Study: Report for Orkney Islands Council and Highlands and Islands Enterprise," 2017, accessed October 11, 2019, http://www.orkney.gov.uk/Files/Committees-and-agendas/Development%20 and%20Infrastructure/DI2017/12-09-2017/I12_App1_Volume_Tourism_Manage ment_Study.pdf.

Gibson, Chris, ed. *Creativity in Peripheral Places.* Abingdon: Routledge, 2013.

HIE. "Creative Industries Strategy 2014–2019 Highlands and Islands Enterprise," 2013, accessed October 11, 2019, from http://timeline.hie.co.uk/media/1361/ creative-industries-creativeplusindustriesplusstrategy.pdf.

Jakob, Doreen, and Nicola J. Thomas. "Firing Up Craft Capital: The Renaissance of Craft and Craft Policy in the United Kingdom," *International Journal of Cultural Policy* 23, no. 4 (2015): 495–511, https://doi.org/10.1080/10286632.2015.1068765.

Lippard, Lucy. "Making Something from Nothing (Toward a Definition of Women's 'Hobby Art')." (1978) In *The Craft Reader*, ed. Glenn Adamson, 483–90 (Oxford: Berg, 2010).

Luckman, Susan. "The Aura of the Analogue in a Digital Age: Women's Crafts, Creative Markets and Home-Based Labour after Etsy," *Cultural Studies Review* 19, no. 1 (2013): 249–70, DOI: https://doi.org/10.5130/csr.v19i1.2585.

———. *Craft and the Creative Economy.* New York: Palgrave Macmillan. 2015.

———. *Locating Cultural Work: The Politics and Poetics of Rural, Regional and Remote Creativity.* London: Palgrave Macmillan, 2012.

———. "Women's Micro-Entrepreneurial Homeworking," *Australian Feminist Studies* 30, no. 84 (2015): 146–60, DOI: 10.1080/08164649.2015.1038117.

Luckman, Susan, and Nicola Thomas, eds. *Craft Economies.* London: Bloomsbury, 2018.

Mahroum, Sami, Jane Atterton, Neil Ward, Allan M. Williams, Richard Naylor, Rob Hindle, and Frances Rowe. *Rural Innovation.* London: NESTA, 2007, https://me dia.nesta.org.uk/documents/rural_innovation.pdf.

Markusen, Ann. "An Arts-Based State Rural Development Policy, Special Issue on State Rural Development Policy," *Journal of Regional Analysis and Policy*

37, no. 1 (2007): 7–10, http://www.jrap-journal.org/pastvolumes/2000/v37/F37-1-markusen.pdf.

Matarasso, Francois. *Stories and Fables: Reflections on Culture Development in Orkney.* January 2012, accessed October 11, 2019, https://parliamentofdreams.com/2012/01/23/stories-and-fables-culture-in-orkney/.

McHattie, Lynn-Sayers, Katherine Champion, and Michael Johnson. "Crafting the Local: The Lived Experience of Craft Production in the Northern Isles of Scotland." *Cultural Trends* 28 no. 4 (2019): 305–16, DOI: 10.1080/09548963.2019.1644791.

National Records of Scotland. *Council Area Profiles*, 2019, accessed October 11, 2019, https://www.nrscotland.gov.uk/statistics-and-data/statistics/stats-at-a-glance/council-area-profiles.

Naudin, Annette. *Cultural Entrepreneurship: The Cultural Worker's Experience of Entrepreneurship.* New York: Routledge, 2018.

Orkney Islands Council. "Orkney's Creative Future." 2017, Orkney Arts Forum, accessed October 11, 2019, https://www.orkney.gov.uk/Files/Community-Life-and-Leisure/Arts/OAF/Orkney_Arts_Development_Strategy_Print.pdf.

Parker, Rozsika. *The Subversive Stitch: Embroidery and the Making of the Feminine.* London: Women's Press, 1984.

Roberts, Elizabeth, and Leanne Townsend. "The Contribution of the Creative Economy to the Resilience of Rural Communities: Exploring Cultural and Digital Capital." *Sociologia Ruralis* 56, no. 2 (2015): 197–219, https://doi.org/10.1111/soru.12075.

Scott, Kirsty, and Maggie Marr. "Shetland Textiles Sector: A Review." June 2012, Shetland Islands Council and Highlands and Islands Enterprise, accessed October 11, 2019, https://www.shetland.gov.uk/economic_development/documents/ShetlandTextileReviewFinalReport.pdf.

Taylor, Stephanie, and Karen Littlejohn. *Contemporary Identities of Creativity and Creative Work.* Abingdon: Routledge, 2016.

TBR. "Measuring the Craft Economy: Defining and Measuring Craft: Report 3." London: The Crafts Council, 2014, https://www.craftscouncil.org.uk/content/files/Measuring_the_craft_economy-v4.pdf.

Thomas, Nicola, David Harvey, and Harriet Hawkins. "Crafting the Region: Creative Industries and Practices of Regional Space." *Regional Studies* 47, no. 1 (2015): 75–88, DOI: https://doi.org/10.1080/00343404.2012.709931.

Chapter Five

Far Out Craft

Andrea Peach

In 1963, on the northernmost coast of the Scottish mainland, Sutherland County Council purchased a disused airbase from the Ministry of Defence. It consisted of a series of derelict, flat-roofed buildings, deemed uninhabitable due to their lack of insulation and basic utilities. Nevertheless, the Council had a vision: to create a thriving community of craftspeople that would address years of depopulation and economic decline in the area. They called it "The Far North Project." A singularly utopian vision, it attracted entrepreneurs and idealists from across the country and abroad.

Many of the Far North Project pioneers were not professionally trained makers, nor were they Scottish. But they received encouragement in terms of generous grants and loans from a variety of Scottish government policies to live their dream. The community reached its height in the counterculture hey days of the late 1960s and early 1970s. For the Far North pioneers however, reality was often far from the dream. Although the project presented an opportunity for adventurous artisans, many hoping to escape from the rat race were quickly disillusioned, and few remained at the village for long.

Still in existence, what is now known as the Balnakeil Craft Village provides an interesting case study of the role government plays in supporting craft communities and encouraging entrepreneurship. In particular, it highlights the relationship between national development strategy and economic sustainability in remote locations, and the subsequent impact of those factors on a maker's desire for creative autonomy. This chapter examines the early years of the Far North Project and draws on archival research from the Highlands and Islands Development Board, oral history interviews, and a 1974 BBC documentary about the Far North Project. It will analyse what attracted these opportunists and idealists from across the country and abroad, and consider how they engaged with the government's policies to link craft with economic regeneration.

THE BRITISH CRAFT REVIVAL

The 1960s and 1970s were a period of considerable reinvention and revival for the crafts across Britain and the Western world.[1] This was a time when the predominant vision for craft was young, contemporary, colourful and conceptual, with a desire to break away from past associations with tradition and function. Its makers included art school graduates with professional aspirations, producing unique one-off objects, or "studio" craft, displayed in gallery settings and commanding high prices. Sharing points of communality with the previous century's arts and crafts movement, and the current revival of interest in craft,[2] this period of craft renaissance gave rise to a new generation of craftspeople and crafts businesses. Not only was there a collective public desire to return to "making," there was also considerable support by way of government funding to promote such activities. Newly created government organizations and their policies played a crucial role in defining and shaping craft as both object and concept at this time.

The best known of these government organizations was the Crafts Advisory Committee (CAC) of England and Wales, founded in 1971. Renamed the Crafts Council in 1979, it continues to support craft today. The CAC was a state-funded, centralised body with responsibility for the development and management of craft activity in England and Wales, and it played a key role in promoting the British craft revival of the 1970s.[3] As the largest organization supporting the crafts in Britain, the CAC provided an ideological template for the promotion of modern craft. Under the stewardship of Lord Eccles (1904–1999), Paymaster General with responsibility for the Arts, the CAC was primarily concerned with promoting craft to the status of fine art. Its funding came from the Arts Branch of the Department of Education, rather than the Board of Trade, as in previous years. This was significant change, as craftspeople were now being acknowledged alongside painters, sculptors, composers and writers for their cultural contribution to society.

By aligning itself with fine art, the CAC ushered in a new era of craft, focusing its attentions on high-end studio craft rather than vernacular, traditional or amateur craft. This change of cultural profile, something Bourdieu would describe as a "dynamic of change in the cultural field,"[4] greatly informed the historical narrative of British craft for this period. The received canon of late twentieth century British craft is told largely through the activities of the CAC.[5] Its governance, however, did not extend beyond England

and Wales, leaving the casual observer to wonder what, if anything, was happening in Scotland. It is largely unacknowledged that at this time Scotland had its own government-funded organizations and cultural policies to support the crafts.[6] This separation in funding bodies is significant to the history of modern British craft, and as this research will demonstrate, led to very different outcomes for the development of Scottish craft, including those involved making and selling it.

THE HIGHLAND PROBLEM

Not only did Scotland have its own government organizations tasked with supporting the crafts in the postwar period, it had a national Craft Centre in Edinburgh and later the Highlands, generous financial aid and development opportunities for Scottish craftspeople, as well as a nationally funded magazine dedicated solely to the promotion of Scottish craft.[7] However, unlike England and Wales, the government organizations responsible for supporting craft in Scotland were not interested in reinventing craft as fine art. Instead, the emphasis was on developing craft as an economic concern. Tasked with addressing Scotland's postindustrial decline and what was described as "the Highland Problem," these government organizations were largely driven by an economic development agenda. Importantly, they saw an opportunity to promote and develop craft as both an industry and a product in remote regions, commodifying "place" as a physical and metaphorical entity. Building on Adamson's thesis that as a form of cultural production "craft is itself a modern invention,"[8] it is argued that this vision led to the invention of modern Scottish craft, as both product and cultural signifier.

There were two national development organizations tasked with economic development after the Second World War: The Highlands and Islands Development Board (1965–1991) (HIDB), now Highlands and Islands Enterprise; and the Scottish Development Agency (SDA) (1975–1991), now Scottish Enterprise. Both the HIDB and the SDA were charged with investigating and promoting viable types of lighter industry, in an effort to reverse Scotland's postwar economic decline. Unlike the rest of Britain, which experienced a postwar economic boom, Scotland suffered in the postwar period. Its socioeconomic problems were the legacy of a crumbling nineteenth-century industrial base which had failed to modernise. Heavily dependent on a narrow range of industry largely located in Scotland's central belt, it failed to keep up with England's diversification into newer, lighter industries.[9]

In the Highlands, there was little manufacturing to speak of. In the postwar period leading up to the 1960s, the majority of the Highland population was reliant on a pluralistic subsistence income closely associated with crofting, which included farming, fishing and tourism. The geographic and social isolation of the Highlands exacerbated the region's economic plight, and for years it suffered from mass emigration, as its younger population sought opportunities elsewhere. By the early 1960s, the Highlands and Islands comprised only 4 percent of Scotland's population, despite geographically making up 40 percent of its landmass.[10] This vicious cycle of depopulation in the Highlands had wide-reaching socioeconomic repercussions, as geographer and regional development theorist Spaven explains:

> the long-term effects have been not only an ageing of the population and a lowering of natural increase but also a lack of enterprise and confidence and a serious weakening of communities already too small and isolated.[11]

In response to the Highland Problem, the Highlands and Islands Development Board (HIDB), an executive body under the Secretary of State for Scotland, was established in 1965. It had the dual purpose of:

> assisting the people of the Highlands and Islands to improve their economic and social conditions and of enabling the Highlands and Islands to play a more effective part in the economic and social development of the nation.[12]

Craft was included in a wider rubric of smaller industries with development potential by the HIDB. Not to be confused with the Highland's more established textiles industry of knitting and weaving, for the HIDB craft encompassed a range of small industrial activity, which might include anything from pottery to jewellery, or indeed any other small batch manufacture. HIDB annual reports and accompanying craft surveys provide evidence of the organization's increasing realisation that Scottish craft, in whatever form, had the potential to be developed as an industry and product. The HIDB's attempts to commodify Scottish craft can be linked to the wider commodification of Scottish heritage and culture, as discussed by McCrone and his coauthors in *Scotland the Brand*:

> [An] aspect of this commodification of heritage and culture relates to the process of economic regeneration, especially at the local level. Local authorities in particular have not been slow to recognise the economic and political potential of heritage.[13]

It is clear that by 1970, craft had become a key part of the Scottish government's wider strategic policy to diversify Scotland's postindustrial economy, create employment opportunities, and regenerate areas of depopulation. This was an ambitious vision which had important ramifications on makers, as well as the objects produced. The HIDB's plans for a commercially viable craft industry also differed dramatically from the CAC's policy for the promotion of craft in England and Wales, the latter distancing itself from anything that could be construed as traditional or obviously commercial.

THE FAR NORTH PROJECT

The Far North Project provides a case study of how national and local agencies encouraged craft commerce and entrepreneurship in remote areas of Scotland, as part of a wider national development policy. As with the rest of the Highlands, Sutherland Council was suffering from The Highland Problem of persistent depopulation and economic decline. Keen to address the problem, the council spotted an opportunity to develop a disused airbase which belonged to the Ministry of Defence. Situated near the village of Durness, the base was built in 1954 and intended to provide housing for staff working at a nearby Nuclear Early Warning System that was never commissioned.[14] By the early sixties, the base had fallen into dereliction—a result of the harsh northern climate and years of neglect—and the site was purchased by the council in 1963 (see Figure 5.1).

Figure 5.1. Balnakeil Craft Village, c. 1976. © Copyright Vanhercke Christiaan and licensed for reuse under the Creative Commons Licence. https://www.geograph.org.uk/photo/2043656.

The council's idea was to use the base to attract small, startup businesses by offering cheap rent and plenty of space.[15] Unsurprisingly, it struggled to draw individuals to the remote location, until it was suggested that "it be converted into a community for artists and craftspeople."[16] Capitalising on the resurgence of interest in the crafts being experienced across Britain, units were advertised nationally and rented to enterprising young craftspeople at a very reasonable rate of £5 a year (about £60 today). The site, which later took on the name Balnakeil Craft Village, attracted applicants from all over Britain and abroad—pioneers keen to "embark on a new experience in living."[17] At the height of the village's popularity, in the 1970s and early 80s, there were twenty-eight units housing various craft businesses. It was noted that the craft village "brought benefits to Durness and the surrounding North West Sutherland region."[18]

The Far North Project attracted individuals, described as "dreamers, wild-schemers, the unorthodox and idealistic."[19] Two of the early pioneers were the Danish ceramic artist Lotte Glob (1944–) and her husband David Illing-worth (1926–2009). Glob, who continues to practice today, learned her craft through hands-on apprenticeships with respected Danish potters including Gutte Erikson and Knut Jensen.[20] Her early life was peripatetic, taking her to Cork aged nineteen and Scotland a year later. She met Illingworth while working at Highland Home Industries Pottery in Mallaig. Upon hearing that a craft village had recently been established in Durness, the two set off in search of adventure and creative autonomy. Eikhof and Haunschild describe this type of aspirational creative producer as a "bohemian entrepreneur." The concept has origins in the nineteenth century and refers to those "living a life-style that is distinct and distinguished from the rest of society, especially the bourgeoisie and business."[21] In the case of the Balnakeil craft entrepreneurs however, their dependence on government support complicated matters, as it ensured that they were never fully creatively autonomous.

Glob was one of the first and also the longest residents of the village.[22] She reflects here on the early years:

> When we first came there were just three or four others and the buildings were totally vandalized. . . . We came on July 24, 1968, at three in the morning, with two babies, a dog, a small electric kiln, a potters' wheel, a ton of clay and five pounds in our pocket. . . . We had a lot of choice of buildings because so many were empty. Windows were broken, doors were broken, the toilet was ripped out and you could look straight into the sewer. There was no power. All the copper pipe was pulled out. . . . We found one room with a door and a window where we settled down with the kids. They were two-and-a-half and six months old. We didn't have electrics for three months and I had to wash nappies in the stream. It was tough.[23]

In 1974, the BBC made a documentary about the village, titled *The Road to Balnakeil*. It opens with presenter Derek Cooper of *Tomorrow's World* and *World in Action* driving a Land Rover along a desolate snow-covered stretch of road towards Durness, reporting grimly: "There's nothing between you and the arctic except miles and miles of sea."[24] The isolation and harshness of the environment are palpable. According to Cooper, Durness shared a "terminal fascination" with similar places such Lands' End or John O'Groats, marking the "end of a holiday road for thousands of visitors."[25] It was this remoteness that initially appealed to makers such as Glob. It also attracted summer tourists, who came to the village out of curiosity and gave its occupants an income.

The early residents of the craft village were largely outsiders, the majority being young English idealists. Like Glob and Illingworth, they were attracted to the cheap rent as well as the idea of communal living and self-sufficiency, "to be unregimented, free to work when they want."[26] As Cooper explains:

The craft village is a haven for those with nothing to declare but their talent, people who aren't afraid of making their own home from scratch, and who are anxious to turn their backs on the amenities and pressures of life in the town.[27]

Residents included individuals such as Alan Dawson and his wife, Jan, who produced an assortment of craft objects to sell to tourists, including corn dollies, ornamental wax candles, and wrought iron fire screens. Maureen Kerr created pressed flower pictures, using local wildflowers that she collected,[28] and also turned her hand to Viking tapestry hessian bags.[29] There was Iain Gunn and his wife, Sue, who sold their house in London to make nursery toys and felt cushions in a range of bright colors. Peter and Liz Harvey were also there, Peter working with leather, although noting "my primary interest was always music . . . leatherwork is more or less incidental."[30] Susan Luckman's research into cultural work in rural areas investigates the impact on incomers like the Harveys, lured by the promise of the good life. As she explains:

incomers [too] bring with them expectations about their new lifestyle which, like the magazines themselves, can gloss over the complexities and realities of life in rural, regional and remote locations.[31]

In the Cooper documentary, Harvey and his wife appear disillusioned and complain about Balnakeil's "sheer isolation" and "disconnection to the world."[32] What seemed like a good idea at the time appears to have given way to what Sue Harvey described as "the harshness of life."[33] Characteristic of many who set up home in Balnakeil, craft was peripheral to what initially lured them there. As Cooper put it:

theoretically you could come all the way up here and handcraft garden gnomes, if that's what turns you on.[34]

One commercially minded couple, Peter and Sylvia Lawry from Cornwall, had a business manufacturing sheepskin rugs by piecing together offcuts. The Lawrys' was the only business that employed labor from the local community, and it was reported in the Cooper documentary that they had recently opened up a second factory in Durness.[35] This more commercial approach appeared contrary to the communal ethos. Asked if he minded being "the odd man out in the community" or "a businessman motivated by profit," Peter Lawry replied:

> I like to look at myself as part craftsman, part artist, but mostly on a commercial scale. It's all very well to make this and that, and do it when you want to, and put a craft label on it, and say 'that's fine, that's enough for bread and butter this week' but that's not how I look at it.[36]

Balnakeil in the early 1970s could be described as a counterculture community comprised of idealistic young people who wanted to "escape the urban rat race."[37] There were similar craft communities emerging in England, and on the West Coast of America,[38] further evidence of the craft revival of this period. For many at Balnakeil, such as the Gunns or the Dawsons, craft was simply a means to an end. But for those who were commercially ambitious, such as the Lawrys, craft was about making a profit using whatever was to hand, in their case repurposing sheepskin offcuts. It can be argued that none of these approaches really had much to do with craft (or indeed Scottish craft), but they were a constituent element of the burgeoning 1970s craft revival. The fact that few of the original Balnakeil residents have continued to practice their craft, or remain at Balnakeil, is telling. For this reason, Lotte Glob and the Far North Pottery were in many ways an exception. As Alan Keegan, who sold her work in his Castewynd Gallery in the 1970s, pointed out, "I sometimes say that Lotte was the only craftsperson that was ever in Balnakeil."[39]

> It was a peculiar selection of people there, some of them were good some weren't. A good ironworker came up. But in general, the people who came were ones who wanted to get away from the rat race, they maybe knew how to do something with their hands, some of them came up and when they got there said 'what am I going to do now.'[40]

The notion of a self-sustaining artistic community appealed to Glob, but unlike many of the other original residents, craft for her was not a means to an end, but a way of life. Glob exemplified what Eikhof and Haunschild describe as the driving force behind the "bohemian entrepreneur," for whom "work in particular was not regarded as a means to earn one's living but as a vehicle for self-fulfilment."[41] However, despite being a self-described "scruffy potter,"[42]

Glob was also very much a professional. She exhibited her work internationally and had trained with some of the finest Danish potters of her generation.
She had come to Balnakeil, not as many of the others as Cooper put it, to simply "to freak out,"[43] but to be a ceramic artist. Glob and Illingworth's artistic
motivations also differed to those encouraged by the HIDB, which prioritised
selling over creating:

> They [Glob and Illingworth] produce functional oven and tableware, which
> they design themselves. They see themselves as basically makers, not sellers.
> They work in close partnership, each doing best, what they do best. But their
> main pleasure derives not from the repetitive work of producing coffee mugs
> or saucers, but the taking of a piece of clay and moulding it into something that
> is no longer just a piece of clay, an activity which for them, brings a great deal
> of happiness.[44]

The Cooper documentary shows a thirty-year-old Lotte throwing a large
vessel on a potter's wheel. Her skills and confidence are evident. The film
cuts to Illingworth, who is now glazing the same pot, along with a number
of other vessels. A production line of sorts, but each vessel bears the mark
of the maker and is unique. This way of working was essential to Glob. As
Illingworth points out in the Cooper documentary:

> We do no conscious design, we don't design on paper at all. It's this way of the
> clay, as it were, showing us what it is capable of, under fire and under the con-
> trol of the fire, as to what we can help to happen, we can't control it entirely.[45]

Glob confirmed this approach when interviewed:

> I still made exactly what I wanted. I always thought, you know, I'd make a cas-
> serole, I'd need a casserole in the house, so I'd make twenty or fifty, (Laughs)
> but they were still all individual because I can't make something I don't like.[46]

This individualistic way of working was at odds with the Highlands and Islands Development Board's policy for the development of craft businesses in
the Highlands. The 1969 *Survey of Craftworkers* commissioned by the HIDB
acknowledged that craft was largely an industry of "luxury or inessential
goods,"[47] but it was convinced that "properly organized, it could tap into new
markets at home and abroad and create new prosperity."[48] For this to happen,
it was crucial that the production of craft objects be viewed as a business.
The HIDB was not interested in "those who engage in craft work solely for
the aesthetic pleasure of occupation."[49] Only producers that had a reasonable
chance of a successful financial return on the sale of their products should
be supported and promoted, as underlined in the 1971 HIDB Annual Report:

Craft enterprises are encouraged to produce goods that sell well and at a price that gives an adequate return. The craft producer who can design for a market taste and produce a regular flow of goods of consistent quality stands every chance of success.[50]

Having recognised that Scottish craft could play a strategic role in the economic regeneration of the Highlands and Islands, the HIDB commissioned a series of reports to investigate the sector. The results were promising, revealing that the total turnover of Highland craft sales was in the region of £500,000 a year, with the potential for this to be more than doubled.[51] The HIDB consequently made improvements to the village and encouraged residents to adopt a more commercial approach to business, as confirmed in their 1973 Annual Report:

In 1971 financial assistance was given on a modest scale to a number of the individual craftsmen who live and work at the Balnakeil craft village, a former armed services camp on the north coast of Sutherland. In 1972 this was followed by a series of meetings with the villagers and County Council, who own the village, with a view to improving living and working conditions in the community and making it more attractive to visiting tourists.[52]

MEMORIES ARE MADE OF THIS

As noted earlier, tourism was considered essential to the economic survival of the craft village, and integral to the Highland Board's policy of developing viable alternatives to heavy industry in the Highlands. Their plan to link craft with tourism by encouraging the production of craft objects as souvenirs was expedient.

In the case of Balnakeil Craft Village, with noted exception of Glob, many of the objects were produced by amateur or hobbyist makers who had not come from art school or an apprenticed background. Many of the makers were not Scottish, and quality was often an issue. There was also the obvious irony, that the people who had come to Balnakeil to avoid "the rat race," were now subsumed in another form of tyranny, that of churning out souvenirs for tourists:

Although most people came here to get away from the pressure of an industrial society, some of them find that a full order book means that their freedom is being diminished and they are being caught up in a self-made production treadmill.[53]

Luckman addresses the lesser researched aspect of tourism and its impact on cultural workers by focusing on rural creativity and the tourist economy in

Cumbria, citing entrepreneurial cultural policy as one of the incentives. But she points out that "for cultural workers themselves, tourism remains a mixed blessing."[54] To meet the demands of tourists, craft workers can be subjected to a "trinketisation" of local crafts.[55] Concerned with issues of quality and a desire to link "authenticity" to the products, the HIDB introduced the "Craftmade" logo scheme 1971 (see Figure 5.2). It was designed to help consumers differentiate between "real" Scottish craft and craft that was imported or mass-produced. Consisting of a stylised Celtic knot with the text "Craftmade" and "The Mark of the Highlands," it came in the form of swing tags and stickers that could be attached to objects, as well as point of sale merchandising including display cards, leaflet dispensers, posters, and window stickers.[56] The symbol soon appeared regularly in HIDB advertising and the promotion of Scottish craft products. The deliberate elision of the words "craft" and "made," rather than "Scottish made" underlined the HIDB's desire to strategically promote craft as an authentic form of cultural production in the Highlands and Islands.

Figure 5.2. Highlands and Islands Development Board Craftmade label, 1971. With permission from Highlands and Islands Enterprise.

The "production of culture" is a theoretical premise which considers how culture is fabricated by people and the institutions to which they belong. In this model, argue Inglis and Hughson: "no form of culture is 'natural' or 'authentic', because it is always fabricated in one way or another."[57] For sociologist Richard Peterson, the production of culture encompasses a wide range of processes, including the product's creation, manufacture, marketing, distribution, exhibition and, ultimately, its consumption. Each of these processes, argues Peterson, plays a defining role in the fabrication of a cultural product's so-called authenticity. However, Peterson goes on to explain, because each of the bodies, or institutions, involved in the processes of creating the product often had competing interests, this would

invariably lead to tensions that would impact upon the type of cultural product produced.[58] In other words, a product that might be considered "authentic"
or "original" would in reality be highly fluid and mutable.

When applied to the cultural policies of the HIDB at the time, the production of culture model provides insight into its approach to craft development,
which differed dramatically to the CAC in England and Wales. In the same
way that Peterson proposes that culture is "not so much society wide and
virtually unchanging" but rather "situational and capable of rapid change,"[59]
so too it is argued that Scottish craft was a complex concoction of competing
ambitions and ideas, shaped by society and by its cultural gatekeepers. It is
maintained that these cultural gatekeepers—namely the national organizations supporting craft in Scotland—had a vested interest in the kind of symbols produced and the contexts in which they are displayed and consumed.

The Craftmade label was therefore designed to reassure consumers that
when purchasing a Craftmade item they were buying both place and authenticity, a practice referred to by Gold and Gold as a form of "place promotion."[60] In reality, the Craftmade label was distributed widely and indiscrimi-
nately across the Highlands. Anyone purporting to be a craftsperson could
obtain and make use of the labels. Therefore, rather than acting as a stamp of
approval in terms of quality, or indeed authenticity, the label conferred only
a tenuous connection to the place of origin, and was no indicator of quality.

Nevertheless, in its 1973 Annual Report the HIDB announced that over
two hundred businesses in the Highlands were now registered as Craftmade
label users, and this included Balnakeil Craft Village. Indeed, in Cooper's
documentary, if you look closely, the Craftmade logo appears in several of
the frames. Glob was not a fan of the Craftmade scheme, preferring her work
"to speak for itself."[61] She was against the idea of labelling her work with any
kind of brand, Craftmade or otherwise:

> everybody, that says they're a craftworker they get a sticker, and that's what
> happened, everybody that said it was craft, they got a sticker. So you could have,
> you know, the most atrocious craftwork with the sticker on. Or fantastic things
> with a sticker on. It was just crazy, I thought.[62]

The Craftmade scheme was deliberate in its promotion of Scottish crafts as
souvenirs, as evidenced in the HIDB's "Memories Are Made of This" advertising campaign (see Figure 5.3). The concepts of memory and souvenirs
are clearly linked here—the word "souvenir" coming from the French "to
remember." The association of craft with souvenirs is, by extension, associated with looking backwards, and in this example connected Scottish craft
to an idealised past. This strategy was again at odds with the promotion of
craft as both highly contemporary and artistic by the CAC across the border.

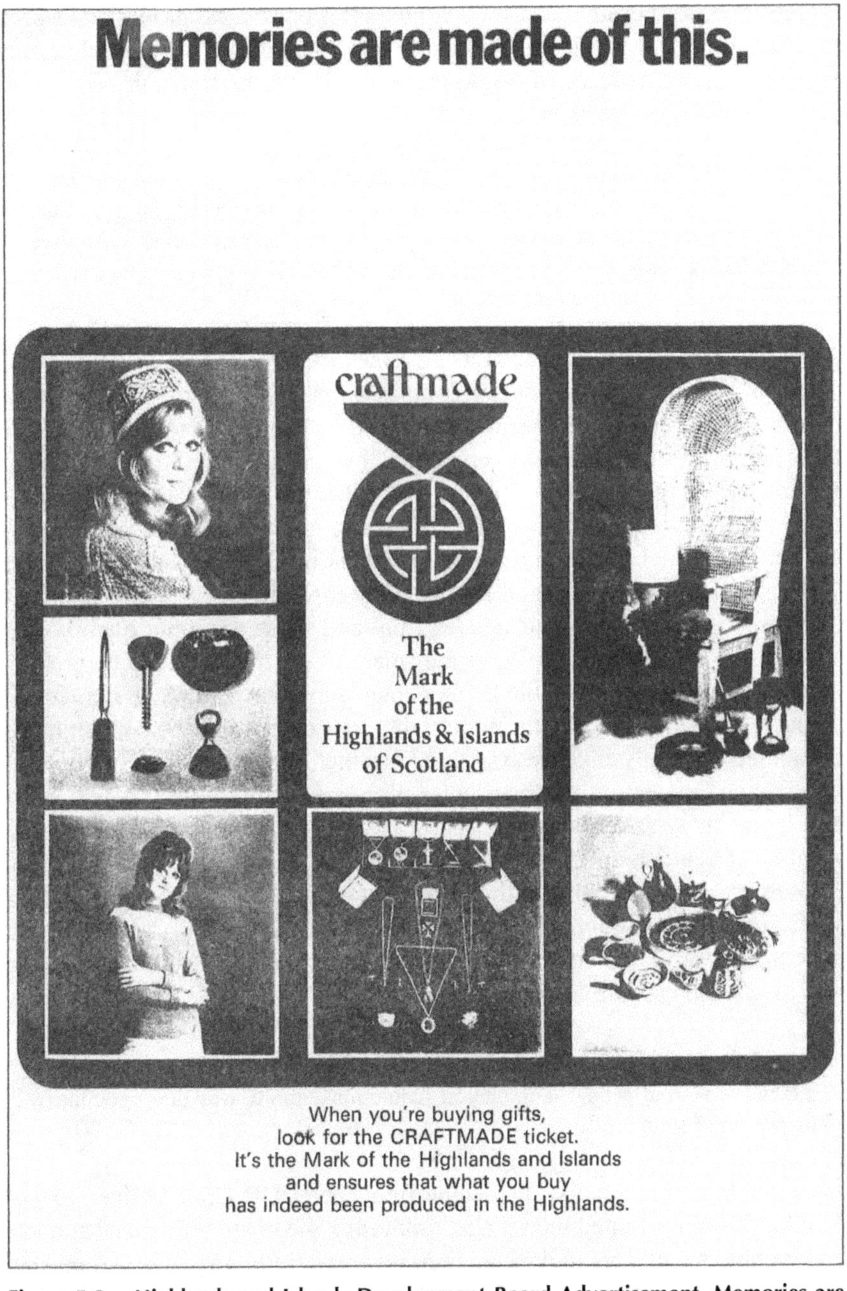

Figure 5.3. Highlands and Islands Development Board Advertisement, Memories are Made of This, 1973. With permission from Highlands and Islands Enterprise.

Literary theorist Susan Stewart writes about this backwards gaze with respect to place, arguing that souvenirs are particularly associated with nostalgia and "the longing for its place of origin."[63] In this sense, the souvenir becomes a powerful and emotive object:

> The souvenir speaks to a context of origin through a language of longing, for it is not an object arising out of need or use value; it is an object arising out of the necessarily insatiable demands of nostalgia. The souvenir generates a narrative which reaches only 'behind', spiralling in a continually inward movement rather than outward toward the future.[64]

As Dean MacCannell, author of *The Tourist: A New Theory of the Leisure Class*, also points out, the souvenir is essentially a "vicarious representation" of a place that has been experienced.[65] Therefore, to be successful these cultural representations, embodied by the souvenir, must be easily recognised by the tourist consumer. Craft theorist Gloria Hickey substantiates this, writing that "souvenir craft must above all be accessible and as such is limited to the understanding of its buyers."[66] In this sense, the souvenir operates as shorthand for place, by capturing its essential qualities in an easily translatable package. A final and most desirable quality of a souvenir is that it physically bears the "mark of the maker," thereby providing an immediate and tangible human connection between the craftsperson, object, and place. By directly linking the craft object and the souvenir, the consumers not only take away a local artefact, they take away a physical and human connection to a particular place—arguably a very potent symbol. It was these salient qualities that the HIDB was trying to articulate and identify in Scottish craft products.

Glob was uncomfortable with the concept of marketing her work as a souvenir and was unwilling to conform to the HIDB's policy of manufacturing a locally recognisable commercial product, even though she admits that she was more than capable of doing so:

> I did make a Loch Ness Monster, I have it somewhere . . . I didn't want to commercialise it. And people said, oh you should make more, why don't you make more? And I said, no.[67]

Incentive to commercialise also came from the HIDB Craft Officer, David Pirnie, who often visited the village, promoting the board's financial support and training for makers to develop their business skills. In particular, makers were encouraged to package their work in ways that would be more appealing to tourists. Glob describes an instance in the 1970s where Pirnie tried to persuade her to make her work more attractive to tourists:

what he [Pirnie] said was, I think we should, you should, we should organise
that you have four soup bowls in a nice package . . . with a little pink ribbon on
and a Craftmade sticker.[68]

Lotte Glob's resistance to the commercialisation of her practice came at
the expense of turning down generous grants being offered by the HIDB.
These grants provided a much-needed lifeline for many craft businesses in
the 1970s. More commercially minded outlets, such as Highland Stoneware
in nearby Lochinver, have attributed their success to early financial support
from the board. As David Grant, founder of Highland Stoneware confirmed
when interviewed by craft journalist Jenny Carter in 1990, much of the success of Highland Stoneware was down to early support from the board:

> We wouldn't be where we are today without the help of the HIDB. They helped
> us financially, with marketing and with our premises. We have help with setting
> up our business systems and we work closely with two management units who
> have helped us to improve our efficiency and have tailor-made software for us.
> We started from nothing and now we employ 30 staff.[69]

Unlike Highland Stoneware, which has built an international reputation for
quality and innovation,[70] not all recipients of HIDB grants used their money
productively, and when interviewed, Glob spoke disparagingly about the
impact of the HIDB funding, particularly on those who misused their grants:
"they [HIDB] put a lot of money into a lot craft people, who either developed
big business or squandered the money and left the country. You know there
was a lot of that, both of that."[71]

As sociologist Howard Becker argues in *Art Worlds* (2008) there is always a
relationship between craft and art practices and the cultural institutions that support them. Indeed, Becker challenges the stereotypical notion of the artist/crafts
person, or cultural producer, working as an autonomous individual, arguing instead that the maker is always embedded in a wider collective network involving
a complex division of labour across numerous cultural institutions, including the
state. The "production of culture" perspectives of Peterson and Becker illustrate
the role that national development organisations had in supporting and developing craft in the 1960s and 70s, and help to explain the various ways in which
individuals such as Glob, and those in Balnakeil Craft Village, reacted to their
policies and strategies, some embracing support and others rejecting it.

In the BBC documentary, Cooper asks Glob's husband, Illingworth,
whether their approach to craft was seen as a disappointment to the Highland
Board. Illingworth replies:

> I am sure features of it are a disappointment for them, yes, because they take
> the simple fact that here is someone producing something that sells, therefore

why don't you make more of it? Why don't you employ six people and increase your output? But of course, it isn't like that at all. If we were to employ even two people I would very soon become a works manager, I would do even less pottery than I am doing now.[72]

In 1980, residents of the craft village were given the option to buy their units from the County Council and it ceased to operate as a commune. The dynamic of the village has changed over the years, particularly with the shift towards private ownership. As the Diggers and Dreamers website (a guide to communal living in Britain) describes:

the compactness of the site and the remoteness lead to a certain feeling of community, the strength of which inevitably varies from time to time.[73]

Currently, there are thirteen businesses registered on the Balnakeil Craft Village site, and include glass, jewellery, ceramics, printmaking, wood turning and painting. The village also boasts a café and a holiday flat. Of interest is the addition of businesses catering to local rather than tourist needs, and these include a hairdresser, a woodwind instrument repair shop, boat and auto services and a plastic recycling workshop.[74] Plans to revitalise the village were mooted in 2014, with a report commissioned in 2014 by Highland and Islands Enterprise (HIE) to look into its regeneration, but nothing to date has been acted upon. Lotte Glob left the village in the 1990s and now practices as an independent ceramic artist from her studio and "sculpture croft" on the shores of Loch Eriboll on the North West Coast in Scotland.[75]

CONCLUSION

This chapter has demonstrated the close relationship between national development strategy and the promotion of craft entrepreneurship and craft communities, challenging the notion of the maker as an autonomous cultural producer. The Far North Project provides evidence of how national craft organisations have attempted to shape the cultural and economic profile of craft to suit their particular agendas and ambitions. By providing financial and ideological incentives to makers, it is argued that government agencies actively influenced the types of craft being produced, as well as encouraged a specific type of consumer.

Newly founded government organizations played a crucial part in the craft renaissance of the 1960s and 1970s. In England and Wales, the CAC (now the Crafts Council), had a singular vision of raising craft to the status of fine art. In Scotland, the HIDB focused its attention on trade, with ambitions that were commercial rather than artistic. For the HIDB, craft was one of a series of industries identified as having development potential, in a bid to address Scotland's postwar economic slump.

The Highland Board's vision for Balnakeil craft village was for it to become self-sustaining through the production of craft souvenirs for tourists. Initiatives such as the Craftmade label scheme provide evidence of how the board actively encouraged the link with Scottish craft and the tourist economy, and attempted to instil "place authenticity" in these products. This emphasis on commodification created tensions within the craft village—embraced by some makers, and wholly rejected by others.

In terms of our understanding of craft entrepreneurship, this case study has demonstrated the active role that national development agencies can play in supporting but also influencing the entrepreneur, in this instance through directly linking craft and tourism by the creation of a craft village. Lured by the promise of creative autonomy and self-sufficiency, a unifying motivation of the early Far North crafter entrepreneurs was a desire to escape. This was congruent with the counterculture ethos of the time. The harsh living conditions and reality of having to earn a living by catering to tourists, however, left many disillusioned.

As the Far North Project case study has shown, the types of object produced and the quality of output varied greatly, and ultimately, the tensions between the craft entrepreneur's desire for creative autonomy and government cultural policy proved incompatible. Today, there is evidence that the community is moving away from a sole reliance on a seasonal tourist market, with less obvious emphasis on the production of Scottish souvenirs. The shift is now on providing a more sustainable balance of craft products and niche craft services, which could appeal to tourists of both the local and wider community. These include contemporary crafts such as ceramics, jewellery and glass, as well as more niche craft products and services, such as musical instrument, boat repairs and upcycling waste materials. The key lesson, as seen in Katherine Champion's chapter examining sustainable strategies of island-based creative practitioners, is the importance of building community resilience through continual adaptation. By adopting responsive entrepreneurial measures, the Far North Project crafting community, now more than fifty years old, continues to evolve.

NOTES

1. Andrea Peach, "What Goes Around Comes Around: Craft Revival, the 1970s and Today," *Craft Research* 4, no. 2 (2013): 161–79.

2. See Tanya Harrod, "Introduction/Craft Over and Over Again," in *Craft*, ed. Tanya Harrod (London: Documents of Contemporary Art, 2018), 12–21; Peach, "What Goes Around"; Alice Rawsthorn, "The Craft Revival," in *Design as an Attitude*, ed. Alice Rawsthorn (Zurich: JRP/ Ringier, 2018), 38–49.

3. Peach, "What Goes Around."

4. Pierre Bourdieu, *The Field of Cultural Production: Essays on Art and Literature* (London: Polity Press, 1993), 19.

5. Tanya Harrod, *The Crafts in Britain in the 20th Century* (New Haven, CT: Yale University Press, 1999).

6. Andrea Peach, "Craft Souvenirs and the Commodification of National Identity in 1970s Scotland," *Journal of Design History* 20, no. 3 (2007): 243–57; Andrea Peach, *The Making of Modern Scottish Craft: Invention and Revival in 1970s Scotland* (PhD diss., Robert Gordon University, 2017).

7. Peach, *The Making*.

8. Glenn Adamson, *The Invention of Craft* (London: Bloomsbury, 2013), xiii.

9. George C. Peden, "The Scottish Economy in Historical Context," in *The Transformation of Scotland: The Economy Since 1700*, eds. Tom M. Devine, Clive H. Lee, and George C. Peden (Edinburgh: Edinburgh University Press, 2005), 6.

10. Gavin McCrone, "The Role of Government," in *The Economic Development of Modern Scotland 1950–1980*, ed. Richard Saville (Edinburgh: John Donald Publishers, 1985), 204.

11. F. D. N. Spaven, "The Concept of Regional Economic Development Expressed in the Highlands and Islands Development Board" (Paper for Colloquium on Regional Economic Development at the Annual Conference of the Canadian Association of Geographers, Newfoundland, 1969), 1.

12. Highlands and Islands Development (Scotland) Act, (Chapter 46, 1965), s.1.

13. David McCrone, Angela Morris, and Richard Kiely, *Scotland—The Brand: The Making of Scottish Heritage* (Edinburgh: Polygon, 1999), 17.

14. Ironside Farrar, "Balnakiel Craft Village—Masterplan," *Report for and on Behalf of Highlands and Islands Enterprise* January 1, 2014, 2; Richard Lansley, *Durness: Past and Present* (Durness Local Studies Group, 1998); Peter Ross, "Back of Beyond: Balnakeil Is Far Out," *The Scotsman*, August 25, 2013, http://www.scots man.com/news/back-of-beyond-balnakeil-is-far-out-1-3061653; "The Original 'Far North' Project," Wordpress, accessed June 19, 2019, https://balnakeil.wordpress .com/the-original-far-north-project/.

15. "The Original 'Far North' Project."

16. Ross, "Back of Beyond."

17. "Balnakeil Craft Village: History," accessed January 3, 2020. https://bal nakeilcraftvillage.weebly.com/history.html.

18. Ironside Farrar, "Balnakiel Craft Village."

19. Ross, "Back of Beyond."

20. Lotte Glob, interview with author, July 16, 2014; Giles Sutherland, "A Dane on Eriboll." *Ceramics Review* 250 (July/August 2011): 33.

21. Doris Ruth Eikhof and Axel Haunschild, "Lifestyle Meets Market: Bohemian Entrepreneurs in Creative Industries," *Creativity and Innovation Management* 15, no. 3 (2006): 234.

22. Courtney Stevens and Ronald Lansley, *Strong Highland Women: Stories from Durness and Balnakeil* (CreateSpace, 2013), 65; Glob, interview.

23. Ross, "Back of Beyond."

24. Cooper, Derek, "The Road to Balnakeil," BBC, March 22,1974, https://www.youtube.com/watch?v=_zi9HRp__KA.

25. Cooper, "The Road."

26. Cooper, "The Road."

27. Cooper, "The Road."

28. Cooper, "The Road."

29. Highlands and Islands Development Board, *Buyers Guide to Retail Products of the Highlands and Islands* (Inverness: Highlands and Islands Development Board, c 1974), 11.

30. Cooper, "The Road."

31. Susan Luckman, *Locating Cultural Work and the Politics and Poetics of Rural, Regional and Remote Creativity* (Basingstoke: Palgrave Macmillan, 2012), 150.

32. Cooper, "The Road."

33. Cooper, "The Road."

34. Cooper, "The Road."

35. Cooper, "The Road."

36. Cooper, "The Road."

37. Cooper, "The Road."

38. Elissa Auther and Adam Lerner, *West of Centre: Art and the Counterculture Experiment in America, 1965–1977* (Minneapolis: University of Minnesota Press, 2012).

39. Alan Keegan, Interview with author, July 31, 2014.

40. Keegan, interview.

41. Eikhof and Haunschild, "Lifestyle Meets Market," 236.

42. Glob, interview.

43. Cooper, "The Road."

44. Cooper, "The Road."

45. Cooper, "The Road."

46. Glob, interview.

47. Highlands and Islands Development Board, *Report Following a Survey of Craftworkers in Shetland, Orkney, Caithness, Sutherland, Ross-shire, Inverness-shire, Argyll* (Inverness: Highlands and Islands Development Board, 1969), 11.

48. Highlands and Islands Development Board, *Highland and Islands Purchasers Survey* (London: NOP Market Research Limited, 1970), 24.

49. Highlands and Islands, *Report Following a Survey*, 9.

50. Highlands and Islands Development Board, *Fifth Report 1 January 1970 to 31 December 1970* (Inverness: Highlands and Islands Development Board, 1971), 23.

51. Highlands and Islands, *Report Following a Survey*, 8.

52. Highlands and Islands Development Board, *Seventh Report 1 January 1972 to 31st December 1972* (Inverness: Highlands and Islands Development Board, 1973), 27.

53. Cooper, "The Road."

54. Luckman, *Locating Cultural Work*, 131.

55. John Urry, *The Tourist Gaze: Leisure and Travel in Contemporary Societies*, 2nd ed. (London: Sage, 2002), 51, cited in Luckman, *Locating Cultural Work*, 135.

56. Highlands and Islands, *Buyers Guide*, 34.
57. David Inglis and John Hughson, *Confronting Culture: Sociological Vistas* (Cambridge, MA: Polity Press, 2003), 210.
58. Richard A. Peterson, *The Production of Culture* (London: Sage, 1976), 14.
59. Richard A. Peterson and N. Anand, "The Production of Culture Perspective," *Annual Review of Sociology* 30 (2004): 312.
60. John R. Gold and Margaret M. Gold, *Imagining Scotland: Tradition, Representation and Promotion in Scottish Tourism Since 1750* (Aldershot: Scholar Press, 1995), 17.
61. Glob, interview.
62. Glob, interview.
63. Susan Stewart, *On Longing: Narratives of the Miniature, the Gigantic, the Souvenir, the Collection* (Durham, NC: Duke University Press, 1993), xii.
64. Stewart, *On Longing*, 135.
65. Dean MacCannell, *The Tourist: A New Theory of the Leisure Class* (London: University of California Press, 1999), 158.
66. Gloria Hickey, "Craft within a Consuming Society," in *The Culture of Craft: Status and Future*, ed. Peter Dormer (Manchester: Manchester University Press, 1997), 93.
67. Glob, interview.
68. Glob, interview.
69. Jenny Carter, "Crafts in the Highlands," in *Highlands and Islands: A Generation of Progress*, ed. Alistair Hetherington (Aberdeen: Aberdeen University Press, 1990), 209.
70. Highland Stoneware, accessed July 8, 2019, https://www.highlandstoneware.com.
71. Glob, interview.
72. Cooper, "The Road."
73. Diggers and Dreamers: The Guide to Communal Living, "Balnakeil Craft Village," accessed June 19, 2019, http://www.diggersanddreamers.org.uk/communities/existing/balnakeil-craft-village
74. "Balnakeil Craft Village: Artists & Businesses," accessed January 3, 2020, https://balnakeilcraftvillage.weebly.com/artists--businesses.html.
75. Lotte Glob: Ceramic Artist in the North West Highlands of Scotland, accessed July 1, 2019, https://lotteglob792300328.wordpress.com.

BIBLIOGRAPHY

Adamson, Glenn. *The Invention of Craft*. London: Bloomsbury, 2013.
Auther, Elissa, and Adam Lerner. *West of Centre: Art and the Counterculture Experiment in America, 1965–1977*. Minneapolis: University of Minnesota Press, 2012.
"Balnakeil Craft Village: History." Accessed January 3, 2020, https://balnakeilcraftvillage.weebly.com/history.html.

Bourdieu, Pierre. *The Field of Cultural Production: Essays on Art and Literature.* London: Polity Press, 1993.

Carter, Jenny. "Crafts in the Highlands." In *Highlands and Islands: A Generation of Progress*, ed. Alistair Hetherington. Aberdeen: Aberdeen University Press, 1990.

Derek, Cooper. "The Road to Balnakeil," BBC, March 22,1974.

Diggers and Dreamers: The Guide to Communal Living, "Balnakeil Craft Village," accessed June 19, 2019, http://www.diggersanddreamers.org.uk/communities/existing/balnakeil-craft-village.

Eikhof, Doris Ruth, and Axel Haunschild. "Lifestyle Meets Market: Bohemian Entrepreneurs in Creative Industries," *Creativity and Innovation Management* 15, no. 3 (2006).

Gold, John R., and Margaret M. Gold. *Imagining Scotland: Tradition, Representation and Promotion in Scottish Tourism since 1750*. Aldershot: Scholar Press, 1995.

Harrod, Tanya. *Craft*. London: Documents of Contemporary Art, 2018.

———. *The Crafts in Britain in the 20th Century*. New Haven, CT: Yale University Press, 1999.

Hickey, Gloria. "Craft within a Consuming Society." In *The Culture of Craft: Status and Future*, edited by Peter Dormer. Manchester: Manchester University Press, 1997.

Highlands and Islands Development (Scotland) Act, (Chapter 46, 1965), s.1.

Highlands and Islands Development Board. *Buyers Guide to Retail Products of the Highlands and Islands*. Inverness: Highlands and Islands Development Board, c 1974.

———. *Highland and Islands Purchasers Survey*. London: NOP Market Research Limited, 1970.

———. *Report Following a Survey of Craftworkers in Shetland, Orkney, Caithness, Sutherland, Ross-shire, Inverness-shire, Argyll*. Inverness: Highlands and Islands Development Board, 1969.

Highland Stoneware, https://www.highlandstoneware.com.

Inglis, David, and John Hughson. *Confronting Culture: Sociological Vistas*. Cambridge, MA: Polity Press, 2003.

Ironside Farrar. "Balnakiel Craft Village—Masterplan," *Report for and on Behalf of Highlands and Islands Enterprise* 1, January, 2014.

Lansley, Richard. *Durness: Past and Present*. Durness Local Studies Group, 1998.

Luckman, Susan. *Locating Cultural Work and the Politics and Poetics of Rural, Regional and Remote Creativity*. Basingstoke: Palgrave Macmillan, 2012.

MacCannell, Dean. *The Tourist: A New Theory of the Leisure Class*. London: University of California Press, 1999.

McCrone, David, Angela Morris, and Richard Kiely. *Scotland—The Brand: The Making of Scottish Heritage*. Edinburgh: Polygon, 1999.

McCrone, Gavin. "The Role of Government." In *The Economic Development of Modern Scotland 1950–1980*, edited by Richard Saville. Edinburgh: John Donald Publishers, 1985.

"The Original 'Far North' Project." Accessed June 19, 2019, https://balnakeil.wordpress.com/the-original-far-north-project/.

Peach, Andrea. "Craft Souvenirs and the Commodification of National Identity in 1970s Scotland," *Journal of Design History* 20, no. 3 (2007): 243–57.

——. *The Making of Modern Scottish Craft: Invention and Revival in 1970s Scotland*, PhD diss., Robert Gordon University, 2017.

——. "What Goes Around Comes Around: Craft Revival, the 1970s and Today," *Craft Research* 4, no. 2 (2013): 161–79.

Peden, George C. "The Scottish Economy in Historical Context." In *The Transformation of Scotland: The Economy Since 1700*, edited by Tom M. Devine, Clive H. Lee, and George C. Peden. Edinburgh: Edinburgh University Press, 2005.

Peterson, Richard A. *The Production of Culture*. London: Sage, 1976.

Peterson, Richard A., and N. Anand. "The Production of Culture Perspective." *Annual Review of Sociology* 30, 2004.

Rawsthorn, Alice. *Design as an Attitude*. Zurich: JRP/ Ringier, 2018.

Ross, Peter. "Back of Beyond: Balnakeil Is Far Out." *The Scotsman*, August 25, 2013, http://www.scotsman.com/news/back-of-beyond-balnakeil-is-far-out-1-3061653.

Spaven, F. D. N. "The Concept of Regional Economic Development Expressed in the Highlands and Islands Development Board" (Paper for Colloquium on Regional Economic Development at the Annual Conference of the Canadian Association of Geographers, Newfoundland, 1969.

Stevens, Courtney, and Ronald Lansley. *Strong Highland Women: Stories from Durness and Balnakeil*. CreateSpace Independent Publishing Platform, 2013.

Stewart, Susan. *On Longing—Narratives of the Miniature, the Gigantic, the Souvenir, the Collection*. Durham, NC: Duke University Press, 1993.

Sutherland, Giles. "A Dane on Eriboll." *Ceramics Review* 250, July/August, 2011.

Urry, John. *The Tourist Gaze: Leisure and Travel in Contemporary Societies*. 2nd ed. London: Sage, 2002.

Chapter Six

Artisan or Designer

Montreal Craft Workers and the Global Discourse on Creativity

Guillaume Sirois[1]

Making crafts products is an activity that has always been situated at the intersection of several fields, raising challenges regarding its definition. Indeed, craft workers have the ambition to create products that are useful in daily life but also endowed with significant aesthetic qualities that distinguish them from industrial products. This double function (utilitarian and aesthetic) places craft workers at the centre of several tensions they must face in positioning their activity in society. One area of tension is the relationship craft workers maintain with the capitalist economy and its consumer culture. On the one hand, making seductive objects that fuel consumers' desire and prompt them to buy beyond their needs may be understood as a contribution to the overconsumption that is strongly associated with capitalist culture. On the other hand, a long tradition of resistance to capitalist dynamics was brought about by father figures who shaped the field,[2] like William Morris who conceived his work as an alternative to the industrial production unfolding at the time. If such a vision is carried forward today by contemporary craft workers, other related issues have emerged with the evolution of the capitalist economy, notably questions related to the environment and sustainable development, or a preoccupation with local production after many manufacturing facilities have moved overseas.

Making craft products can be conceived as the activity by which everyday objects endowed with distinctive aesthetic qualities are designed and manufactured following a small-scale production mode and often building on traditional savoir faire. Pursuing such an activity today implies dealing with several considerations, including artistic and aesthetic choices; technical skills and traditional knowledge; economy and entrepreneurship dynamics; environment and sustainable development and social and labour conditions.

If individual craft workers have to define their own practice vis-à-vis these elements, two archetypes may be used to characterise the work of people making craft products: the artisan and the designer. The ideal-typical model of the artisan[3] would be the craftsperson who works independently, making objects from the raw material to the end product, working with one or a few preferred materials and offering the product in a small shop that also serves as a workshop. The artisan business is usually organised around a master who has vast experience in making a specific kind of objects and works alongside a small team of workers who are involved in every step of the process. This creates a suitable environment for an apprenticeship, which is the main method by which knowledge is transmitted. By contrast, the ideal-typical model of the designer[4] corresponds to a practice centred on the conception of objects in which drawing is perceived as the favoured way to express ideas before their materialisation. The designer is not necessarily attached to a specific material or a preferred making process but focused on developing the best product to solve a problem or answer a need of various clients. Designers find their inspiration from diverse sources, as design is now a worldwide practice, and exchanges between national contexts are common. Today, education in design is strongly institutionalised, with college and university programs training students in every branch of product design.

In my research on the craft sector in Montreal, I used these two archetypes as opposite ends in a spectrum of craftsmanship conceptions. The two ideal-typical conceptions provide a tool to understand various positions taken by craft workers vis-à-vis creativity and entrepreneurship. If there is a milieu of artisans and a milieu of designers living side by side in Montreal—occasionally crossing each other—the question is not so much to have craft workers choosing their camp but rather to use the opposite positions to reflect on the development of craftsmanship in a city. In this investigation, I was interested in understanding how the craft community positions itself vis-à-vis the discourse on creative economy that has been widely promoted by the city of Montreal, as well as their relation to design, which is presented as a strategic sector of this new economy. Thus, the investigation was structured in two distinct steps. During the first phase, I analysed official policy documents to understand how creativity and entrepreneurship is promoted by city officials. A list of the main policy documents consulted is presented in Appendix A. In the second phase, I turned to craftworkers themselves. First, I built a database of people who conceive and produce objects locally, drawing on two directories assembled by local organisations.[5] From this database, I selected a representative sample of ten craftspeople, with whom I conducted semi-structured interviews.[6] All craftspeople in the sample are mid-career professionals who work full time on their practice. The sample covers a diversity of craft practices and encompasses companies of various sizes that are at different stages in their development. Appendix B presents some of the characteristics of the selected companies. During the interviews, I was especially interested in their position on creativity and entrepreneurship, as my previous work on creative entrepreneurship[7] has clearly demonstrated how creators tend to use contrasted logics—creative, entrepreneurial, and social—when they describe their work and its place in the city.

The whole research process provided the opportunity to confront the vision of creativity and entrepreneurship promoted by the City of Montreal and the experience of craftspeople working in the city. It reveals a tension in the vision of creative entrepreneurship: whereas the municipal administration promotes the model of the designer as the epitome of the contemporary creator at the heart of its "cool"[8] and competitive economy, the craft community rather conceive their work as the incarnation of an alternative economy that is based on a set of values, which are often purposely opposed to a crude version of globalised capitalism.

MONTREAL, CREATIVITY, AND DESIGN

In the last two decades, cultural development in the city has been largely driven by two interrelated policy streams: the first one aims at transforming the city into a "cultural metropolis of the 21st century," and the second one led to Montreal's designation as a "UNESCO City of Design." In its definition of design, the city administration adopts a large conception of the discipline. "For the City of Montreal, design is an activity of ideation, creation, planning, production and management that influences the quality of its living environment, makes its economy more competitive, participates in its cultural expression and strengthens its identity and that of its businesses."[9] Therefore, the definition comprises all branches of design, including several practices dedicated to the conception of objects. If the language of craftsmanship is rarely explicitly used in these policies, a large part of Montreal's craft community nevertheless feels included in the definition of the sector.

A Cultural Metropolis and a City of Design

The story of these policies started in 2002 when Gérald Tremblay, the newly elected mayor of Montreal, invited civil servants and civil society leaders to participate in the "Sommet de Montréal," a large-scale event intended to create a new vision for the development of the city. The event provided the setting for a group of cultural leaders to pitch their vision of city development based on arts and culture. During the same period, this group of cultural leaders founded an art advocacy organisation called Culture Montréal, which quickly became a dominant player in the cultural sector and the main vehicle to promote their conception of arts and culture as a powerful development tool. Their vision was summarised in a simple phrase, which proposed to turn Montreal into "a cultural metropolis of the 21st century." The phrase became a slogan municipal officials and cultural sector representatives still use today. The message was heard from the beginning by city officials who started to prepare a first cultural development policy, which was adopted in 2005 under the title "Montréal, métropole culturelle." However, the ambition attached to the vision carried by Culture Montréal commanded the association of other partners and, in 2007, high officials in the provincial and federal governments and representatives of the business community agreed to participate in another summit dedicated to this project of building a cultural metropolis. Following the summit, a ten-year action plan (2007–2017) involving all partners was issued. The plan (which was revised in 2012 and 2014) retains the three main priorities of the cultural policy adopted in 2005 (democratisation of culture, support to creators and improvement of infrastructure qualities) and adds two supplementary objectives: enhancing Montreal's status in Canada and internationally and securing the means of a cultural metropolis. Following this decade of development, the city of Montreal issued a new cultural policy in 2017 under the same label "Montréal, métropole culturelle."

This vision, which promotes cultural activities as a holistic development tool, is deliberately rooted in the discourse of the creative economy that was developing at the time. Indeed, policies put in place by the UK's labour government at the end of the 1990s[10] were generally perceived around the world as an easy-to-import model of development, a new way to revive economic activities in city centers. In the following years, creativity became a key element to spearhead urban and economic redeployment for several governments around the world, fuelled by a popular and academic discourse on "creative economy," "creative city," and "creative class."[11] The work of Richard Florida was particularly influential in the development of such a view. Even if his work has been heavily criticised in academic literature for its approximative use of the notion of class and several flaws in methodologies,[12] Florida's vision remains very popular among city officials.[13] The American scholar was particularly influential in Montreal as he came to the city, at the invitation of Culture Montréal, to study the city's potential for creativity growth. His analysis[14] concluded that the city is perfectly situated to take advantage of various factors to attract creative people, which are said to be at the forefront of economic development.

Since the beginning, it was also clear for promoters of the cultural metropolis that such a vision must be translated in visible changes in the city so the new creative identity becomes clear to its citizens and visitors. To advance this priority, the city of Montreal invested in the multifaceted practice of design as it appeared to be a key creative discipline by which the cultural metropolis status can be showcased to the public. In 2006, the municipal administration took two steps to increase various practices of design in the city. In line with its international aspirations, the city presented an application to be designated a "UNESCO City of Design" and, at the same time, created the "Bureau du design," to promote the discipline in the city. In the perspective of presenting a global portrait of design in the city, the application file borrows from several creative disciplines that can be associated with the broad term of design, which include craftsmanship and showcase some of its notable creators and institutions. Throughout these years, the discourse on creativity and design has evolved in the city, and many young craft workers now identify with the community of designers.

Two elements emerging from these policy documents must be briefly outlined here, as they represent the vision of creativity put forward by the municipal administration: a continuing preoccupation with its international profile and the rise of the language of entrepreneurship.

International Competitiveness

The project of transforming Montreal into a "cultural metropolis" has always been attached to an international ambition. On this aspect, the influence of Richard Florida's work is particularly strong. For example, the first cultural policy enumerates the most notable assets the city can count on to compete with other "world's major cities." Such references to the international competition among cities of the world are everywhere in these policy documents. However, with time, the city seems to be more positive about its place on the international scene. The first plan in 2007 simply set a goal by formally including the objective to raise Montréal's international profile. In the conclusion, it states, "in the globalized economy of the 21st century, it is also necessary to understand where the 'Montreal brand' now stands and what actions should be taken to improve how it is perceived in Canada and abroad."[15] The two subsequent versions of the plan note encouraging progress on that front. For example, in 2014, the plan claims that "objectively speaking, Montréal is advantageously positioned to accentuate its creativity and knowledge, its artists, enterprises and cultural institutions, and to see them spread far and wide around the world."[16] In the last version of its cultural policy, in 2017, the city proclaims that "Montréal is comparable to Paris, New York, Berlin and a few other major cities, with an exceptional concentration of creators, artists and cultural and creative companies."[17]

In this context, the practice of design was the perfect field to develop Montreal's new creative image. Indeed, the designer appeared as the idealised worker of the future[18] as a designer is flexible and innovative while being constantly in touch with what is going on around the world. The decision to seek the international "UNESCO City of Design" was a clear indication of that ambition. Therefore, the application file to UNESCO attempts to demonstrate that Montréal has deployed considerable efforts over the years "to make Montréal a world-class design centre."[19] Since that date, officials responsible for developing design have been remarkably active on the international scene, making good use of the creative city network they have joined. However, as observed in the last action plan for design, issued in 2018, the market for local designers remains "mostly local," as these creators "have difficulty qualifying internationally."[20] Thus, Montreal's international reputation in this domain stays essentially institutional, as UNESCO commends the implication of the city in its network, while international development efforts have not yet reached those who practice design in this city.

Creative Entrepreneurship

Design was a key sector for the cultural development of Montreal in part because it is a sector of entrepreneurs and, as such, it is not constantly dependent on public subsidies. By contrast to the city's international ambitions, the language of entrepreneurship has emerged much more recently in Montreal. Indeed, before 2012 there was no real discussion about cultural or creative entrepreneurship in the policy documents. The only mentions of enterprises or entrepreneurs are made in relation to a general description of the cultural sector, based on the classical dichotomy between the not-for-profit and incorporated sectors. However, the 2012 action plan introduced a new topic: the quest for new financing models for the arts and culture. At the time, many discussions in the cultural sector revolved around the sclerosis of the state funding model being too rigid and incapable of answering young creators' needs, as most of the budget was already attributed to established artists and practices.

One way out of this crisis was to look for alternative funding models, which often involved the business sector. Therefore, much of the policy attention in the cultural sector was dedicated to further developing the "alliance between the art and business communities."[21] If this alliance was first imagined as a way to strengthen philanthropy, it soon became a much broader endeavour in which communalities between the two communities were found. As a result, the city of Montreal seems to have fully embraced the conception of the creator as an entrepreneur, since its last cultural policy dedicates a chapter to the topic. "The more our cultural and creative entrepreneurs can adapt to consumers' expectations, the more they will have the means to take risks in research and development."[22] Once again, design appears as an emblematic sector for such development, as it is situated at the intersection of various priorities for Montreal's cultural development. Not surprisingly, the newly issued development plan of the sector seeks to develop both entrepreneurship and the international market,[23] as it seems the right way forward for a sector that incarnated Montreal's cultural ambitions.

Thus, recent development plans and cultural policies have turned Montreal creators into agents of its economic development and international influence. Indeed, the vision that is presented in these policy documents is built on the belief that creators have a key role to play in the economic development of the city, especially in relation to its ambitions to compete with other major creative cities on the planet. In this perspective, the creator is turned into an entrepreneur that follow trends to successfully build his business in a highly competitive and globalised capitalist economy.

MONTREAL CRAFT WORKERS

If policies in Montreal indicate a clear direction for its cultural development, the position of craft practitioners vis-à-vis creativity and entrepreneurship is much more nuanced. Indeed, craftspeople develop their business around their own creativity, but also a whole set of values that incarnate their vision of their practice and the place it should occupy in the city. The following sections explore, first, how craftspeople see creativity in relation to the ideal-typical models described in the introduction—artisan and designer—and, second, how this conception is translated in their entrepreneurial vision. This analysis leads to a discussion of the main values that are at the heart the craft activity in Montreal.

The Artisan-Designer

When asked to present themselves, craft workers in Montreal use a wide variety of terms that are indicative of their relation to their practices and the place they occupy in Montreal's creative landscape. Indeed, some respondents used a term related to a subcommunity of craftspeople, like "ceramist" or "illustrator," whereas others emphasise that they are a "maker" or a "manufacturer." Despite the prevalence of the discourse on design in the city, only two respondents use, at the outset, the term "designer" to describe themselves. This diversity shows that the community of craftspeople in Montreal is fragmented and more complicated that the two archetypes presented in the introduction. Yet, the two models are fruitful analytical tools to dig deeper into the conception of creativity of these craftspeople.

On one side, craftspeople who emphasise the "making" aspect of their activity are closer to the artisan archetype. From this perspective, making objects locally in a small shop is a form of resistance to industrial production that has alienated our relation to objects. One respondent, who learned shoemaking through apprenticeship, comments, "With mass production, people forget. They lose the relation to a [good] shoe and how it is made"[24] (respondent 2). For these craftspeople, their practice is rooted in a traditional savoir faire (e.g., shoemaking, fine woodworking, sewing) they cultivate as the hallmark of their production. "The quality of fabrication, the quality of assembling, the level of details, being precise and meticulous . . . we work in a minimalist aesthetic here, but with minimalism, it takes details that are handled with care" (respondent 3). Similarly, the practice of many craftspeople is strongly associated with a specific material—fabric, leather, wood or concrete—to the point that it would be difficult for them to consider making objects without this material. Moreover, their knowledge of this specific material becomes an integral part of their expertise. Many talk about the richness of their preferred material and how its properties guide their creative process. For example, a craftsman who specialises in concrete talks about the complexity of the substance: "It is a material with a large number of variables, and I mean a lot of variables, and it is a bit maniac to try to control everything, but I am maniac" (respondent 9). A similar relation to the material exists for the ceramist: "The material informs me about its potential and it is with this information that I can make a good design. It is very simple, but ceramics is very complex" (respondent 1).

On the other side, design is generally perceived as being more remote from savoir faire or the materiality of the production. In fact, the two respondents who use that term as the first description of their identity (respondents 4 and 8) are both farther from the production. The first one uses the metaphor of the conductor to describe how he works with his team of designers, whereas the second one conceives custom objects for her clients, selecting a specific set of collaborators for each project. However, while only two respondents fully endorse the term, several others use the term later in the conversation or use similar terms like "conceptor" or "creator" to talk about this aspect of their activity. No matter what term they use, all respondents are strongly attached to the idea of retaining exclusive control over the aesthetic aspect of the objects they produce in their workshops, even for those who run medium to large companies or those who have worked with the same collaborators for many years. In its traditional conception, the creative activity of design should be more abstract, as noted indirectly by the lamp maker: "I think I am a designer . . . but at the same time, I have never worked as much with material, I mean raw material" (respondent 4). This observation that opposes the work of the designer to the material reveals how conception is thought of as an intellectual process in which drawing is the preferred means to express ideas. In this regard, it seems that drawing has kept an aura in this community of creators. One respondent reports a conversation she had with another well-known designer during which they both admitted they do not have sketchbooks and do not necessarily conceive their pieces through drawing. However, she claims, it remains taboo as drawing is the classical conceptual tool of the designer. For her part, she prefers to work directly with the material, as does the other respondent who says: "It happens often that I do not draw, I do the pattern directly, and I do [the piece] in fabric. I draw sometimes, but it is more because the clients want it" (Respondent 7).

While the lines between the work of the artisan and the designer are not clear, both milieus nevertheless provoke strong reactions from some craftspeople. Several respondents are reluctant to call themselves artisans, as the term feels dated, even if their work has a strong link to the artisan culture. Indeed, they perceive the milieu of artisans as a community associated with old craftmanship culture dating back to the 1970s. Younger craftspeople may not necessarily want to be associated with this milieu (respondent 2), as they do not share the "same vision" (respondent 7) or perceive it as being too strongly rooted in traditional techniques and aesthetics that are not expressive enough (respondent 1). In this regard, younger craftspeople are closer to the vision promoted by Montreal policies, as they prefer the term designer, which conveys a more contemporary image of creativity. Therefore, some respondents try to reconcile both sides in their practice, like this craftsman who produces contemporary pieces of furniture: "We have tried to take our distance from the idea of the artisan. We are still an artisanal company, as we manufacture one piece of furniture at a time. We are not on the production line or into big production. There is still an artisanal aspect in terms of production, but in terms of conception, I consider the company more as a design company" (respondent 3).

Conversely, association with the designer community may also provoke a push-back reaction from some respondents who do not feel included in this community. Here again, the reaction is based on a certain image of design that is widely promoted these days in Montreal. Indeed, several respondents associate the design community with the idea of fashion and trends,[25] and even global trends. Such a vision divides the craft community in Montreal. For two respondents (5 and 6), their business is based on current trends in lifestyle and home interior design, and they try to stay up-to-date with the latest trends or even precede them. "I do research. I am very curious about the trends. I am looking for what is going on around me. And I think about the products that I could develop" (respondent 5). If, for these craftspeople, staying in touch with the zeitgeist is paramount, the exact opposite is at the heart of the vision of other craftspeople who are generally sceptical of the city's efforts to promote design. "I have a flair for trends, and I do not like them. When I see them, I say to myself, 'okay, we do not do this'" (respondent 1). For these creators, their originality comes from their independence: "I do not look at what is going on around me. I do not look for trends in magazines and blogs. There is a side of me that likes to function in my own bubble, so my creative universe is not influenced by that" (respondent 7). For these creators, the rejection of trends is consistent with their goal to craft timeless objects that could be recognised for their qualities regardless of time or context.

In summary, the relation between the artisan and design archetypes reveals a strong tension in the craft community. It is the tension between the conception of objects that should be associated with originality and innovation and the manufacturing of these objects that should demonstrate a high level of mastery in some traditional techniques and knowledge related to a specific material. The former requires looking forward, and the latter a knowledge of the past. At the heart of this tension lies the elaboration of a new "maker culture" which attempts to mix traditional knowledge with innovative ideas and processes in order to answer today's needs. Such a culture, which has been studied in other cities, like New York[26] or Portland,[27] is conceived as a counteroffensive against globalisation, which tend to standardise and dehumanise the world. Therefore, for the local craftspeople working in Montreal, the challenge is to create a business that incarnates such an alternative to the global economy.

The Entrepreneur

The negotiation between the artisan and the designer position is also reflective of how craftspeople envision entrepreneurship. In contrast to the hesitations that characterise their creative identity, all respondents are comfortable with calling themselves entrepreneurs. Furthermore, as is the case in other creative sectors,[28] this kind of entrepreneurship is often described as an adventure, fraught with challenges and strongly coloured by precariousness, but an adventure in which the creative pursuit becomes a justification for difficult working conditions.[29] Thus, several respondents see commonalities between attributes of the entrepreneur and those of the creator. For example, a craftswoman said about entrepreneurship, "It is extremely creative, this aspect of the job. This is what I like. In financial management for example, one always needs to find solutions. What I don't like is routine" (respondent 7). In such an adventure, a person's creativity is solicited not only to create the product but also to develop the entrepreneurial vision. Thus, many respondents described the creative entrepreneur as being constituted of two distinctive parts that make up the good candidate for the job. "I think of myself as a hybrid between the two. There are creators or artists that are able to calculate and who like the business part of it. I think I definitely have this entrepreneurship profile. I have always been good at mathematics, economy and finance in school, and I have always been good in visual arts" (respondent 10). This special kind of entrepreneurship, which has been described as "bohemian entrepreneurship,"[30] is not without internal conflicts. Indeed, the two sides of the profession may find themselves in conflict from time to time. This is the most common mistake made by young entrepreneurs who only "want to be an artist" (respondent 8) and forget that they have something to sell. Nevertheless, even for the successful craft entrepreneur, striking the right balance between the creative and entrepreneurial parts of the job remains a challenge, with most of the respondents reporting that their creative time is constantly constrained by business tasks.

If craft entrepreneurship is a special kind of business, this is primarily because there are strong values at the core of the business activity. Indeed, all respondents are striving to conceive, produce and sell objects that are creative, sustainable and locally produced. These three elements form the core values of their version of craft entrepreneurship and as such, they are worth exploring further as they may sometime enter into conflict with the business imperative.

Creativity, Sustainability, Locality

The first value to which all respondents are strongly attached is creativity, since they see it as the main resource through which their business can distinguish itself. However, the requirements of creation are not necessarily easy to reconcile with the crude realities of business. This is what one respondent expresses when she says she would prefer to be liberated from the obligation to make a living out of her craft activity. She gives the following example: "There is a call for submissions for an exhibition right now. We would like to propose four pairs of shoes with unusual materials. We could put a sole in wood, mold another sole in ceramic, we could print in 3D, or work with other material like concrete. This is very interesting as we could unleash our artistic side" (respondent 2). While the business side of her activity is experienced mainly as a limitation for this craftswoman, who is still at the start-up stage of her company, it takes a whole different meaning for another respondent, who has been very successful lately. For him, the business side is a real driver of his creativity. "I don't like things that are frozen in time. I like projects. I am an entrepreneur by heart, and I am looking for ways to bring projects to my company. So, as soon as I finish a model, I am like: what's next?" For him, success in business means more possibilities for creation. "I like to make money, not for the sake of it, but to feed the workshop, to get new means, to be able to buy new tools, give better salaries. All this makes me want to have a viable business" (respondent 4). In a way, each craft entrepreneur talks about the tension between the two side of the business and the necessity to find the right balance, whether it is by maintaining the production of their best-seller products while proposing more experimental products (respondents 5 and 9), creating new products along the same lines of previous ones for loyal customers (Respondent 3), abandoning production that is too complicated for more promising projects (respondent 1) or developing new partnerships to renew the production (respondent 10). Yet, despite all compromises, creativity remains a key value for these craftspeople. This is what one respondent expresses when she says, "If you want to be creative, you cannot start by asking yourself: will it sell? This is not how it works!" (respondent 1).

Beyond the primary value of creativity, two complementary values are common in the craft community and strongly colour the production: sustainability and locality. Indeed, the strong relation that many craftspeople have developed with the material and savoir faire becomes an integral part of their business. Fabricating objects in high-quality material, following a well-mastered technique, together with a small team of local craftspeople is a way to propose an alternative to our consumer culture. If such a position has developed from a critical perspective on the capitalist economy, a whole market for sustainable goods, respectful of environmental and ethical principles, has developed. Many craft businesses in Montreal are intentionally situating themselves in this market segment. Nevertheless, the integration of such values in a business model is not without contradictions. One good example is provided by respondent 2, who is attached to the idea of producing shoes that are made to last at least ten years. By doing so, she wants to bring her brand in the "slow fashion movement" that has developed in reaction to the "fast fashion" which is increasingly prevalent. To do so, they use the traditional material of shoemaking, leather, which raises other concerns related to the environment. "The use of leather is an important debate: vegan leather versus animal leather. But vegan leather is in fact plastic. So, in the end, I don't know what's best."

A similar tension over material is reported by another respondent who is specialised in producing goods from recycled material. "When you recycle

material, it takes a lot of energy: you need to find the material, clean it, sort it.
... If you work with material that is not noble, you won't be able to justify the
price. Often, young creators start to recycle jeans or jute, but these initiatives
collapse because the business model is not working" (respondent 10). In her
case, she developed a successful business model by working predominantly
with fur, a material that can raise similar questions to leather from an environmental point of view, but for which a certain price can be justified. These
two cases show how the relation to the material is subject to contradictory
values that sometimes confront each other in a craft project. In the end, the
values promoted must always be balanced with market reality. In most cases
studied here, it means developing a luxury product, which contradicts the ac-
cessibility ideal many craftspeople also pursue.

Similar dilemmas can be found in the respondents' strong attachment to
local production. Many of the respondents praise their team of dedicated
workers (respondent 7), their long-time collaborators (respondent 1) or even
their network of local suppliers (respondent 8). Producing locally allows
these craftspeople to keep an eye on the production and make sure that the
quality they want is met. "I prefer to have a smaller company but to be able to
keep control over the quality" (respondent 3). However, this engagement with
local production goes beyond the business aspect when company becomes
rather a community. "This is the social fabric that we create here, the way
employees talk about the enterprise culture. There are new couples forming
here, babies, families. This is where it makes sense for me" (respondent 4).
If supporting the community can be both a driver and a stressful pressure for
these entrepreneurs, some of them are wondering to what extent they should
stick to the principle. Is it important, for example, to produce the packaging
locally? Should they find a local supplier even for parts that have nothing to
do with the aesthetic aspect of the product? And in the end, to what extent is
it important for the customer anyway?

CONCLUSION

Finally, for the Montreal craft community, being an entrepreneur means
developing a practice that is based on creativity, sustainability and locality
while being able to find suitable market outputs for their products. This is
revealing of tension between market reality and the core values at the heart
of craftsmanship each craftsperson must face to be successful from a business
point of view but also faithful to their beliefs.

This investigation has exposed the "maker culture" that is currently developing in Montreal, in which the craft community has an important role

to play. As it is framed in part by cultural policies, this culture implies a forward-looking vision in which creators are painted as innovators and developers, but also a movement towards the revival of ancestral techniques and traditional knowledge. This vision redraws the contours of object-making in the city and proposes an alternative version of market economy in which objects are not appreciated only for their price but also for their intrinsic qualities and the values they carry. If the intention of the Montreal craft community is not necessarily to change the world for good with their objects, they nevertheless attempt to bring about a world that is more creative, more sustainable and more ethical and human.

The maker culture that is unfolding in Montreal takes place within our current market economy. Yet, it does not mean that the craft community has to be entirely subordinated to the market needs, and several of its members have the ambition to make the business sector evolve through their action. As it has been noted, craft products constitute a form of "contested commodity"[31] which questions our relation to our current consumer culture. In this perspective, many craftspeople insist on the necessity of educating customers about their field, whether it is the quality of the material, the fabrication process or the sustainability of products. In their view, such education has the potential to transform the way people see objects and make them more appreciative of high-quality craftsmanship. The craft community is nevertheless fully aware that Montreal remains a very small market, even if it becomes more educated on good craftsmanship. Yet many of its members are wondering if their future as entrepreneurs lies in an ever-expanding market, as such a vision might be too close to the capitalist orthodoxy that these unconventional entrepreneurs constantly challenge.

APPENDIX A

Policy Documents, City of Montreal

Ville de Montréal. (2005). *Montréal, métropole culturelle: Politique de développement culturel 2005–2015*. Ville de Montréal.
Ville de Montréal. (2006). *Montréal, ville UNESCO de design* (dossier de candidature). Ville de Montréal.
Ville de Montréal. (2007). *Plan d'action 2007–2017: Montréal, métropole culturelle*. Ville de Montréal.
Ville de Montréal. (2012). *Plan d'action 2007–2017: Montréal, métropole culturelle, édition 2012*. Ville de Montréal.
Ville de Montréal. (2012). *Chantier Montréal ville UNESCO de design en actions et en chiffres: Compte -rendu 2006–2012*. Bureau du design, Ville de Montréal.

Ville de Montréal. (2014). *Plan d'action 2007–2017: Montréal, métropole culturelle, édition 2014.* Ville de Montréal.

Ville de Montréal. (2016). *Rapport d'activités / Montréal ville UNESCO de design.* Bureau du design, Ville de Montréal.

Ville de Montréal. (2017). *Montréal, métropole culturelle: Conjuguer la créativité et l'expérience culturelle citoyenne à l'ère du numérique et de la diversité: Politique de développement culturel 2017–2022.* Service de la culture, Ville de Montréal.

Ville de Montréal. (2018). *Créer Montréal: Plan d'action en design.* Bureau du design, Ville de Montréal.

APPENDIX B

Table 6.1. List of Respondents

	Specialization	Foundation	Number of Employees
Respondent 1	Ceramist	1996	6
Respondent 2	Shoemaking	2017	2
Respondent 3	Woodworking	2003	20
Respondent 4	Lamp making	2010	60
Respondent 5	Stationery	2011	4
Respondent 6	Household linen	2014	1
Respondent 7	Toys in fabric	2005	3
Respondent 8	Custom objects	2009	1
Respondent 9	Concrete objects and architectural elements	2001	8
Respondent 10	Recycled clothes and accessories/ Millinery	1993	8

NOTES

1. The author acknowledges the financial support of Fonds de recherche du Québec—Société et culture.

2. Alexandra Midal, *Design: Introduction à l'histoire d'une discipline* (Paris: Pocket, 2009).

3. Caroline Mazaud, "Artisan, de l'homme de métier au gestionnaire?," *Travail et emploi* no. 130 (2012).

4. Lucila Carvalho, Andy Dong, and Karl Maton, "Legitimating Design: A Sociology of Knowledge Account of the Field," *Design Studies* 30, no. 5 (2009).

5. Répertoire des designers du Bureau du design, Ville de Montréal and Répertoire des artisans professionnels du Conseil des métiers d'art du Québec.

6. Semi-structured interviews were conducted between May 2 and June 5, 2019, with ten craftspeople. Generally, the interviews took place in their workshops or boutiques.

7. Guillaume Sirois and Guy Bellavance, "Organisations émergentes du monde de l'art: Une analyse de l'hybridité des logiques d'action," *Recherches en communication* no. 47 (2018).

8. Jim McGuigan, *Cool Capitalism* (London: Pluto, 2009).

9. *Montréal, ville UNESCO de design* (dossier de candidature) (2006),

10. Robert Hewison, *Cultural Capital: The Rise and Fall of Creative Britain* (London: Verso, 2014).

11. David Throsby, *The Economics of Cultural Policy* (Cambridge: Cambridge University Press, 2010).

12. Jamie Peck, "Struggling with the Creative Class," *International Journal of Urban and Regional Research* 29, no. 4 (2005): 740–70; Andy Pratt, "Creative Cities: The Cultural Industries and the Creative Class." *Geografiska Annaler* 90, no. 2 (2008): 107–17.

13. Elsa Vivant, *Qu'est-Ce Que La Ville Créative ?* Paris: Presses universitaires de France, 2009.

14. Kevin Stolarick, Richard Florida, and Louis Musante, *Montréal, ville de convergences creatives: Perspective et possibilités* (Catalytix, 2005)

15. *Plan d'action 2007–2017: Montréal, métropole culturelle* (2007), 16.

16. *Plan d'action 2007–2017: Montréal, métropole culturelle* (2014), 10.

17. *Montréal, métropole culturelle: Conjuguer la créativité et l'expérience culturelle citoyenne à l'ère du numérique et de la diversité: Politique de développement culturel 2017–2022* (2017), 23.

18. Pierre-Michel Menger, *Portrait de l'artiste en travailleur: Métamorphoses du capitalisme* (Paris: Seuil, 2002).

19. *Montréal, ville UNESCO de design* (dossier de candidature) (2006), 5.

20. *Créer Montréal: Plan d'action en design* (2018), 18.

21. *Plan d'action 2007–2017: Montréal, métropole culturelle* (2014), 11.

22. *Montréal, métropole culturelle: Conjuguer la créativité* (2017), 39.

23. *Créer Montréal* (2018), 23.

24. All interviews were conducted in French. All quotes provided here are my translation from the original in French.

25. Guillaume Erner, *Sociologie Des Tendances* (Paris: PUF, 2008).

26. Richard E. Ocejo, *Masters of Craft: Old Jobs in the New Urban Economy* (Princeton, NJ: Princeton University Press, 2017).

27. Steve Marotta and Charles Heying, "Interrogating Localism: What Does 'Made in Portland' Really Mean?" in *Craft Economies*, Susan Luckman and Nicola Thomas, eds., 141–49 (London: Bloomsbury, 2018).

28. Andrea Hausmann, "German Artists between Bohemian Idealism and Entrepreneurial Dynamics," *International Journal of Arts Management* 12, no. 2 (2010).

29. Angela McRobbie, *Be Creative: Making a Living in the New Culture Industries* (Cambridge: Polity, 2016).

30. Doris Ruth Eikhof and Axel Haunschild, "Lifestyle Meets Market: Bohemian Entrepreneurs in Creative Industries," *Creativity and Innovation Management* 15, no. 3 (2006): 234–41.

31. Susan Luckman and Nicola Thomas, eds. *Craft Economies* (London: Bloomsbury, 2018).

BIBLIOGRAPHY

Bajard, Flora. "Du travail d'atelier au collectif: L'inscription professionnelle ambivalente des 'céramistes-créateurs.'" *Sociologie de l'art* 21 (2012): 43–64.

Carvalho, Lucila, Andy Dong, and Karl Maton. "Legitimating Design: A Sociology of Knowledge Account of the Field." *Design Studies* 30, no. 5 (2009): 483–502.

Eikhof, Doris Ruth, and Axel Haunschild. "Lifestyle Meets Market: Bohemian Entrepreneurs in Creative Industries," *Creativity and Innovation Management* 15, no. 3 (2006).

Erner, Guillaume. *Sociologie des tendances.* Paris: PUF, 2008.

Hausmann, Andrea. "German Artists between Bohemian Idealism and Entrepreneurial Dynamics." *International Journal of Arts Management* 12, no. 2 (2010): 17–29.

Hewison, Robert. *Cultural Capital: The Rise and Fall of Creative Britain.* London: Verso, 2014.

Jourdain, Anne. "La construction sociale de la singularité: Une stratégie entrepreneuriale des artisans d'art." *Revue française de socio-économie* 2, no. 6 (2010): 13–30.

Lipovetsky, Gilles, and Jean Serroy. *L'esthétisation du monde: Vivre à l'âge du capitalisme artiste.* Paris: Gallimard, 2013.

Luckman, Susan, and Nicola Thomas, eds. *Craft Economies.* London: Bloomsbury, 2018.

Marotta, Steve, and Charles Heying. "Interrogating Localism: What Does 'Made in Portland' Really Mean?" In *Craft Economies*, edited by Susan Luckman and Nicola Thomas, 141–49. London: Bloomsbury, 2018.

Mazaud, Caroline. "Artisan, de l'homme de métier au gestionnaire?." *Travail et emploi*, no. 130 (2012): 9–20.

McGuigan, Jim. *Cool Capitalism.* London: Pluto, 2009.

McRobbie, Angela. *Be Creative: Making a Living in the New Culture Industries.* Cambridge: Polity, 2016.

Menger, Pierre-Michel. *Portrait de l'artiste en travailleur: Métamorphoses du capitalisme.* Paris: Seuil, 2002.

Midal, Alexandra. *Design: Introduction à l'histoire d'une discipline.* Paris: Pocket, 2009.

Ocejo, Richard E. *Masters of Craft: Old Jobs in the New Urban Economy.* Oxford: Princeton University Press, 2017.

Peck, Jamie. "Struggling with the Creative Class." *International Journal of Urban and Regional Research* 29, no. 4 (2005): 740–70.

Pratt, Andy. "Creative Cities: The Cultural Industries and the Creative Class." *Geografiska Annaler* 90, no. 2 (2008): 107–17.

Sirois, Guillaume, and Guy Bellavance. "Organisations émergentes du monde de l'art: Une analyse de l'hybridité des logiques d'action." *Recherches en communication* no. 47 (2018): 89–107.

Stolarick, Kevin, Richard Florida, and Louis Musante, *Montréal, ville de convergences creatives: Perspective et possibilités.* Catalytix, 2005.

Throsby, David. *The Economics of Cultural Policy.* Cambridge: Cambridge University Press, 2010.

Vial, Stéphane. *Le design.* Paris: PUF, 2017.

Vivant, Elsa. *Qu'est-Ce Que La Ville Créative ?* Paris: Presses universitaires de France, 2009.

Part II

Challenges of Craft Entrepreneurship

Chapter Seven

"I Can't Put That Out There as Me"

Exploring the Relationship between Creative Identity and Intellectual Property in the Representation of Contemporary Craft Online

Lauren England

Studies on cultural and creative labour have highlighted the centrality of creative identity in the pursuit of creative work and self-expression as a motivator for creative behaviours.[1] Recent work on craft micro-entrepreneurship has also highlighted the importance of finding and expressing a distinctive personal voice, to attract and communicate with audiences and consumers through self-representations. These often integrate aspects of both personal and professional life,[2] particularly when using online retail platforms and social media.[3] There is currently limited discussion of how this manifestation of identity is managed by early career contemporary craft makers representing their work online in relation to intellectual property (IP).

This chapter investigates this connection, specifically the links between IP and the development of a recognisable style or "fingerprint," and the relationship this has with IP for early career makers. In particular, this chapter reflects on the issues that arise for these nascent craft entrepreneurs in the representation and marketing of their work online and via social media. This is an important consideration in the craft context where narrative construction and visual self-representation are integral to both creative[4] and entrepreneurial practices.[5] Craft work is more readily associated with a love of making and the pursuit of autonomy and job satisfaction[6] than with entrepreneurship and the generation and exploitation of IP. Nevertheless, these are important considerations for craft makers operating in increasingly competitive creative markets both online and offline[7] and in relation to how craft is understood and positioned[8] within the wider Creative Industries context when developing training, business advice and policies to support sustainable sector development.

The chapter begins with an introduction to the literature on craft identities, makers' use of social media and how IP relates to craft. After presenting the approach to this research, the chapter draws from the perspectives of early career makers to explore the identity link between craft producers and their products or artefacts and its relationship with IP protection. Three key themes are presented here: the delicate boundary between inspiration and copying when engaging in craft work and how makers self-regulate against copying in the pursuit of original creative self-expression; that the protection of an individual's creative identity has both a moral and economic dimension; and that greater exposure and creating a recognisable signature or creative "fingerprint" could assist in informal protection and policing by audiences. It is highlighted that these practices are primarily conducted outside of the formal framework of copyright and often bypass legal protection. Issues arising from the use of social media in craft enterprise and the self or audience-regulation of online spaces are discussed in relation to these core themes. The chapter concludes with a call for further research on contemporary craft and early career management, and greater clarity on makers' intellectual property rights (IPRs), particularly in relation to the increasing representation of craft and makers online.

CRAFT IDENTITIES, SOCIAL MEDIA AND IP

Crafting Identity

Self-representation within creative work in the form of a creative identity is well documented in the literature. Glăveanu and Tanggaard[9] define creative identites as "representational projects emerging in the interaction between self (the creator), multiple others (different audiences), and notions of creativity informed by societal discourses." Meanwhile, Gotsi et al.[10] describe the pursuit of this as a creative's "desire to see themselves as distinctive in their artistry, passion, and self-expression." This approach emphasises the intrinsic drivers and rewards associated with creative practice and craft work specifically.[11]

While creative identity is understood to be socially constructed and mediated,[12] the concept of creativity as individualised, unique and focused on novelty is pervasive in contemporary discourse about craft and disseminated widely by policy and cultural and educational institutions.[13] In the context of craft entrepreneurship, the process of narrative construction and visual self-representation[14] is acknowledged as a form of self-branding through which makers can position and market original craft products.[15] It is also noted that storytelling on social media can help to construct a narrative that increases consumer appreciation for craft work and develops an understanding of its associated cultural and monetary value.[16]

What has so far been underexplored is the link between this representation of creative identity and IP, particularly in relation to how this identity is presented and shared on global digital platforms. This chapter therefore seeks to develop our understanding of how craft entrepreneurs negotiate their creative identity and present this online as part of building brand awareness and reputation.[17] From this perspective we can explore the subsequent entanglement of creative identity and online representation with IP concerns and consider the challenges and opportunities that social media platforms present craft entrepreneurs in marketing, selling and protecting their work.

These issues are particularly interesting to investigate during the early career period, as presented in this chapter, as this is a formative stage[18] in which a professional body of work is created and promoted.[19] It is therefore a point where IP may become important as the maker seeks to assert their position in the market. However, it is also a period where creative identity is still being developed.[20] The construction and legitimisation of entrepreneurial identity is understood to be particularly challenging for nascent entrepreneurs.[21] As such, early-career craft makers are likely to experience particular challenges in the negotiation of their online creative identity and in securing IP protection.

Crafting Online

Social media is now an integral component in craft entrepreneurship; self-representation across multiple online platforms (websites and various social media platforms) has become the new normal, a professional baseline[22] for those looking to create and sustain a craft business. Thomas et al.[23] identify online and digital tools as enabling: "social exchange; access to educational resources; audiences; peer support; marketing and online selling; just-in-time production/bespoke manufacturing; customer engagement and bespoke customization." Yair[24] also highlights how storytelling on social media can be used to add value to craft products while Patel[25] identifies social media platforms as sites for signalling creative and cultural expertise in order to secure work in increasingly competitive marketplaces.

Research into online communities of craft practice[26] presents social media platforms as sites for craft engagement, collaboration and support,[27] the sharing of skills and knowledge[28] and debates around ideology and practice.[29] However, in the increasingly competitive and globalised market for contemporary craft, makers face growing challenges when disseminating their creative and professional identities online in standing out from the crowd, staking a claim to work made in a particular style, getting there before someone else and effectively communicating ones' creative identity in a visual format. Arguably this leads makers to take a highly individualised approach to social media promotion. While a valuable tool for creatives, social media can however have negative consequeses for mental health.[30] In the craft context this can be seen in relation to pressure to maintain an online presence and feeling exposed[31] and vulnerable in showing work in progress or getting public feedback on work.

Craft and IP

The growing representation of craft work online and its promotion via social media also has significant implications for IP protection. IP is defined as "creations of the mind, such as inventions; literary and artistic works; designs; and symbols, names and images used in commerce."[32] IP protection can be used for financial benefit, but also to gain recognition for a creation through moral rights attribution.[33] One form of IP protection is copyright, "a legal term used to describe the rights that creators have over their literary and artistic works."[34] To gain copyright protection the first requirement is originality.[35] This is split into two components; the work must be "independently created by the author and not copied from other works" and it must possess "at least some minimum degree of creativity."[36] While automatic, copyright protection only applies to works that have been "fixed in a tangible medium or expression"[37] and therefore only the physical artefact rather than the idea is protected.

For design-based craft work, protection is also automatically gained for the shape and configuration of objects through "Design right," although formally registering a design can achieve better protection for its appearance, physical shape, configuration and decoration.[38] Alternatively, product makers can apply for a patent to protect their work, although there is a requirement to demonstrate technical innovation. Trademarks for brand names and logos have also been used by larger scale producers such as Wedgewood ceramics and Murano glass to assert authenticity and distinguish from imitation products.[39]

A heightened sense of individualism in craft work and a growing concern with IP[40] is interesting as craft has historically been "integrally associated with openness, collaboration and sharing."[41] This is in part due to a reliance on the sharing of techniques, knowledge and skills[42] and the tacit knowledge element of craft practices that have depended on personal interactions in order to pass on techniques.[43] However, the growing number of self-taught makers using resources such as YouTube to learn and develop their craft skills and pass them on digitally[44] presents an alternative to this physical community and challenges the co-location requirement.

It is important to consider whether the increased interest in IP is beneficial to craft makers and craft practices, or whether it is a response to the "positioning of IPRs as an increasingly important economic strategy for Global

North nations"[45] and the status of crafts within the Creative Industries. IP is central to the definition of Creative Industries given by the DCMS as those originating from "individual creativity, skill and talent," with "potential for wealth and job creation through the generation and exploitation of intellectual property."[46]

Public debates on copyright and legal settlements are fairly rare in contemporary craft circles,[47] perhaps due to uncertainty in craft communities about their rights.[48] However, as online representation and e-commerce becomes more important for craft entrepreneurs,[49] the relationship between craft and IP arguably becomes increasingly complex and a greater consideration for craft makers. Several issues arise from the position of craft within copyright law; first, while they may be artistic, the utilitarian nature of some craft objects (i.e., furniture or tableware) can disqualify them from copyright protection under the category of "works of artistic craftmanship," as functional objects require patent protection. Second, claiming ownership over a particular manifestation of artistic expression in a craft work can be challenging when such works use techniques derived from traditional craft skills, which are designed to be shared.[50]

Yood and Warmus present that craft continues to reside in "that curious zone between influence, homage and theft,"[51] while Adamson[52] states that "all culture is, to some degree animated by ideas borrowed from elsewhere," resulting in significant problems both in the application of copyright protection and cultural appropriation. It has further been argued that copyright "is a specifically modern institution,"[53] which subsequently has difficulty accounting for traditional forms of craft work such as quilts and practices like glassblowing whose technical and cultural origins predate copyright.[54]

Cultural entrepreneurship is associated with moral principles followed in the pursuit of "good" work, rather than the pursuit of profit.[55] The act of claiming attribution and asserting the moral rights component of copyright can therefore be used to further this endeavour and develop cultural and social capital. However, there is also potential to convert this into economic capital[56] as status and reputation are also influential in the development of artistic careers.[57] This is supported by Yood and Warmus who state that the craft market operates on a system of author recognition and reward, as exemplified by its ability to identify authorship and dictate market prices accordingly—they suggest that we can "trust in the marketplace and in history, and believe that people in the long run will distinguish and privilege originality over emulation."[58] The idea that the market and craft consumers could self-regulate against copying outside of costly legal frameworks is supported by Luckman et al.[59] who suggest that "copycats" could be discouraged through community policing and public, online "shaming" practices.

Luckman et al. also note a belief that staying ahead of trends and actively promoting work would position the maker above copycats.[60] This is important for craft entrepreneurs in establishing and sustaining a market position and has been demonstrated in recent social media shaming of large homeware and fashion retailers by artists and designers who have had their work copied.[61] In this instance community policing appears to have been somewhat effective in that products have been removed or discontinued, although not all have resulted in compensation or prevented further infringement. The cost of copyright enforcement is, however, not to be overlooked and may contribute to the lack of consideration it is given by most craft makers, particularly when going up against multinational corporations: "Justice is expensive, which means that it can become a tool of the rich, by the rich, for the rich."[62]

This chapter expands on the ideas presented earlier to explore both audience-policing and self-regulation against copying. The focus here is on this experience from the perspective of early-career makers in relation to their creation and online promotion of craft works that are intended as expressions of their creative identity.

APPROACH

This chapter builds on data collected as part of wider research on craft higher education and early career practice, considered here as the first four years of active professional practice.[63] While definitions of craft vary,[64] the focus of this chapter is on the production of 3D contemporary craft objects/artefacts in core craft materials: ceramics, furniture, glass, jewellery, metal crafts, silversmithing and textiles.[65] Interviews were conducted between 2016 and 2018 with thirty-four early career crafts practitioners (six male and twenty-eight female) pursuing independent careers in the UK. Participants all had formal further or higher craft education training (diploma, undergraduate and masters level) and the majority of participants were white. It is therefore acknowledged that experiences specific to diverse makers[66] and those who have not received a formal craft education may not be fully represented in this study and requires further research. The interviews focused on makers' experiences of developing and sustaining their professional practice as nascent craft entrepreneurs. Thematic analysis was applied to the interviews with iterative rounds of coding to specifically consider the way interviewees articulated the relationship between their creative identity, its online representation and IP. All participants in this study are anonymous and are distinguished here by their material discipline and a participant number.

FINDING YOUR FINGERPRINT

As discussed previously, craft communities can provide "natural protection" and self-police work that is seen to be too derivative, particularly in close-knit discipline groups such as glassmaking.[67] When discussing their concern or lack of concern with IP in relation to their creative practice and business, participants highlighted their awareness of issues around copying, gained either from personal experience or secondhand from friends, university tutors or the media. A delicate boundary was identified between being inspired by another maker's work and directly copying, and participants emphasised that it was important to know the market and what others were making in order to avoid unconscious as well as conscious copying, referred to as "crossing boundaries" or "treading on toes."

Certain characteristics of craft work mean that this boundary can be blurry; some participants acknowledged the challenge of working with traditional or ubiquitous craft materials and processes (i.e., throwing clay or blowing glass) in that their work used well known and used techniques which in turn created a greater likelihood of crossover between their work and others'. Here, the way in which skills are passed down between makers, and the somewhat derivative nature of craft work[68] created a feeling that there were "no original ideas left." For some this negated concern over unintended copying. As expressed by a glassmaker, concern over this form of unintentional similarity was further diminished by a belief that no legal action would be taken.

> it's like something that you can't get out of. Because you'll always find somebody who's work looks similar to yours, and you can be right at the end of making it and then find that person on Instagram. And you're like "argh what do I do now?" And you just think well who cares you know, he's not going to sue me. (glassmaker 1)

Nevertheless, even when engaging with traditional or well-utilised techniques, participants explained how they focused on applying these in a novel way in order to differentiate themselves. Here the importance was placed on achieving a recognizable style, or as one participant described it, "finding my fingerprint" (ceramicist 2). This included developing distinctive approaches to traditional techniques—"making it your own"—as expressed here: "we are all inspired by people and that's not a problem at all, but you make it your own you know, there's a million sgraffito artists but I make it my own, you need to make it your own" (ceramicist 1). This is particularly significant for early career makers as this is a period where inspiration will often be drawn from the work of others, including both established artists and other emerging makers.[69] As such, the risk of falling on the wrong side of the fine line between drawing inspiration and copying may be heightened.

In spaces such as shared or open-access studios, the potential for imitation can also be exacerbated by the proximity of makers and display of work (finished and in progress) in the studio, and through the use of common materials, as noted here—"we use the same clay so it can be hard to tell the difference, and we use a lot of same glazes" (ceramicist 4). This creates issues around market saturation and network lock-in, particularly when makers are selling or exhibiting similar work in the same venue.[70] Early career makers without the resources or expertise to set up their own studio may be more reliant on such shared workspaces and therefore more likely to experience this issue.

However, the desire to create work that authentically displayed their creative identity also prevented makers from producing, marketing or selling work that was considered to be too close to the work of others. This suggests that these makers were self-regulating against copyright infringement, usually related to a respect for other creatives whose work they admired. Below, a jeweller describes an experiment which they chose not to pursue further as they felt it bore too great a resemblance to the work of another jeweller who they respected.

> There was just traits of it that looked more like [another maker's] than it did mine . . . knowing that that was already something that was out there I thought well I can't put that out there as me. Number one I don't wanna tread on [their] toes, but I wanna make sure that what I'm putting out there will, you can tell it's my work. (jeweller 1)

Although it was acknowledged that they had not consciously copied their work, it was felt that the final product did not bear a strong enough connection to their own creative identity to stake a claim over it. There was also concern that this new item might be associated more readily with the other maker as it lacked a distinct sense of their own creative identity. This suggests that the concern with the representation of an authentic creative identity has both a moral (attribution) and a commercial dimension.

MORALS AND MONEY:
PROTECTING CREATIVE IDENTITY

Where participants *were* concerned with their IPRs there was little reference to financial motivations such as exploiting their IP to generate income, as advocated for in creative industries policy.[71] Rather, their concern was for protecting their creative identity and the visual connection between the maker and their designs, as articulated here: "I had it happen once and had a bit of a falling out with somebody and it's, it's horrible but yes I suppose really you do need to know where you stand with your work don't you and protect it, protect your creative identity" (ceramicist 3).

A commercial dynamic was however observed in the distinction made between copying that took place between hobby-level and professional-level makers; it was seen as more acceptable to imitate another maker if the product was for personal use or enjoyment, but the sale of such works crossed a line. A ceramicist stated that "if someone makes something and you really like it and you just made one for yourself at home, that's ok, I mean that can happen. But if you sell it, that's not ok" (ceramicist 5).

This distinction also applied to online spaces; the intention to sell a product that had been copied from another maker was determined by whether it appeared on a personal or business page on Facebook, Instagram or a website. As reflected in the following quotation, here it is the commercial business that is being protected rather than the creative identity of the maker. The growing use of online platforms for craft retail[72] can be seen as exacerbating this problem as it creates greater competition between hobbyist and professional makers.[73]

> Somebody had just ripped off my work . . . she'd put it on her business page. Had it not been on her business page fine . . . I had to be like, ok but don't sell them! And then it got a bit worse so I had to be like I'm sorry, cease and desist. (ceramicist 1)

However, it was often articulated that a makers' ability to protect their work, morally or financially, was limited to sending a cease and desist notification. This was primarily associated with the high costs of obtaining legal advice or more formal protection, as articulated here: "there's not much point in me sort of forking out the money to protect my designs, unfortunately that's the way it is. But I can't afford to do that at the moment" (jeweller 2).

MANAGING ONLINE PRESENTATION
AND AUDIENCE-REGULATED PROTECTION

One way in which graduates identified that they could informally protect their work (for free) or negate the negative effects of being copied was in actively and openly promoting their work to a wide audience so as to create an association between the style or creative identity of the maker which could be recognised by an audience. Following the suggestion of Yood and Warmus[74] and the findings of Luckman et al.,[75] this would then allow for a distinction between an "original" and a "rip off" product. As expressed here, achieving the greatest exposure possible was an advantage as it created an association between the maker and the product or a particular visual style: "You've just gotta do, do the thing first and better and more exposed. You've gotta do it bigger than anyone else" (furniture maker 1). This included promoting their work via social media as an aspect of their entrepreneurial practice. In this way the audience were used to policing copying, both in relation to their own purchasing choices, but also in notifying makers of similar works, again supporting the work of Luckman et al.[76] and following media reports on the copying of craft and design works.[77]

Alternatively, some makers actively limited the online presence of finished works out of concern for copying: "I don't share a lot of my work online . . . there's always that thought of what if I put something online and then see it the day after and someone else has made it" (jeweller 3). Alternative strategies for reducing others' ability to copy their designs included restricting the visibility of final products by only posting "snippets of things, or stuff that doesn't really matter" (ceramicisit 4), or focusing on sharing the making process rather than the final product. One maker also described their practice of signing, dating and sealing original copies of designs/drawings as proof of creative authorship that could be used in the event that designs were copied. Although the effectiveness of this method had not been tested in a legal setting, it had proved effective in deterring a major UK fashion label in using one of their jewellery designs that had been appropriated by an intern without the need for legal action. This experience is described in the following extract.

> Before I post it [a drawing] online I'll always put it into an envelope with a stamp on it, post it, it will come back to my house but it will have a date on it . . . so if it did go to court for whatever reason then obviously I could give that to court and then they'd see sealed in the envelope with the stamp with a date on it. Luckily I had that and it was resolved, I got an apology, I got a gift card and everything! (jeweller 4)

The function of self-managing product representation online or gaining exposure via social media and using audience-regulation were both often related to makers' perceived lack of ability to pursue legal avenues due to their cost, complexity and ineffectiveness as mentioned earlier. This message had also been reinforced by lectures given as part of degree programmes and CPD training, and by legal and craft sector professionals, as articulated in the following quote:

> All the legal people basically said like yeah you can't do anything! The thing they suggested, just if you come up with something, uh just make it the best, do

it the best and just get the most coverage for it so if anyone rips it off it's like oh he's ripping of that guy! (furniture/product maker 2)

This supports the idea that online exposure for creatives and makers can help them achieve the status and reputation which is understood to be influential in the development of artistic careers,[78] and that craft audiences are expected to self-regulate against copy-cats[79] by recognizing "rip-offs" as having lower market value. However, it also serves to highlight potential barriers to legal advice and representation faced by early career makers.

CONCLUSION

This chapter has sought to develop our understanding of how creative identity relates to IP and social media representation in the context of craft entrepreneurship. Here the need to share online to promote one's craft work and generate sales is positioned in tension with the need to protect designs and limit what is shared in order to reduce the likelihood of copying. Practices of self-regulation against copyright have also been identified as makers self-select the work they claim as their own, or alternatively feel where this connection is not strong enough that "I can't put that out there as me" (jeweller 1). This draws attention to the delicate and blurred boundary between inspiration and copying in relation to the use of craft materials and processes.

This can be considered as a characteristic of craft work which is particularly significant for early career craft entrepreneurs who are are still developing their professional work, constructing their creative identity and establishing their place in the market. However, it is also relevant for craft entrepreneurs at a variety of career stages in relation to their IPRs and how they market and sell their works online.

It is argued here that the successful creation of a recognisable visual signature or "fingerprint" and the consistent dissemination of creative identity, both on and offline, acts as an informal method of IP protection through audience-driven policing and attribution. However, rather than being limited to non-economic, intrinsic rewards,[80] it is suggested that there are both moral and financial incentives for the attribution of craft work, particularly online. It is however argued that makers' strategies for regulating against copyright (both personally and through the support of audiences) are conducted outside of the formal frameworks of IP legislation and often bypass legal protection. While this can be considered to be a feature of craft entrepreneurship, it may be particularly important during the early career period when makers may lack the financial means to pursue formal IP protection or have not yet developed a product that meets legislative requirements.

These findings have implications for craft education and business development support in relation to strategies for social media marketing, IPRs and the formal and informal regulation of online spaces. There are also policy implications as the IP of craft entrepreneurs does not appear to be formally protected or exploited, thereby contesting the emphasis on this in Creative Industries policy.[81] Nevertheless, it is important to consider the potential benefits of increased protection for craft, as income generation through IP exploitation could improve the sector's status within the Creative Industries. Further research on contemporary craft and makers' IP rights is therefore required, including access to IP protection, legal advice and the relevance of current legal frameworks. This is particularly important in relation to the increasing representation of craft work and craft entrepreneurs online.

The focus here has been on how this is experienced by early career makers. It is suggested that the negotiation of creative identity online is especially challenging for this group of craft entrepreneurs as they seek to establish themselves in increasingly competitive markets where digital platforms offer opportunities to sell craft work and build a brand, but also carry risks. It is also argued that barriers to IP protection are greater for this group given the financial implications and limited professional experience or networks from which to draw support from. Further research into how these issues are experienced and addressed by makers with both developing and established brand identities is, however, needed to support the sustainable development of the sector.

NOTES

1. Vlad Petre Glăveanu and Lene Tanggaard, "Creativity, Identity, and Representation: Towards a Socio-Cultural Theory of Creative Identity," *New Ideas in Psychology* 34 (2014); Manto Gotsi et al., "Managing Creatives: Paradoxical Approaches to Identity Regulation," *Human Relations* 63, no. 6 (2010); Ed Petkus, "The Creative Identity: Creative Behavior from the Symbolic Interactionist Perspective," *Journal of Creative Behavior* 30, no. 3 (1996); Stephanie Taylor and Karen Littleton, *Contemporary Identities of Creativity and Creative Work* (Farnham, Surrey: Ashgate, 2012).
2. Susan Luckman, *Craft and the Creative Economy* (Springer, 2015).
3. Susan Luckman, Jane Andrew, and Tracy Crisp, "Crafting Self: Promoting the Making Self in the Creative Micro-Economy," (Adelaide: School of Creative Industries, University of South Australia, 2019).
4. Emma Bell et al., *The Organization of Craft Work: Identities, Meanings, and Materiality* (London: Routledge, 2018).
5. Luckman, *Craft and the Creative Economy*.
6. Mark Banks, "Craft Labour and Creative Industries," *International Journal of Cultural Policy* 16, no. 3 (2010).

7. Luckman, *Craft and the Creative Economy*.

8. Doreen Jakob and Nicola Thomas, "Firing Up Craft Capital: The Renaissance of Craft and Craft Policy in the United Kingdom," *International Journal of Cultural Policy* 23, no. 4 (2017).

9. Glăveanu and Tanggaard, "Creativity, Identity, and Representation," 12.

10. Gotsi et al., "Managing Creatives," 781.

11. Richard Sennett, *The Craftsman* (New Haven, CT: Yale University Press, 2008).

12. Glăveanu and Tanggaard, "Creativity, Identity, and Representation."

13. Chris Bilton, "Valuable Creativity: Rediscovering Purpose," in *The Palgrave Handbook of Creativity at Work* (New York: Springer, 2018).

14. Bell et al., *The Organization of Craft Work*.

15. Luckman, Andrew, and Crisp, "Crafting Self."

16. Ibid.

17. Susan Luckman and Nicola Thomas, *Craft Economies* (London: Bloomsbury, 2018).

18. Will Hunt, Linda Ball, and Emma Pollard, *Crafting Futures: A Study of the Early Careers of Craft Graduates from UK Higher Education Institutions* (London: Crafts Council, 2010).

19. Richard Caves, *Creative Industries: Contracts between Art and Commerce* (Cambridge, MA: Harvard University Press, 2000).

20. Taylor and Littleton, *Contemporary Identities of Creativity and Creative Work*.

21. Karen Williams Middleton, "Becoming Entrepreneurial: Gaining Legitimacy in the Nascent Phase," *International Journal of Entrepreneurial Behavior and Research* 19, no. 4 (2013).

22. Luckman, Andrew, and Crisp, "Crafting Self."

23. Nicola Thomas, Fiona Hackney, and Katie Bunnell, "Connected Communities: Connecting Craft and Communities" (Online: AHRC, 2011), 6.

24. Karen Yair, *How Makers and Craft Organisations Are Using Social Media Effectively* (London: Crafts Council UK, 2012).

25. Karen Patel, "Expertise and Collaboration: Cultural Workers' Performance on Social Media," in *Collaborative Production in the Creative Industries*, ed. James Graham and Alessandro Gandini (London: University of Westminster Press, 2017).

26. Leonardo Bonanni and Amanda Parkes, "Virtual Guilds: Collective Intelligence and the Future of Craft," *Journal of Modern Craft* 3, no. 2 (2010).

27. Karen Patel, *Supporting Diversity in Craft Practice through Digital Technology Skills Development* (London: Crafts Council UK, 2019).

28. Simon Moreton, "Craft as Community," 2011, http://www.craftcommunities .com/craft-as-community.html.

29. Kristen A. Williams, "'Old Time Mem'ry': Contemporary Urban Craftivism and the Politics of Doing-It-Yourself in Postindustrial America," *Utopian Studies* 22, no. 2 (2011).

30. Katerina Lup et al., "Instagram# instasad?: Exploring Associations among Instagram Use, Depressive Symptoms, Negative Social Comparison, and Strangers Followed," *Cyberpsychology, Behavior, and Social Networking* 18, no. 5 (2015).

31. Patel, *Supporting Diversity in Craft Practice.*

32. World Intellectual Property Organisation, "What Is Intellectual Property?," WIPO, https://www.wipo.int/about-ip/en/.

33. The assertion of the Right of Attribution is not automatic and requires positive action by the creator, usually in the form of a statement in a written document such as a licensing contract.

34. World Intellectual Property Organization, "Copyright," WIPO, https://www .wipo.int/copyright/en/.

35. Douglas M. Nevin, "No Business Like Show Business: Copyright Law, the Theatre Industry, and the Dilemma of Rewarding Collaboration," *Emory LJ* 53 (2004).

36. Ibid., 1537–38.

37. Ibid., 1539.

38. GOV.UK, "Intellectual Property and Your Work," https://www.gov.uk/intel lectual-property-an-overview/protect-your-intellectual-property.

39. A. P. Russo and Giovanna Segre, "Collective Property Rights for Glass Manufacturing in Murano: Where Culture Makes or Breaks Local Economic Development," (2005).

40. Kirsty Robertson, "Embroidery Pirates and Fashion Victims: Textiles, Craft and Copyright," *Textile* 8, no. 1 (2010).

41. Amy Holroyd, "Why It's Important to Be Open," Crafts Council UK, https:// www.craftscouncil.org.uk/articles/why-its-important-to-be-open/.

42. Ash Amin and Joanne Roberts, "Knowing in Action: Beyond Communities of Practice," *Research policy* 37, no. 2 (2008).

43. Scott D. N. Cook and Dvora Yanow, "Culture and Organizational Learning," *Journal of Management Inquiry* 2, no. 4 (1993).

44. Luckman, *Craft and the Creative Economy*; Luckman, Andrew, and Crisp, "Crafting Self."

45. Robertson, "Embroidery Pirates and Fashion Victims," 87.

46. DCMS, "Creative Industries Mapping Document," (London: DCMS, 2001) 5.

47. James Yood and William Warmus, "Dialogue: Is Copyright Protection a Good Thing for Studio Glass?," *Glass: The UrbanGlass Art Quarterly* (2010).

48. Robertson, "Embroidery Pirates."

49. Luckman, *Craft and the Creative Economy.*

50. Holroyd, "Why It's Important to Be Open."

51. Yood and Warmus, "Dialogue," 52.

52. Glen Adamson, "Cut and Paste," *Crafts*, 2019, 22.

53. Mark Rose, *Authors and Owners: The Invention of Copyright* (Cambridge, MA: Harvard University Press, 1993), 3.

54. Robertson, "Embroidery Pirates."

55. Mark Banks, "Moral Economy and Cultural Work," *Sociology* 40, no. 3 (2006).

56. Pierre Bourdieu, *The Forms of Capital (1986)*, ed. I Szeman and T Kaposy, vol. 1, *Cultural Theory: An Anthology* (Chichester: Wiley, 2010).

57. Pierre-Michel Menger, "Artistic Labor Markets and Careers," *Annual Review of Sociology* 25, no. 1 (1999).

58. Yood and Warmus, "Dialogue," 52.

59. Luckman, Andrew, and Crisp, "Crafting Self."

60. Ibid.

61. Foster Kamer, "Are Brooklyn Fashion Designers Being Ripped Off by Urban Outfitters?," The Village Voice, 2010, https://www.villagevoice.com/2010/05/27/are-brooklyn-fashion-designers-being-ripped-off-by-urban-outfitters/; Linkins, "Urban Outfitters Continues Their Grand Tradition of Ripping Off Designers [Updated]." Huffington Post, 2011. https://www.huffingtonpost.co.uk/2011/05/26/urban-outfitters-steal_n_867604.html

62. Yood and Warmus, "Dialogue," 53.

63. Crafts Council UK, "Hothouse 2019: Eligibility, Programme and Financial Information" (Online: Crafts Council UK, 2019).

64. Glen Adamson, *Thinking through Craft* (London: Berg, 2007); Alex Langlands, *Craeft: How Traditional Crafts Are about More Than Just Making* (London: Faber & Faber, 2017); Sennett, *The Craftsman*.

65. Crafts Council UK, "Studying Craft 16: Trends in Craft Education and Training" (2016).

66. Patel, *Supporting Diversity in Craft Practice*.

67. Luckman, Andrew, and Crisp, "Crafting Self," 74.

68. Yood and Warmus, "Dialogue."

69. Caves, *Creative Industries*; Susan Orr and Alison Shreeve, *Art and Design Pedagogy in Higher Education: Knowledge, Values and Ambiguity in the Creative Curriculum* (London: Routledge, 2017).

70. Lauren England and Roberta Comunian, "Support or Competition? Assessing the Role of Heis in Professional Networks and Local Creative Communities: The Case of Glassmaking in Sunderland," *Beyond the Campus: Higher Education and the Creative Economy* (London: Routledge, 2016).

71. DCMS, "Creative Industries Mapping Document."

72. Yair, "How Makers and Craft Organisations Are Using Social Media Effectively."

73. Luckman, *Craft and the Creative Economy*.

74. Yood and Warmus, "Dialogue."

75. Luckman, Andrew, and Crisp, "Crafting Self."

76. Ibid.

77. Kamer, "Are Brooklyn Fashion Designers Being Ripped Off by Urban Outfitters?"; Linkins, "Urban Outfitters Continues Their Grand Tradition of Ripping Off Designers [Updated]."

78. Menger, "Artistic Labor Markets and Careers."

79. Luckman, Andrew, and Crisp, "Crafting Self."

80. Mark Banks, "Craft Labour and Creative Industries."

81. DCMS, "Creative Industries Mapping Document."

BIBLIOGRAPHY

ACID. "Spot the Difference." ACID, https://www.acid.uk.com/about/spot-the-difference.

Adamson, Glen. "Cut and Paste." *Crafts*, 2019, 1.
———. *Thinking through Craft.* London: Berg, 2007.
Amin, Ash, and Joanne Roberts. "Knowing in Action: Beyond Communities of Practice." *Research Policy* 37, no. 2 (2008): 353–69.
Banks, Mark. "Craft Labour and Creative Industries." *International Journal of Cultural Policy* 16, no. 3 (2010): 16.
———. "Craft Labour and Creative Industries." In *Creativity and Cultural Policy*, 81–98. New York: Routledge, 2014.
———. "Moral Economy and Cultural Work." *Sociology* 40, no. 3 (2006): 455–72.
Bell, Emma, Gianluigi Mangia, Scott Taylor, and Maria Laura Toraldo. *The Organization of Craft Work: Identities, Meanings, and Materiality.* New York: Routledge, 2018.
Bilton, Chris. "Valuable Creativity: Rediscovering Purpose." In *The Palgrave Handbook of Creativity at Work*, 483–500. New York: Springer, 2018.
Bonanni, Leonardo, and Amanda Parkes. "Virtual Guilds: Collective Intelligence and the Future of Craft." *Journal of Modern Craft* 3, no. 2 (2010): 179–90.
Bourdieu, Pierre. *The Forms of Capital (1986).* In *Cultural Theory: An Anthology.* Edited by I. Szeman and T. Kaposy. Vol. 1. Chichester: Wiley, 2010.
Caves, Richard E. *Creative Industries: Contracts between Art and Commerce.* Cambridge, MA: Harvard University Press, 2000.
Cook, Scott D. N., and Dvora Yanow. "Culture and Organizational Learning." *Journal of Management Inquiry* 2, no. 4 (1993): 373–90.
Crafts Council UK. "Hothouse 2019: Eligibility, Programme and Financial Information." Online: Crafts Council UK, 2019.
Crafts Council UK. "Studying Craft 16: Trends in Craft Education and Training," 2016.
DACS. "Works of Artistic Craftsmanship." DACS, https://www.dacs.org.uk/knowledge-base/factsheets/works-of-artistic-craftsmanship.
DCMS. "Creative Industries Mapping Document." London: DCMS, 2001.
England, Lauren, and Roberta Comunian. "Support or Competition? Assessing the Role of Heis in Professional Networks and Local Creative Communities: The Case of Glassmaking in Sunderland." In *Beyond the Campus: Higher Education and the Creative Economy*, 145–63. London: Routledge, 2016.
Glăveanu, Vlad Petre, and Lene Tanggaard. "Creativity, Identity, and Representation: Towards a Socio-Cultural Theory of Creative Identity." *New Ideas in Psychology* 34 (2014): 12–21.
Gotsi, Manto, Constantine Andriopoulos, Marianne W, Lewis, and Amy E Ingram. "Managing Creatives: Paradoxical Approaches to Identity Regulation." *Human Relations* 63, no. 6 (2010): 781–805.
GOV.UK. "Intellectual Property and Your Work." https://www.gov.uk/intellectual-property-an-overview/protect-your-intellectual-property.
Holroyd, Amy. "Why It's Important to Be Open." Crafts Council UK, https://www.craftscouncil.org.uk/articles/why-its-important-to-be-open/.
Hunt, Will, Linda Ball, and Emma Pollard. "Crafting Futures: A Study of the Early Careers of Crafts Graduates from Uk Higher Education Institutions." Institute for

Employment Studies, Brighton/University of the Arts London, London/The Crafts Council, London, 2010.

Jakob, Doreen, and Nicola J. Thomas. "Firing Up Craft Capital: The Renaissance of Craft and Craft Policy in the United Kingdom." *International Journal of Cultural Policy* 23, no. 4 (2017): 495–511.

Kamer, Foster. "Are Brooklyn Fashion Designers Being Ripped Off by Urban Outfitters?" The Village Voice, 2010 https://www.villagevoice.com/2010/05/27/are-brooklyn-fashion-designers-being-ripped-off-by-urban-outfitters/.

Langlands, Alex. *Craeft: How Traditional Crafts Are about More Than Just Making.* London: Faber & Faber, 2017.

Linkins, Jason. "Urban Outfitters Continues Their Grand Tradition of Ripping Off Designers [Updated]." Huffington Post, 2011. https://www.huffingtonpost.co.uk/2011/05/26/urban-outfitters-steal_n_867604.html.

Luckman, Susan. *Craft and the Creative Economy.* New York: Springer, 2015.

Luckman, Susan, Jane Andrew, and Tracy Crisp. "Crafting Self: Promoting the Making Self in the Creative Micro-Economy." Adelaide: School of Creative Industries, University of South Australia, 2019.

Luckman, Susan, and Nicola Thomas, eds. *Craft Economies.* London: Bloomsbury, 2018.

Lup, Katerina, Leora Trub, and Lisa Rosenthal. "Instagram# instasad?: Exploring Associations among Instagram Use, Depressive Symptoms, Negative Social Comparison, and Strangers Followed." *Cyberpsychology, Behavior, and Social Networking* 18, no. 5 (2015): 247–52.

McAuley, Andrew, and Ian Fillis. "Careers and Lifestyles of Craft Makers in the 21st Century." *Cultural Trends* 14, no. 2 (2005): 139–56.

Menger, Pierre-Michel. "Artistic Labor Markets and Careers." *Annual Review of Sociology* 25, no. 1 (1999): 541–74.

Moreton, Simon. "Craft as Community." Online: Craft Communities, 2011.

Nevin, Douglas M. "No Business Like Show Business: Copyright Law, the Theatre Industry, and the Dilemma of Rewarding Collaboration." *Emory LJ* 53 (2004): 1533.

Orr, Susan, and Alison Shreeve. *Art and Design Pedagogy in Higher Education: Knowledge, Values and Ambiguity in the Creative Curriculum.* New York: Routledge, 2017.

Patel, Karen. "Expertise and Collaboration: Cultural Workers' Performance on Social Media." In *Collaborative Production in the Creative Industries*, edited by James Graham and Alessandro Gandini, 157–76. London: University of Westminster Press, 2017.

Patel, Karen. *Supporting Diversity in Craft Practice through Digital Technology Skills Development.* London: Crafts Council UK, 2019.

Petkus, Ed. "The Creative Identity: Creative Behavior from the Symbolic Interactionist Perspective." *Journal of Creative Behavior* 30, no. 3 (1996): 188–96.

Robertson, Kirsty. "Embroidery Pirates and Fashion Victims: Textiles, Craft and Copyright." *Textile* 8, no. 1 (2010): 86–111.

Rose, Mark. *Authors and Owners: The Invention of Copyright.* Cambridge, MA: Harvard University Press, 1993.

Russo, Antonio Paolo, and Giovanna Segre. "Collective Property Rights for Glass Manufacturing in Murano: Where Culture Makes or Breaks Local Economic Development." (2005).

Sennett, Richard. *The Craftsman.* New Haven, CT: Yale University Press, 2008.

Taylor, Stephanie, and Karen Littleton. *Contemporary Identities of Creativity and Creative Work.* Farnham, Surrey: Ashgate, 2012.

Thomas, Nicola, Fiona Hackney, and Katie Bunnell. "Connected Communities: Connecting Craft & Communities." Online: AHRC, 2011.

Williams, Kristen A. "'Old Time Mem'ry': Contemporary Urban Craftivism and the Politics of Doing-It-Yourself in Postindustrial America." *Utopian Studies* 22, no. 2 (2011): 303–20.

Williams Middleton, Karen L. "Becoming Entrepreneurial: Gaining Legitimacy in the Nascent Phase." *International Journal of Entrepreneurial Behavior and Research* 19, no. 4 (2013): 404–24.

World Intellectual Property Organisation. "Copyright." WIPO, https://www.wipo.int/copyright/en/.

World Intellectual Property Organisation. "What Is Intellectual Property?" WIPO, https://www.wipo.int/about-ip/en/.

Yair, Karen. "How Makers and Craft Organisations Are Using Social Media Effectively." London: Crafts Council UK, 2012.

Yood, James, and William Warmus. "Dialogue: Is Copyright Protection a Good Thing for Studio Glass?" *Glass: The UrbanGlass Art Quarterly* 2010, 3.

Chapter Eight

Diversity Work and "Niceness"

Addressing Racism in the Knitting Community

Karen Patel

It has been exhausting. It's exhausting to consistently have to defend your position as a POC [person of colour]. It is exhausting to fight back on hundreds, thousands of years of wrong-doings and normalizing behavior that is damaging to different groups and groups of people. It is easy for non-POC to say, "I don't have to worry about this" or "not my problem" and it's difficult to point out, "yes, yes it is your problem." Your actions, whether you are aware or not, can either continue or end racism, discrimination, etc.[1]

This quote is an excerpt from an Instagram post by a knitter of colour, Tina. say.knits, in January 2019. It is one of thousands of posts on the social media platform referencing the issue of racism in knitting. Though some knitters of colour had used the platform in the past to highlight their experiences, this activity intensified when a prominent white knitter and blogger from the United States, Karen Templer, published a blog post about her ambition to visit India in January 2019. In the blog post, Templer describes how when she was younger, being offered a trip to India by her friend's family "was like being offered a seat on a flight to Mars."[2] That comment in particular sparked an online backlash from knitters of colour, which in turn led to some white knitters defending Karen. In an attempt to collate experiences and ostensibly highlight the scale of the issue, another knitter of colour, su.krita, asked her Instagram followers to share their experiences of racism in the community. She collated them in a series of Instagram Stories, which include experiences of being followed or patronised in local yarn stores and receiving inappropriate comments about race and ethnicity in local knitting groups.

These online stories and related posts are the primary focus of this chapter, which explores the work of knitters of colour from predominantly the UK,

US and Australia who shared their experiences of racism in the knitting community on Instagram throughout 2019. Hundreds of Instagram images and posts were collated into Instagram Stories and shared by su.krita. A number of other women makers of colour also invest their time and energy into collating and sharing the stories of others on Instagram, as well as dealing with thousands of comments of both a positive and negative nature. They do this alongside running a craft business, and thus their professional online presence becomes entangled with the race debates which profoundly affect them. Some of these users call out what they describe as "niceness" in online craft communities, where the line between personal and professional for many is clearly defined. This chapter highlights the diversity work[3] a group of knitters of colour engage in as they attempt to address racism in the knitting community. While online platforms can provide a means through which experiences can be highlighted and important stories told, they are sites where "offline" inequalities are seemingly reproduced. As I will show, this has implications for the wider sphere of craft entrepreneurship, where makers are increasingly reliant on social media activity and online presence in order to succeed.

INEQUALITIES IN CRAFT AND CHALLENGES FOR WOMEN MAKERS OF COLOUR ONLINE

The online debates about racism in the knitting community on which this chapter focuses are part of the wider issue of inequalities in craft and the creative industries. Much has been made of inequalities in creative work in general[4] but there has been relatively little focus on the specificities of the craft sector and the impact on craft entrepreneurship. In the UK, Spilsbury draws on employment statistics to highlight that the majority of people working in craft occupations full time are white, male, and older than the average across all occupations in the UK.[5] In previous works I have highlighted the experiences of women makers of colour in the UK,[6] identifying some of the challenges and barriers they can face when trying to establish their craft enterprises, with a focus on social media use. Based on interviews with seventeen makers, these challenges included the perception of craft and creative practice as not being a viable career choice, and a lack of confidence with using social media and online spaces, either through lack of knowledge of the platform or not wanting to open themselves up to criticism. Many of those interviewed were still trying to establish themselves as craft entrepreneurs (making a living from their craft), while negotiating a predominantly white and middle-class sector alongside the challenges and pressures of social media. Indeed, the role of social media in craft entrepreneurship remains underexplored.

Existing work on social media and racism/oppression highlights the extent to which online platforms such as Twitter, Facebook and Instagram can be hostile spaces for women of colour, regardless of their job or status. Amnesty International reported in 2018 the scale of abuse, or "trolling" that women face on Twitter. The report highlights that black women are disproportionately targeted for online abuse, being 84 percent more likely than white women to be subject to abusive tweets. Women of colour (including Asian, Latinx and mixed-race women) were 34 percent more likely than white women to receive abuse on the platform.[7] Litchfield et al. carried out a study of social media abuse aimed at black sportswomen, finding that tennis player Serena Williams was subjected to the most abuse, particularly on Twitter. They found that racism formed a significant part of the online abuse, highlighting how the "everyday racism'"[8] which pervades white-dominated spaces is exacerbated online. "Everyday racism" is described by Essed[9] as involving systematic, recurring practices and behaviours which become socialised. Litchfield et al. note that "Online environments, such as Twitter, can provide a complete abandonment of social restrictions that might otherwise be present in face-to-face interaction, providing a fertile space for abuse to occur."[10] As I will show, there are examples of "everyday racism" within the knitting community, and the stories shared demonstrate its pervasiveness in both offline and online spaces.

METHOD

To analyse the online racism debates and the subsequent storytelling from women knitters of colour, I took screenshots of Instagram Stories which were created by five women who referred directly to either Karen Templer's blog post or the subject of racism in knitting. The five Instagram users were su.krita, thecolourmustard, Tina.say.knits, astitchtowear and oceanbythesea. These five makers were the most prominent voices in the online debates, and are based in the UK, US and Australia. Screenshots needed to be taken of the Instagram Stories which consist of a curated collection of images or videos which appear for a few seconds, and so they needed to be captured in an "offline" format for closer analysis. This in the end was a crucial exercise because as of February 2020, su.krita and oceanbythesea had deleted all of the posts and Instagram Stories which related to issues of racism in knitting. It is not known why they did it, but I will discuss the implications of this in greater detail later on.

A total of 231 posts were collected from Instagram Stories and posts by the users. An ethical consideration for taking posts "offline" is that images and stories can be taken out of context, particularly as some users would have submitted their experiences not knowing where their posts might end up.[11] Any users who contributed to the online debates who are not one of the five prominent makers are anonymised in this chapter. I decided not to anonymise the five makers featured here because their profiles are in the public domain, and I felt they should receive credit for the work they have done to raise awareness of racism in the knitting community, even if the evidence is no longer online in some cases.

The screenshots consisted of a mixture of photos, "selfies" with captions, annotated extracts from Karen Templer's blog post and plain text. The content of the Instagram Stories and posts were thematically analysed, identifying similarities in the content and nature of the posts. From the analysis, two key themes emerged which centre on the main complaints[12] from the five prominent users—emotional labour and diversity work, and "niceness" online.

EMOTIONAL LABOUR AND DIVERSITY WORK

> Talking about racism means dealing with the racism articulated in response to what you are talking about. Which also means: you end up doing more emotional labour the more you talk about doing emotional labour.[13]

In this quote Sara Ahmed is referring to her conversations with academics of colour who have attempted to complain about institutional racism and discrimination in higher education. Ahmed points to the emotional labour of both dealing with racism and its response. I use the term emotional labour to describe the work of the makers of colour because it was referred to frequently in discussions on Instagram, and also because the emotional labour that makers of colour invest in platforms such as Instagram is exploitable and productive for platform owners.[14]

I argue that for makers of colour involved in these debates, the affordances of social media platforms can intensify the emotional labour of dealing with racism and dealing with the response to racism online. This is exacerbated by the "always on" nature of social media communication where users can be notified about new messages or comments on their posts as soon as they appear. People can choose not to look at Instagram or turn notifications off, but the sheer volume of responses received by the users in this research leaves them with a lot to deal with. Thecolourmustard shared a post by a user who thanked her, su.krita, oceanbythesea and astitchtowear for their labour. The post stated the following:

Recognize that they are performing emotional labour that THEY SHOULD
NOT HAVE TO. Recognize that it is TRAUMATIZING TO HAVE TO JUS-
TIFY YOUR EXISTENCE AND EXPLAIN YOUR PAIN AND ANGER TO
THOSE WHO ARE HURTING YOU.

In the same Instagram Story (which is no longer available online), Thecolourmustard shared a post by another user which said that the same prominent
users "are performing a lot of emotional labour right now, always, and not
just in the fiber community." Both posts go on to urge other knitters to "learn
from them" and "educate yourself, it's not their job but they're doing it."
These other users, who are predominantly makers of colour, acknowledge the
emotional labour that Thecolourmustard, su.krita and others are performing to
call out racism online and offline. This labour involves creating and curating
Instagram Stories which highlight the problem, but also responding to people
attempting to defend Karen Templer and play down the harm that such posts
can cause to makers of colour. This playing down of harm serves to exacer-
bate the negative affect of racism they experience. Indeed "pain" and "harm"
was frequently referenced in the posts when people recalled their experiences
of racism in the knitting community. Some users described how dealing with
discrimination or poor treatment in the community, offline and online, is
"exhausting" as mentioned by Tina.say.knits at the beginning of this chapter.
In reference to the racism debates, Oceanbythesea said on Instagram that she
had been "triggered" by what is going on, and said: "I live this every. Single.
Day. All of these micro-aggressions add up." The exhaustion, pain, hurt and
anger described in the posts are seemingly an attempt to educate white knitters about the felt consequences of their actions. Naming emotions online can
also serve to create "communities of feelings"[15] which other knitters of colour
can rally around, which is possibly why some users felt the need to share and
acknowledge the emotional labour of su.krita and the others.

These women's attempts to educate others about their experiences of racism and inequalities on Instagram is a form of diversity work. Diversity work
is "the work we do when we are attempting to transform an institution; and
second, diversity work is the work we do when we do not quite inhabit the
norms of an institution."[16] This could be applied to the work these women are
doing in calling out racism in the knitting community—which is the "institution" in question. Thecolourmustard posted the following on Instagram some
time before the online debates emerged in relation to the Templer blog post.
Here she is beginning to share her apprehension about the knitting community; the post has since been deleted.

I love this community; by exposing me to such a beautiful craft, it has helped
me through the happiest and roughest of times, and it is so generous, kind, fun,

and inspiring . . . but whenever I enter a yarn store here in my 80.5% white city, and I find that I am the only Asian immigrant inside, or when I hear about knit nights or festivals near me and my first instinct is to ask myself "but who is going?" or when I rarely see women like me modelling the latest knitting patterns or designing or sharing their making on Instagram . . . I can't help feeling like I'm only an outsider looking in.

Sara Ahmed describes how institutions take shape "as an effect of what has become automatic."[17] Within knitting, we could say that whiteness is automatic. This is because knitters of colour such as Thecolourmustard still feel like outsiders; because many of the users describing their experiences on Instagram mentioned their hesitance with attending events, going into local yarn stores and so on. As one user said, the knitting community "has been white for a v. long time." The women's experiences described in the posts are a consequence of the automatic whiteness of the knitting "institution." As Ahmed describes, within institutions there becomes an ease with the "becoming background"—the idea that an institution's workings are "how we do things here." This ease also takes the form of "incredulity or naiveté or ignorance of the newly arrived or outsiders."[18] Some of this online activity can be seen as a result of the predominant whiteness of the knitting institution. Ahmed describes how diversity work is difficult because it involves doing work within institutions which "what would not otherwise be done *by* them."[19]

Following Ahmed's argument, those carrying out the diversity work in the knitting space are seemingly required to be persistent, because considering issues of racism and inequality is not "automatic" within the knitting community. As a result, many of them describe the pain and harm they have experienced while engaging in these debates in online spaces. Some of the emotions they described were not always caused by outright trolling or online abuse. Instead they were caused by activity which some knitters were said to engage in to protect their reputation. I describe this as "niceness" and silencing.

"NICENESS" AND SILENCING ONLINE

In the knitting world, there is this very insidious undertone of "niceness"—how many times have we seen a difficult topic brushed off with "we all knit to relax" or "if you don't like what she is saying, you can just scroll past."

Many of the prominent knitters of colour described the "niceness" pervasive in online knitting spaces. The previous excerpt is from a (now deleted) post by su.krita. There were many posts from within the sample which directly addressed white knitters, asking where they were in these debates, that their "silence" was just as harmful to them. In an Instagram Story, Thecolourmustard posted: "So, to all you white makers out there who tout diversity and representation and allyship, where the hell are you? Where is your outrage? Why aren't you checking this nonsense?" This is a reference to the lack of visibility of white knitters who did not appear to have responded to the Karen Templer blog post and the subsequent backlash towards makers of colour. It affirms Sara Ahmed's idea that diversity work is almost always carried out by the people who do not quite inhabit the norms of the institution in question. In this case, non-white knitters. In another post, su.krita said that there is a sense within the online knitting community of "not wanting to rock the boat" because of the "niceness." She described the "overall sense of the crafting community being held accountable less than another industry because it's 'just a hobby' even though we're talking about the words/actions of business owners who make a living through the community." She also commented that because the online knitting community is mostly women, that may also contribute to the "compulsion of being nice."

For many creative entrepreneurs, social media platforms are central as a means through which they network, sell their work, signal their expertise[20] and manage reputation.[21] Susan Luckman describes craft entrepreneurs' maintenance of their online presence as "self making" which is "a required strategy of presenting a particular integrated sense of self as both maker (the professional craft worker) and the broader person, as part of a rounded performance of a seemingly successfully balanced self."[22] The "compulsion of being nice" online as described by su.krita is most likely linked to the perceived need to perform this balanced, seemingly successful self. Therefore, participating in online debates about race, politics or otherwise presents a risk to online presence.

At the same time, staying silent within the community as part of a culture of passive "niceness" can limit the potential for change, as highlighted by Pitcan, Marwick, and boyd (stylised lowercase) in their analysis of "respectability politics" enacted in online environments. They argue that the tactics and strategies people employ to "perform a vanilla self" in order to gain upward mobility results in a regulation of "norms and status, thereby helping maintain structural divisions rooted in structural oppression."[23] The politics of respectability in this context suggests that craft entrepreneurs have an imagined online audience, which may include people or organisations which could determine future opportunities, such as sales. This puts craft entrepreneurs of colour involved in racism debates in a difficult position. This is because the pervasive online respectability politics—which are determined by hegemonic norms—mean that "digital media can provide new opportunities for mobility, but confers greater risk upon those with tenuous social positions."[24]

Thecolourmustard shared posts by white knitters who acknowledge that racism in the community needs addressing. One white maker said, "It's time, as white people, to use our privilege for good instead of allowing racism and discrimination to occur which is even perpetuated when we stay silent."

In attempting to facilitate change by raising awareness of racism in knitting, the five knitters frequently mentioned the culture of "niceness" online. This sometimes led to knitters of colour feeling like their views were being dismissed, or their "tone" was being "policed." Thecolourmustard referenced makers attempting to police her tone. Astitchtowear posted: "if my humanity depends on your approval of my tone, then you are not an ally. Anger is a completely valid response to oppression . . . so if you don't like my tone because it lacks the deference that you believe you are entitled to, that is a personal issue."

Su.krita posted screenshots of direct messages from white makers accusing her of being a bully, and saying that they feel the need to "tiptoe" and second guess everything they post online. A real point of contention within the online debates was that when makers of colour expressed anger about racism in the community, the response of some white makers was to perceive it as an attack towards them, a form of bullying, or claim "reverse racism" which was mentioned in several posts. Such a response is an example of what Audre Lorde describes as "when women of colour speak out of the anger that laces so many of our contacts with white women," we are often told that we are "creating a mood of hopelessness," "preventing white women from getting past guilt," or "standing in the way of trusting communication and action."[25] Audre Lorde argues that to dismiss the anger of women of colour "is merely another way of preserving racial blindness, the power of unaddressed privilege, unbreached, intact." Astitchtowear's post on Instagram encapsulates this sentiment within the context of the knitting community:

> When someone within our community does harm we want to believe that it was unintentional because we don't want to damage that shared bond of community. It follows that we want to believe that if they just became aware of the harm that they would find a way to correct it and do better. Instead they defend their behaviour. They curate a space where others not only defend their original behaviour but insist that there was no harm in the first place . . . some of you don't see the people that you have hurt as valid members of the community. This is just a discussion to be hosted and then dismissed when it has overstayed its welcome. So that the community can return to its true purpose. Its true colours.

In these online spaces, knitters of colour are using the platforms to voice their anger, yet they face attempts to police or silence it, seemingly to maintain a culture of "niceness" and preserve the existing norms and conditions of the "institution" of knitting. As Sara Ahmed notes, "Racism becomes something bad that we can't even speak of, as if to describe x as racist is to damage or even hurt x. The organization becomes the subject of feeling, as the one who must be protected, as the one who is easily bruised or hurt. When racism becomes an institutional injury, it is imagined as an injury to whiteness."[26] In this case the "organization" or "institution" is the knitting community, where the "status quo" of the white and relatively privileged is seemingly upheld and maintained. The "institution" does not only include other knitters, but also suppliers, guilds, customers, craft organisations and fairs which can all play a part in the success, or otherwise, of craft entrepreneurs.

To uphold the institution, those in privileged positions, by and large, remained silent throughout these debates, which sparked some of the anger voiced by makers such as su.krita. Sara Ahmed notes how, within institutions, "you have to silence someone because they are talking or because they are talking in the wrong way, perhaps in a way that has too many implications for the organisation." In relation to staying silent, she notes that silence can be a way of performing collegiality. "Indeed how complaints are suppressed might point in the same direction to what we hold dear: working with others; having a sense of a shared project; being part of something, part of a feminist 'we' even."[27] In this sense, Ahmed is suggesting that the sense of collegiality enacted through silence—which is how complaints are often suppressed—can also be enacted through complaint, as evidenced on Instagram among these prominent knitters of colour and the collegiality and solidarity it has fostered.

The importance of "self-making" and putting across a professional business image online, not "rocking the boat," is seemingly at odds with participating in debates about race online. Ultimately most craft entrepreneurs need to think about their online image and commercial priorities, hence why they tend to keep their personal views separate from their business presence. As a result, the emotional labour of the makers of colour involved in these debates is ultimately only really appreciated within a small, engaged online community. Despite the powerful stories told, these issues have received relatively little media coverage.[28]

DISCUSSION

The stories shared by the makers featured in this chapter all come from the knitting community, which is only a small part of the craft economy. What does this mean for craft entrepreneurship? As mentioned near the beginning of this chapter, it is not unreasonable to say that the craft workforce is dominated by white, middle-class makers, despite many forms of craft originating from Africa, Asia and South America. Traditional crafts entailed a great deal of expertise which is devalued and denigrated not only because it was carried out by people of colour, but by women in domestic spaces, and this continues today. As I have argued in other works, the concept of expertise is gendered and classed[29] and I would also argue it is racialised. The rise in craft entrepreneurship is concurrent with increased consumer interest in authentic, handmade products and a fascination with the "aura of the analogue."[30] Yet, as Susan Luckman and Richard Ocejo have shown, the contemporary, hipster-driven "maker movement" represents a certain type of craft practice considered to involve a great deal of expertise, but it is also overwhelmingly white and middle class.[31]

Craft entrepreneurship in this contemporary guise in Western contexts could be perceived as representing a type of patriarchal, hierarchical "institution" within which some makers of colour are performing diversity work in an attempt to be visible and appreciated within it. Craft organisations such as Crafts Council UK are working towards supporting greater diversity in craft practice,[32] but as we have seen from the global stories shared on Instagram, there is a long way to go. The Instagram Stories shared by the makers in this research highlight unconscious biases which stem from deep-rooted problems within society, and which relate not only to race, but also to gender, class, ability and sexuality.

It is suggested in research that the structural inequalities which exist offline are reproduced in online spaces.[33] Social media platforms provide a space for people to air their prejudices anonymously, and Twitter and YouTube[34] can be fertile sites for abuse, trolling, and misogyny.[35] However, su.krita's exercise of asking people to share their experiences of racism within the wider knitting community, and the response she received, suggests that platforms such as Instagram can provide a space for people to speak out. Makers who shared stories of being mistreated in yarn stores also tended to mention that they either walked out of the store, or carried on with what they were doing without saying anything. In this sense, the online space is relatively "safe" for disclosure (anonymously at least), and some people are willing to share their experiences once they have reflected on the treatment they have received in offline contexts. The idea of "coming forward" is significant here, but it requires someone like su.krita to do the online diversity work of gathering responses, anonymising them and publishing them in Instagram Stories. Furthermore, this sharing of others' stories appeared on the Instagram profile which she also uses to share her knitting. For her and the other makers featured in this chapter, their diversity work can be visible on their social media page, and sits alongside images of their work for sale, or work in progress. That is, at least, until they choose to delete the posts as su.krita, Thecolormustard, and oceanbythesea did at the time of writing. This may be an attempt to mitigate the risks of online presence by instead appearing more work-focused. It might also potentially enhance entrepreneurship opportunities and allow them to compete with white makers who are not required to carry out diversity work. On the other hand, the makers may have simply become drained from the emotional labour of dealing with racism and its response online. Unfortunately, the fact these posts have been deleted means that the views and experiences of makers of colour are effectively erased from the online debate. This raises questions about how effective social media platforms could actually be for facilitating change, when those who are marginalised end up being silenced anyway.

The deletion of posts also presented an ethical challenge for me when writing this chapter, as the analysis was carried out when the posts were still online. I could have instead anonymised the users, but I still wanted their diversity work to be recognised because it remains important work that at least started a conversation and raised awareness of the issues of racism in knitting. That the posts aren't online anymore points to the volatility of social media as an object of research, and the complexities of data collection and ethics when posts are deleted.

The online space is clearly fraught with risk for craft entrepreneurs and the efficacy of platforms for facilitating positive change remains in question. However, platforms do allow people to start a conversation and mobilise in other ways. For example, as a result of these discussions and the engagement she received, su.krita has established a safe knitting space in Sydney for makers of colour, called "Sydney is cancelled." According to the group's Facebook page, Sydney is cancelled is "creating a space that is safe for marginalised makers. BIPOC [Black, Indigenous People of Colour] have experienced ongoing and systemic alienation in mixed spaces within the fibre art community. We centre the voices & experiences of BIPOC here."[36] This group is an example of how online communities can lead to the establishment of physical safe spaces. However, it seems to be spearheaded by one person, who has already invested a lot of time and energy into raising awareness of racism in her field. While these efforts are welcome and much needed, one wonders how sustainable it is for a maker who is simultaneously running a craft business. In this sense, where online diversity work is entangled with online presence, if such efforts extend into physical safe spaces the effort it takes to create a group and organise events will spill into the day-to-day demands of running a craft business. What does this mean, then, for women makers of colour involved in both diversity work and craft entrepreneurship? Being able to juggle many different tasks at once is a part of being an entrepreneur in any field, none more so than in creative work which is characterised by precarious, piecemeal working.[37]

But as I have shown in the case of the knitting community, diversity work is additional work which, at the moment, is carried out predominantly by women makers of colour. Further research should explore in depth how diversity work is carried out in the day-to-day routines of craft entrepreneurs, and how they negotiate the demands on their time, energy, online presence and entrepreneurship opportunities.

CONCLUSION

Online discussions about racism in the knitting community certainly gathered momentum after Karen Templer published *2019: My Year of Colour*. However, as indicated by some of the users featured in this chapter, makers of colour have been experiencing racism in the craft sector for a very long time. Microaggressions occurring in daily life and even outright aggression in online spaces can chip away at a maker's ability to run a business in a predominantly white and middle-class sector. Online abuse continues despite the work of the knitters featured in this chapter. For example, a screenshot of racist abuse occurring on Facebook within a knitting group was shared by Jeanette Sloan, another maker of colour on Instagram. Her accompanying caption included the following:

> I've chosen to turn off comments on this post because they currently stand at over 600 which, as you'll appreciate, is a huge number to reply to or moderate in addition to being emotionally exhausting for me or anyone to read. I would ask just two things of everyone continuing to read and share this post who is shocked by the fact that incidences like this still happen in 2019.
>
> 1. There have been so many heartbreaking and depressing experiences shared by BIPOC over the last 9 months so WHY are you still shocked?
> 2. What are you going to do about it?[38]

The caption emphasises the demand—both in terms of time and emotionally—of online diversity work. Jeanette's admission that moderating comments is "emotionally exhausting" expresses the emotional labour of attempting to address racism in the knitting community, then dealing with its response. These demands, I argue, undoubtedly disadvantage makers of colour involved in diversity work, encroaching on the time and energy required for running a craft business, when they could be searching for opportunities, promoting their work or working on their craft practice.

The next step, which is arguably the most difficult, is for makers doing this diversity work to try and mobilise more makers, to reach wider audiences and hope that their work will help to educate others and challenge institutional bias in the sector. Craft organisations, suppliers and stores also need to take racism seriously and be willing to call it out. While social media can be useful for mobilising online movements relating to racism,[39] it does not help that the regulation of online abuse remains woefully below standard, and that marginalised groups continue to be silenced online. It is also a huge concern that hate speech is allowed to proliferate on the same platforms which ostensibly aim to "give people the power to build community and bring the world closer together."[40] Social media platform owners should do more to help people doing the diversity work online, otherwise social media's potential to create meaningful change will always be limited.

NOTES

1. Instagram post by Tina.Say.knits, Instagram, posted January 9, 2019, https://www.instagram.com/p/BsbG_NWl8ph/.

2. Karen Templer, "2019: My Year of Colour," accessed July 11, 2019, https://fringeassociation.com/2019/01/07/2019-my-year-of-colour/.

3. Sara Ahmed, *On Being Included: Racism and Diversity in Institutional Life* (London: Duke University Press, 2012).

4. Mark Banks, *Creative Justice: Cultural Industries, Work and Inequality* (London: Rowman & Littlefield International, 2017); also see Dave O'Brien, Kim Allen, Sam Friedman, and Anamik Saha, "Producing and Consuming Inequality: A Cultural Sociology of the Cultural Industries," *Cultural Sociology* 11, no. 3 (2017): 271–82.

5. Mark Spilsbury, "Who Makes? An Analysis of People Working in Craft Occupations," Crafts Council UK, February 2018, accessed July 11, 2019, https://www.craftscouncil.org.uk/documents/892/Who_makes_2018.pdf Accessed 30 Sept 2020.

6. Karen Patel, "Supporting Diversity in Craft Practice through Digital Technology Skills Development," Crafts Council UK, February 2019, accessed July 11, 2019, https://www.craftscouncil.org.uk/documents/1173/19-03-19_Supporting_Diversity_in_Craft_Practice_report_FINAL.pdf Accessed 30 Sept 2020.

7. "Crowdsourced Twitter Study Reveals Shocking Scale of Online Abuse against Women," Amnesty International, accessed July 11, 2019, https://www.amnesty.org/en/latest/news/2018/12/crowdsourced-twitter-study-reveals-shocking-scale-of-online-abuse-against-women/.

8. Chelsea Litchfield, Emma Kavanagh, Jaquelyn Osborne, and Ian Jones, "Social Media and the Politics of Gender, Race and Identity: The Case of Serena Williams," *European Journal for Sport and Society* 15, no. 2 (2018): 154–70.

9. Philomena Essed, *Understanding Everyday Racism: An Interdisciplinary Theory* (Newbury Park, CA: Sage, 1991).

10. Litchfield et al., "Social Media and the Politics of Gender," 166.

11. Alice Marwick and danah boyd [lowercase intentional], "I Tweet Honestly, I Tweet Passionately: Twitter Users, Context Collapse, and the Imagined Audience," *New Media and Society* 13, no. 1 (2011): 114–33.

12. Sara Ahmed, "Complaint as Diversity Work," *Feminist Killjoys*, November 2017, accessed July 11, 2019, https://feministkilljoys.com/2017/11/10/complaint-as-diversity-work/.

13. Sara Ahmed, "White Friend," *Feminist Killjoys*, May 2019, accessed July 11, 2019, https://feministkilljoys.com/2019/05/31/white-friend/.

14. Mark Coté and Jennifer Pybus, "Learning to Immaterial Labour 2.0: MySpace and Social Networks," *Ephemera* 7, no. 1 (2007): 88–106; Kylie Jarrett, *Feminism, Labour and Digital Media: The Digital Housewife* (London: Routledge, 2015).

15. Adi Kuntsman, "Introduction: Affective Fabrics of Digital Cultures," in *Digital Cultures and the Politics of Emotion*, 6 (London: Palgrave Macmillan, 2012).

16. Ahmed, *On Being Included*, 91.

17. Ahmed, *On Being Included*, 25.

18. Ahmed, *On Being Included*, 25.

19. Ahmed, *On Being Included*, 25.

20. Karen Patel, *The Politics of Expertise in Cultural Labour: Arts, Work, Inequalities.* (London: Rowman & Littlefield International, 2020).

21. Alessandro Gandini, *The Reputation Economy: Understanding Knowledge Work in Digital Society* (London: Springer, 2016).

22. Susan Luckman, *Craft and the Creative Economy* (London: Springer, 2015), 113.

23. Pitcan, Marwick, and boyd, "Performing a Vanilla Self," *Journal of Computer-Mediated Communication* 23, no. 3 (2018): 168.

24. Pitcan, Marwick, and boyd, "Performing a Vanilla Self," 176.

25. Audre Lorde, *Sister Outsider: Essays and Speeches* (Berkeley, CA: Crossing Press, 1984), 131.

26. Ahmed, *On Being Included*, 147.

27. Sara Ahmed, "Damage Limitation," *Feminist Killjoys*, February 2019, accessed July 11, 2019, https://feministkilljoys.com/2019/02/15/damage-limitation/.

28. The only notable article is by Jaya Saxena, "The Knitting Community Is Reckoning with Racism," Vox, February 2019, accessed July 11, 2019, https://www.vox.com/the-goods/2019/2/25/18234950/knitting-racism-instagram-stories.

29. Patel, *Politics of Expertise.*

30. Luckman, *Craft and the Creative Economy.*

31. Richard Ocejo, *Masters of Craft: Old Jobs in the New Urban Economy* (Princeton, NJ: Princeton University Press, 2017).

32. Addressing the lack of diversity in craft is one of Crafts Council UK's key strategic objectives. See "New Audiences, New Makers, New Making: Business Plan 2018–2022," Crafts Council UK, accessed July 11, 2019, https://www.craftscouncil.org.uk/content/files/Crafts_Council_2018_-_2022_business_plan_webversion.docx.

33. Kaitlynn Mendes, Jessica Ringrose, and Jessalynn Keller, *Digital Feminist Activism: Girls and Women Fight Back against Rape Culture* (Oxford University Press, 2019).

34. Anthony McCosker, "Trolling as Provocation: YouTube's Agonistic Publics," *Convergence* 20, no. 2 (2014): 201–17.

35. Jamie Bartlett et al, "Misogyny on Twitter", 2014. Accessed 12 October 2020, https://www.demos.co.uk/files/MISOGYNY_ON_TWITTER.pdf?1399567516.

36. https://www.facebook.com/sydneyiscancelled/.

37. Rosalind Gill and Andy Pratt, "In the Social Factory? Immaterial Labour, Precariousness and Cultural Work," *Theory, Culture and Society* 25, no. 7–8 (2008): 1–30.

38. Instagram post by Jeanette Sloan, June 4, 2019, https://www.instagram.com/p/ByR_odEJEhd/.

39. Marcia Mundt, Karen Ross, and Charla M Burnett, "Scaling Social Movements through Social Media: The Case of Black Lives Matter," *Social Media and Society* 4, no. 4 (2018): 1–14.

40. "Mission Statement," Facebook Investor Relations FAQ, accessed July 11, 2019, https://investor.fb.com/resources/default.aspx.

BIBLIOGRAPHY

Ahmed, Sara. "Complaint as Diversity Work." Feminist Killjoys, November 2017, accessed July 11, 2019, https://feministkilljoys.com/2017/11/10/complaint-as-diversity-work/.

———. "Damage Limitation." Feminist Killjoys, February 2019, accessed July 11, 2019, https://feministkilljoys.com/2019/02/15/damage-limitation/.

———. *On Being Included: Racism and Diversity in Institutional Life*. London: Duke University Press, 2012.

———. "White Friend." Feminist Killjoys, May 2019, accessed July 11, 2019, https://feministkilljoys.com/2019/05/31/white-friend/.

Amnesty International. "Crowdsourced Twitter Study Reveals Shocking Scale of Online Abuse Against Women." December 2018, accessed July 11, 2019, https://www.amnesty.org/en/latest/news/2018/12/crowdsourced-twitter-study-reveals-shocking-scale-of-online-abuse-against-women/.

Banks, Mark. *Creative Justice: Cultural Industries, Work and Inequality*. London: Rowman & Littlefield International, 2017.

Bartlett, Jamie; Richard Norrie; Sofia Patel; Rebecca Rumpel; Simon Wibberley. "Misogyny on Twitter", 2014. Accessed 12 October 2020, https://www.demos.co.uk/files/MISOGYNY_ON_TWITTER.pdf?1399567516,

Coté, Mark, and Jennifer Pybus. "Learning to Immaterial Labour 2.0: MySpace and Social Networks." *Ephemera* 7, no. 1 (2007): 88–106.

Crafts Council UK. "New Audiences, New Makers, New Making: Business Plan 2018–2022," Crafts Council UK, accessed July 11, 2019, https://www.craftscouncil.org.uk/content/files/Crafts_Council_2018_-_2022_business_plan_webversion.docx.

Essed, Philomena. *Understanding Everyday Racism: An Interdisciplinary Theory*. Vol. 2. Newbury Park, CA: Sage, 1991.

Facebook. "Mission Statement," Facebook Investor Relations FAQ, accessed July 11, 2019, https://investor.fb.com/resources/default.aspx.

Gandini, Alessandro. *The Reputation Economy: Understanding Knowledge Work in Digital Society*. London: Springer, 2016.

Gill, Rosalind, and Andy Pratt. "In the Social Factory? Immaterial Labour, Precariousness and Cultural Work." *Theory, Culture and Society* 25, no. 7–8 (2008): 1–30.

Jarrett, Kylie. *Feminism, Labour and Digital Media: The Digital Housewife*. London: Routledge, 2015.

Kuntsman, Adi. "Introduction: Affective Fabrics of Digital Cultures." In *Digital Cultures and the Politics of Emotion*, 1–17. Palgrave Macmillan, London, 2012.

Litchfield, Chelsea, Emma Kavanagh, Jaquelyn Osborne, and Ian Jones. "Social Media and the Politics of Gender, Race and Identity: The Case of Serena Williams." *European Journal for Sport and Society* 15, no. 2 (2018): 154–70.

Lorde, Audre. *Sister Outsider: Essays and Speeches.* Berkeley, CA: Crossing Press, 1984.

Luckman, Susan. *Craft and the Creative Economy*. London: Springer, 2015.

Marwick, Alice E., and danah boyd. "I Tweet Honestly, I Tweet Passionately: Twitter Users, Context Collapse, and the Imagined Audience." *New Media and Society* 13, no. 1 (2011): 114–33.

McCosker, Anthony. "Trolling as Provocation: YouTube's Agonistic Publics." *Convergence* 20, no. 2 (2014): 201–17.

Mendes, Kaitlynn, Jessica Ringrose, and Jessalynn Keller. *Digital Feminist Activism: Girls and Women Fight Back against Rape Culture*. Oxford University Press, 2019.

Mundt, Marcia, Karen Ross, and Charla M. Burnett. "Scaling Social Movements through Social Media: The Case of Black Lives Matter." *Social Media and Society* 4, no. 4 (2018): 1–14.

O'Brien, Dave, Kim Allen, Sam Friedman, and Anamik Saha. "Producing and Consuming Inequality: A Cultural Sociology of the Cultural Industries." *Cultural Sociology* 11, no. 3 (2017): 271–82.

Ocejo, Richard. *Masters of Craft: Old Jobs in the New Urban Economy*. Princeton, NJ: Princeton University Press, 2017.

Patel, Karen. *The Politics of Expertise in Cultural Labour: Arts, Work, Inequalities.* London: Rowman & Littlefield International, 2020.

———. "Supporting Diversity in Craft Practice through Digital Technology Skills Development." Crafts Council UK, February 2019, accessed July 11, 2019, https://www.craftscouncil.org.uk/documents/1173/19-03-19_Supporting_Diversity_in_Craft_Practice_report_FINAL.pdf Accessed 30 Sept 2020.

Pitcan, Mikaela, Alice Marwick, and danah boyd. "Performing a Vanilla Self: Respectability Politics, Social Class, and the Digital World." *Journal of Computer-Mediated Communication* 23, no. 3 (2018): 163–79.

Saxena, Jaya. "The Knitting Community Is Reckoning with Racism." Vox, February 2019, accessed July 11, 2019, https://www.vox.com/the-goods/2019/2/25/18234950/knitting-racism-instagram-stories.

Spilsbury, Mark. "Who Makes? An Analysis of People Working in Craft Occupations." Crafts Council UK, February 2018, accessed July 11, 2019, https://www.craftscouncil.org.uk/documents/892/Who_makes_2018.pdf Accessed 30 Sept 2020.

Templer, Karen. "2019: My Year of Colour." Accessed July 11, 2019, https://fringeassociation.com/2019/01/07/2019-my-year-of-colour/.

Chapter Nine

From Amateur to All-Business

Women on the Verge of Craft Entrepreneurship

Mary Kay Culpepper and David Gauntlett

At first, and for a while, losing her job was a calamity for Holly.[1] Her career as a graphic designer was central to the way she defined herself. She was always as proud of her work as she was her ability to take care of herself and her family from the profession she had chosen when she was a teen. Without it, she felt untethered, which compounded the distress she felt from the lack of a paycheck.

One thing she did have was spare time. When her in-laws suggested that Holly, her spouse, and their two children accompany them for a week at the beach, she figured she might as well, since she had heard nothing from the dozens of job applications she had sent out.

The trip brightened both her outlook and her prospects. As she rinsed off in the outdoor shower after a morning at the shore, a knot in the wooden door sparked a thought. "The pun 'Wood you be mine?' popped into my head," she recalled. "As soon as I toweled off, I ran inside and sketched a card design." She shared the finished product—hand-drawn and hand-cut on kraft card-stock that was blanket-stitched up the left side in red embroidery floss—on Instagram and Facebook. Hours later, her friends and followers craved that card and were willing to pay her for it. So began Holly's second career: craft entrepreneur.

Holly was one of six such women we met in the process of a larger study ($n = 48$) of the identities and motivations of amateur makers—that is, people who pursue activities from making drones to making dinner—in the US and UK. Like Holly, each of them experienced a turning point that prompted them to begin welding something they loved doing to something they might make money doing.

MAKING SENSE OF THE BEGINNING

Despite the robust amount of empirical work devoted to women who practice craft entrepreneurship, scant information exists on those who are just at the point of turning a hobby into a business.[2] Until recently, the focus instead often fell on the products of eminent women makers or those who have been successful in craft-based ventures; time and circumstance arguably cloud their recollections of getting started.[3]

The oversight points to a missed opportunity, which this volume seeks to set right. Naudin's chapter later on examines the insights and experiences of craftswomen in the ambiguous midst of their entrepreneurial lives. This chapter, by contrast, tracks the stories of craftswomen contemplating the first tentative steps towards converting a hobby into a profession. In the range of these narratives lies an understudied spectrum of women's craft entrepreneurship.

"I often wished for someone who could have helped me through this, but I just got to this point on my own," said Laila, another of the women in our project. People who are, like her, contemplating craft-based businesses of their own could benefit from the stories of those also in the throes of deliberation. For them, perceptions from women just about to take the plunge could prompt new assessments essential to deciding whether to follow suit.

Women would-be craft entrepreneurs could also profit from understanding more about the environmental constraints and supports that they must negotiate to not only produce creative products but to experience the creativity necessary to begin envisioning a business. We find that affordance theory[4]— considered as part of a broader framework that also incorporates identity, agency and action[5]—offers a promising means for viewing the resources that promote creativity as well as entrepreneurship.[6]

To initiate the narratives of the women in our research who were on the verge of craft entrepreneurship, we used a method honed in our teaching and research practices: We asked them to make something in their medium, think about how they first felt creative working with it, and then talk to us about the thoughts and feelings that making engendered. As we reviewed their stories, we looked closely at how they moved from being people who felt that they had creative identities to those who developed the agency to make things (including, eventually, businesses). In the process of creating, they encountered affordances that they either surmounted or capitalised on to emerge with a marketable product. In this chapter, we argue that their way forward was a result of their encounters with creative identity, agency and affordances in the action of making.

BRAIDING THEORIES

As researchers interested in everyday creativity, we take a multidisciplinary approach[7] in theorising creative identity and process.[8] For example, the personality-based construct of self-efficacy, built on Albert Bandura's social cognitive theory, is useful in considering why people engage in everyday creativity.[9] Likewise, Anthony Giddens's theory of structuration is an aid for studying the agency of individuals in relation to the power of social structures.[10] Recent work with the constructs of creative self-efficacy[11] and creative personal identity strike a theoretical balance useful in understanding what leads someone to contemplate starting a craft-based business.[12]

THE PSYCHOLOGICAL AND SOCIAL

The concepts of self-efficacy and structuration complement each other but do not mean the same things. In Bandura's account, self-efficacy—a person's belief in their abilities—is one of the most important determinants of outcomes in human behavior. Even so, self-efficacy is not entirely straightforward:

> Efficacy in dealing with one's environment is not simply a matter of knowing what to do. . . . Rather, efficacy involves a generative capability in which cognitive, social, and behavioral subskills must be organized into integrated courses of action to serve innumerable purposes. Success is often attained only after generating and testing alternative forms of behavior and strategies, which requires perseverant effort. Self-doubters are quick to abort this generative process if their initial efforts prove deficient.[13]

But people do not exist independently of social forces, and Giddens's theory of structuration serves as a sociological counterpoint to social cognitive theory. At its essence, structuration characterizes people's actions as framed by rules—some more explicit, like laws and regulations, and some more invisible, such as a general sense of what things are or should be like—and resources. By living within these structures, people continually test rules and resources. New rules and resources emerge from continued interaction and are tested in ever-increasing social interactions. The repeated cycles have a knock-on effect: Social interaction alters or modifies rules and resources, while the rules and resources subvert or reinforce social interaction. Small-scale change can eventually become societal-level change.

In the business of living and making things, people filter this constant change. As they construct their identities—a process which is not necessarily very conscious or explicit—they survey their thoughts, actions and emotions. For Giddens, this construction reveals itself as reflexivity, bridging personal and social transformations.[14] People rarely experience reflexivity outright because much of what happens in social life is routine. It's the extraordinary, though—those breaks in routine—that create the opening for creativity.

Giddens says that such identity-shaping moments transpire throughout a lifetime: "Fateful moments are those when individuals are called on to take decisions that are particularly consequential for their ambitions, or more generally for their future lives."[15] Under these circumstances, the making of a personal identity—rather like the making of a craft-based business—is a continual series of self-actualising projects.

Creative self-efficacy arises when someone believes they can produce creative things, and Framer and Tierney maintain that belief can predict, moderate and mediate creative action.[16] Creative identity is the product of self-beliefs, such as creative self-efficacy that determine whether someone thinks of themselves as creative.[17] Making something and seeing the outcome as creative goes at least part of the way towards conferring both creative self-efficacy and creative identity.

Further, the construct of entrepreneurial self-efficacy, gaining traction in business and management studies, shifts the focus from a person's creative ability to their capability in using problem-solving skills to start and run a business.[18] Biraglia and Kadile argue that creativity, along with entrepreneurial passion, is essential to entrepreneurial self-efficacy for home brewers who aspire to build a business.[19]

Whether their focus is entrepreneurial or every day, creators constantly and reflexively act to reaffirm their identities. Fortunately, creative personal identity is adaptable enough to suit an array of situations and contexts. In a passage that particularly applies to creatives, Giddens maintains that people frame identity as a kind of biographical project, an evolving story that incorporates personal, cultural and societal contexts:

> The existential question of self-identity is bound up with the fragile nature of the biography which the individual 'supplies' about herself. A person's identity is not to be found in behavior, nor—important though this is—in the reactions of others, but in the capacity *to keep a particular narrative going.*[20]

Keeping the narrative alive can involve work in itself. As Glăveanu and Tanggaard relate, some creators create so they can maintain their creative identities, while others are enticed to create to avoid marginalisation.[21] To be sure, creators sometimes do both things at once.

Compelling though it may be at times, the creative identity project is not always top of mind, as Giddens's delineation of the levels of consciousness would suggest. Glăveanu and Tanggaard agree that creative identity does not grow when it is thought about and shrink when it is not. It does, however, come into focus when someone undertakes a mode of creative expression, and then communicates with others about that expression.[22]

THE ROLE OF MAKING

In our work, these complementary constructs give context that unites the act of making objects with that of constructing identities. We have found a fruitful method in asking research participants to make things as part of the process, and to reflect and speak about these things, so that participants can work on representations of identity more thoughtfully (rather than just generating spontaneous speech on that topic). We have asked them to make things in their favourite or preferred media,[23] as well as in prescribed objects such as video, collage and playfully crafty materials such as LEGO, yarn and pipe cleaners.[24] The resulting narratives are richly revealing about the individuals' inner lives. When individuals answer a question by making something and then reflect on the process, the process enables them to chronicle their stories and recount their experiences differently.

Their narratives suggest to us that the way to make a creative identity is to make something. While that sentence reads like a syllogism, it bears the ring of truth: These people have told us time and again that deciding to make is the first act in a long series of constructions for the creative person.

FROM AGENTIC MOTIVATION TO
ACTION AND AFFORDANCES

The next act, of course, is the agency to proceed. In our research, participants have used words such as "determine," "discipline" and "focus" to describe their drive to create. This vocabulary and the activities it implicates recall the self-determination and intrinsic motivation that social psychologists such as Ryan and Deci[25] have written about in terms of free will and that Amabile brought to creativity studies.[26] What we mean when we speak of agency is an individual's propensity to make their own choices. That definition squares with those of the social psychologists[27] as well as with Giddens. Agency, then, stems from both identity and self-efficacy.

As a next step, action is the proving ground for creative identity, thanks in no small measure to the affordances—the constraints and supports of their environment—that people encounter when they make things. We have found the concept of affordances central to an individual's process of making—although environmental affordances do not make up *all* of the explanations for a successful creative practice, which is why we also consider identity and self-efficacy.

Gibson coined the word and the theory behind it in the 1970s as a precept in perception in the field of environmental psychology.[28] He maintained that affordances were those aspects of an organism's environment that affected it, helping or hurting its progress. That sounds perfectly reasonable unless the organism—in our example, a maker—is unsure whether what they encounter is helpful or harmful. That is because affordances have no value until they are confronted, Gibson declared. Moreover, an organism's perception of the affordance determines whether the aspect delivers "caresses or blows, contact comfort or contact injury, reward or punishment, and it is not always easy to perceive which will be provided."[29] That ambiguity constitutes the break from routine that Giddens described, and likewise presents a chance for creativity to surface.

In the nearly fifty years since its debut, affordance theory has found purchase in human-computer interaction, neuroscience and economics. More recently, creativity theorists—notably Glăveanu[30] and Moeran[31]—have devised theoretical models to describe how the perception of affordances affect people who make things.[32]

Anything in an organism's environment can be an affordance, from substances and surfaces to designs and configurations. While this description seems amorphous at first, it does cover the uncertainty in the question all makers face: What to make now?

In Glăveanu's sociocultural model of an affordance theory of creativity, affordances represent actions a person *could* take, interleaving with the intentionality they *would* take, and normativity they *should* take. These norms and intentions, Glăveanu holds, can limit or heighten the creativity exhibited by a person through a made object. Affordances have the potential to counter those limits, which makes a person's perception affordances as significant to a creative outcome as the affordance itself. Glăveanu further maintains that creativity resides not in a tangible creative product, but in the act of confronting affordances.[33]

Moeran's explication focuses on the kinds of affordances creative people face. In his categorisation, affordances fall into six categories: time, space, money, tools and materials, social networks and representation. Yet the categories are hardly static. Every affordance relates to the others, and this pinging of affordance against affordance adds up to what Moeran calls "circuits of affordance," which suggests the neural circuits that light up with creative thinking.[34]

While most of the components of the circuit are self-evident, representation calls for further comment. Moeran based his model on his research into cultural creatives in Japan working in magazines and design.[35] For them, assessing representational affordances requires fluency in genre, form and the field's typical way of doing things, a line of thought that hearkens back to Glăveanu's notation of normativity.[36]

That said, amateur makers—particularly those contemplating a craft-based business—may or may not know or even care about the norms. For them, representation has more to do with how they feel about what they are doing. As a kind of stock-taking, representation is essential to the processing of affordances in the service of action. Appropriately for affordance theory, this is an environmental perception turned inward. Because the resulting perspectives can fan the creative flame or extinguish it outright, we reason they can be accurately labeled representational.

THE RETURN TO IDENTITY

Locating creative affordances within the action of making mimics the transformation that occurs within the creative process. For the creative person, the engagement with action means that not only has something tangible been made, but a creative identity has been transformed—either enlarged or diminished—as well. As the woodworker Peter Korn writes in his memoir of a life of furniture-making, a key creative breakthrough came when he realised that the characteristics that he sought to cultivate in his creations—which he had already identified as "integrity, simplicity and grace"—were in fact descriptors of the life he wanted to make for himself.[37]

For Ryan and Deci, this agency-action-affordance progression is central to the cultivation of identity:

That is, the development of an identity depends to some extent on the cultural affordances available to the person. [Social determination theory] specifically suggests that those affordances include not only exposure, but also autonomy, competence, and relatedness supports. Of course, this is true to identities in every domain . . . especially because the very construct of identity is social in nature.[38]

They go on to say that an environment that supports a maker's needs is essential, and we add that the opportunity for both creativity and creative identity lies within how affordances—or the lack of them—are met by that maker.

Producing the kind of creative identity necessary for would-be craft entrepreneurs (and every maker, for that matter) to thrive is an ongoing creative project. As Ryan and Deci argue, it arises from a "process of self-discovery and growth—that is, an ongoing attempt to find life roles and self-definitions that are congruent with their predispositions, interests, and integrated values and that will thus afford need satisfaction and support flourishing."[39]

The six women on the brink of craft entrepreneurship in our interviews could then be said to be in the thick of their identity projects, just as they were in the middle of their schemes for new businesses and the making of the products they hoped would bring them success. We turn to their narratives to see how the patterns of identity, agency, action and affordances in making come to life.

FROM SIX STORIES, EXPONENTIAL INSIGHTS

Our case memos, written in 2016 shortly after each of the roughly hour-long interviews at the women's homes and studios, sketch the most basic details of their stories.

Ann is a white, forty-something figurative still-life painter in the US. She studied art and textiles in college, though painting was always a presence in her creative life. Now that her children are at university, she spends a lot of time painting. She has a gallery exhibition scheduled within the year.

Baylie, whose family is Scots-Irish, is an American in her late fifties. She started making handbags because she wanted one made especially for her. She began thinking about becoming a craft entrepreneur when friends began asking her for a purse, telling her they'd pay her for the work and materials. Baylie was a freelance photographer who found her assignments increasingly less satisfying, and the notion of doing something different was an appealing next step.

Ellen is a white American in her late thirties. After she lost her teaching job in a round of budget cuts, she began facilitating corporate conferences and business meetings. Ellen struggled with advice from experts to keep her cartooning she loved separate from her consulting, but her intuition told her to blend them with graphic recording—making live sketches during facilitation. She found social media a way to document her cartoons and build a following.

Holly, in her early forties, is an American of Cherokee, German and Irish descent. She was laid off from her job as a graphic designer, and she now makes hand-cut and hand-illustrated greeting cards with amusing messages. She spoke of the affordances that helped her begin her business, and how ideas can mushroom when you train yourself to think of them. She plans to have at least 350 designs available on Etsy.

Laila, whose family is South Asian, is in her early thirties and pulling together a business making and selling jewellry in England. She trained in art school and knew that she would never have a traditional career. She works part time in design firms to make ends meet. Besides jewellry, other things she makes include choreography, furniture, textiles, glass and sculpture.

Salma, an Iranian immigrant in her late fifties, shares a consulting business with her husband in England. She also has a side gig making jewellry from metal clay and teaching classes on technique. When we spoke, she was contemplating another at-home business—crocheting bath linens from luxury fibers. Her experience in other businesses helped her with the decision-making in this new one.

CONNECTING COMMON THEMES

Unifying topics emerge from these synopses. First, these women were middle-aged, and in the midst of their working lives. Moreover, they all had work experience before considering starting craft-based businesses of their own. They also all centered their notional enterprises on things they already enjoyed making. That is, their identities as painter, bag-maker, card creator, cartoonist, jeweller and crocheter existed well before our interviews.

The qualifying question for the entire research project was, "Do you feel creative when you make something in your preferred medium?" Participants who answered yes were included in the research project. Ellen spoke for many of them when she said, "I don't think I could not be creative. For me, it's essential to have that everyday outlet." Laila described the durability of a creative identity when she said, "I don't clock in and clock out of doing this. Even when I'm sleeping, I'm still a jewellry designer."

AGENCY

With the existence of their creative identities established, how did these women talk about the agency to create that those identities enabled? Their observations sometimes emerged from their descriptions of how they faced the affordances they encountered on the way to developing a creative identity. Other times, they were speaking aloud about what spurs them to create. Regardless of the direction, they used words such as *motivation, intent, discipline* and *determination* to identify the drive they had to make their fledgling businesses.

Ann spoke of the motivation her business goals helped her generate. She would, she said, produce enough paintings for an exhibition, price them for sale, and post them on social media. "Meeting goals keeps your determination front of mind," she said.

Baylie's motivations were also externally focused, allowing her to zero in on the aspects of making she preferred. "Now my goal is to design, cut, do that first bag for production and continue with cutting and punching," she said as she discussed her business plan. "But I will farm out all the stitching because the part I love best is designing it and figuring it out and how this is going to work together." For these women, the drive to make things led to their establishing a business as a vehicle for their enthusiasms.

AFFORDANCES IN ACTION

Making a product—say, a handbag—is not unlike making a craft-based business. Both undertakings stem from the action of *doing* something, whether the doing is fitting a rivet or creating a marketing plan. Actions then culminate into more significant projects. Yet before actions can culminate, all makers must face the affordances embedded in creating.

We devised six sub-codes for different kinds of affordance—representation, social, techno-material, time, space and money. Reading the accounts of the affordances these women encountered helps bring the concepts to life. Consider:

- *Representation*, outlined earlier in this chapter, focused on participants' interior perspectives of their creative pursuits. Extreme likes and dislikes sometimes informed their comments; sometimes, they liked what they made; other times, they did not, or were uncertain of the outcome. That said, there was no mistaking how they felt. Baylie, for example, expressed love for the materials she works with, while Holly said she delights in the act of stitching her cards together.

  The ability to view mistakes as a path towards innovation was a theme that emerged from several interviews, as did the idea of creating uncertainty as a catalyst for new directions. Their conceptions of representational affordances also reflected the inevitability of creative expression. As Salma said, "The most important thing is that you want to do something, and in my experience, that thing must happen." Laila put it in more dramatic terms: "If you don't make the thing that demands to be made, you feel like someone strangling you. You have to let it out."

- Describing their *social affordances*, these women often talked about making and posting the things they made on sites such as Etsy or Instagram. For Ellen, regular posting was a way of measuring her progress: "Social media gives me a structure and a platform, I guess you could say, and a way of evaluating how I'm doing." For Holly and Salma, it provided a means to advertise and sell their goods.

Family and friends also make up a person's social network, either developing or undermining the maker's attempts. Baylie's handbags could trace their beginnings to a bag her friend had made, and Baylie traded a photo portrait session with the friend's daughter for lessons on how to work with leather. In a case where friends did not deliver, Holly recounted that a friend who was working at a lifestyle magazine asked her to design some cards on spec for a photo shoot. "I never heard back, and was bummed," she said, "but sometimes that stuff happens."

Salma's and Laila's family and friends influenced their crochet and jewellry, suggesting design flourishes and materials. Meanwhile, Ann talked about what she did to counteract the inherent loneliness of painting. "I'm in here in my studio, day after day, alone," she said. "I do meet people for lunch, but most of the day, it's just me. The radio announcer became my closest friend for a little while there. But that's what it takes to create the show that I envision."

- The women discussed *techno-material* affordances in terms of quality, especially for tools and raw materials. Ellen spoke of the happiness she felt when she works with simple materials such as felt-tipped markers and colored paper. Laila delighted in organizing the pearl beading of a necklace, so it fell particularly gracefully around the wearer's shoulders.

Others described how the insider knowledge they had accumulated about their craft fulfilled them, and some said that this gave them the confidence to consider taking their creative pastime into a business. Salma recalled that her ability to master crochet freed her from having to use patterns. Baylie was adamant that her handbag tastes—luxurious leather paired with streamlined hardware—attracted buyers who responded to her pared-down aesthetic. After Holly solved the problem of getting her logo on the back of each card—using two sheets instead of one, she laser-printed the logo on one and carved the design into the other—her solution became her edge. What started as a material necessity became a signature.

- *Time* showed up in their narratives in a variety of ways: plans, sequences and deadlines, as well as their timelines. Ellen reckoned she could "easily finish ten drawings in an hour." Baylie's handbag concern could only flourish, she said, when her schedule held fewer photography assignments. Ann held off on pursuing painting until her children were self-sufficient enough for her to transfer her attention to creativity.

These women were willing to juggle their schedules to accommodate projects. Laila said a jewellry design would often awaken her from a deep sleep, and she found the payoff for getting out of bed and starting the piece worth the inevitable grogginess the next morning. "The best feeling for me is to spend hours doing something and stand back and think 'Wow, I made that.'"

- Finding *space* was often an ongoing concern for these women, and they developed a range of ways to find it. Once it was secured, they were freer to follow up on their entrepreneurial dreams.

Holly reclaimed the attic when her children went away to school. When she was away from her desk at home, Ellen drew on airplanes as she flew to work assignments. Laila rented a place she could set up her jewellry bench, and Baylie leased a house in her neighborhood when her handbags demanded more space than her home allowed.

In the wake of a catastrophic house fire, Ann devised the space above her garage as a painting studio. "When we put in the windows, I saw how great a creative space it could be," she said. "I painted this floor white to reflect all that great light, and I claimed this space for myself." It was the best place she could launch her business as an artist, she said, because it was hers.

- Although it was mentioned less frequently than other affordances in the participants' discussions, *money* was often the subtext in their narratives. At times, they directed their efforts towards saving it. As noted earlier, Baylie bartered photographs for lessons in leatherworking. Laila saved money by occasionally rummaging through dumpsters. "I got a Singer sewing machine from a skip, and I'll find offcuts of fabric and ribbon from a few select ones in the fashion district near my office," she said.

Salma lives near a store whose yarns inspired her creative imagination. After buying one or two skeins and realising that she needed more to finish a project, she discovered that yarns need to be purchased from the same dye lots to ensure uniformity of color. Her problem was solved—and her fledgling business boosted—when she discovered she could get three facecloths from a single skein of linen. Then, her experience pricing her jewellry line helped her determine the feasibility of a facecloth business. "Each facecloth costs me, in terms of yarn, about £2.50," she said. "With the packaging, it comes to £5. Then I can sell it for £10 to £15."

All of the women agreed they were grateful to use their creativity to make money. "At first, I had no intention to make a business from this," Baylie remembered. "But when my photography assignments began to fall off, I saw that I could replace some income with these handbags. I have to tell you, that felt good."

These perceptions reveal how affordances shape the ways each woman proceeds with starting a business, while at the same time shaping her creative identity. Their stories illustrate the tangles of affordances they faced, as time impinged on social networks and money, and space influenced the tools and materials they used. That they were following through on a dream to turn their creative pursuits into craft-based businesses demonstrates how well they engaged with their circuits of creative affordance—particularly representation, which plays an outsized role in whether people capitalise on the offerings presented by the intersections of other affordances. In essence, through experience and reflexivity, they had burnished their creative identities to the point where they could accommodate a new facet of being.

ENTREPRENEURSHIP

Reflexivity appeared to enhance these women's stores of creative self-efficacy. But what led to their developing entrepreneurial self-efficacy—that is, their belief in their abilities to reach goals and weather the highs and the lows of starting a business?[40] It could be the same drive for self-expression and creative expression that motivated them to begin making things in the first place. Such attributes could bolster someone's initiative, risk tolerance and persistence—essential attributes of successful entrepreneurs.[41] These women honed those qualities by developing the creative identity that urged them to make something in the first place. Fortunately for them, they also possessed the self-knowledge that could help them capitalise on the tasks ahead.

Baylie, for example, was confident that parts of the process that appealed more to her than others, resulting in the decision to hire a small staff. "I didn't get into this to make the same bag over and over, because I'm not that person," she said. "So it's a win-win for me to get other people involved."

Ellen's self-knowledge was sufficient enough to help her weigh the value of advice from a mentor. "The first thing she said was, 'Ellen, before you hear anything I say, you have to know that there are no rules. We're all just making it up.' I think that did it for me. Maybe I don't know what I'm doing exactly, but I don't have to spend my time looking for that one right answer."

Interestingly, self-knowledge often led to the realisation that making money, while an alluring prospect, was not necessarily the motivation for starting a business. Instead, personal satisfaction—a by-product of creative self-efficacy—was. As Holly said, "I never thought I was going to be rich, and that's not why I'm doing it. I just enjoy it, and if people want to buy it, that's great."

That was certainly the case for Laila and Ann. Sharing creative expression with others who identify with you and your style, they both maintained, came with its rewards: professional growth, peer recognition and the chance to keep making things they love. Indeed, even as Salma sized up the competition in her segment, she was clear about her entrepreneurial ambition. "In Etsy, I saw a lot of people doing this sort of thing, but none of them have linen as I do," she said. "It's my hobby. I'm doing this just to get it out the world so I can crochet some more."

MAKING AS AFFORDANCES, IDENTITY AND ACTION

By identifying as creators and pursuing a craft that could start a business, these six women had to confront the way they felt about becoming craft entrepreneurs. Like all creators, they were following Raymond Williams's prescription for creative growth: "For creativity and social self-creation are both known and unknown events, and it is still from grasping the known that the unknown—the next step, the next work—is conceived."[42]

Being able to take this step required a particular alignment of identity, self-efficacy, and affordances—a mix which came in a few different flavors, but was not especially common or easy to arrive at. This explains why there may be quite a lot of people who think that they might turn their craft or hobby into a business "someday," but relatively few who actually do.

As we have identified the creative journey as a project of the self, for entrepreneurs just as much as for artisans, this also points to why it is difficult—and plainly sometimes painfully risky—to try to turn that project into an outward-facing, money-seeking business venture. In everyday life, our narrative of the self can remain private and much of the time shrouded in things unsaid. But when the project of the self is put at the beating heart of a commercial enterprise, the spotlight of attention is directed straight towards it. Although the success or failure of a business will always feel personal to an entrepreneur, a craft or artisan business built on one person's creative self-expression will feel especially exposing—in a sense, self-identity *itself* is "on the line," at the mercy of other people's tastes and opinions, and the unruly marketplace of competing products and creative visions.

CONCLUSION

At the beginning of this chapter, we suggested that the accounts of women "about to take the plunge" might prove informative for other would-be entrepreneurs. And although that may be the case, there is a cheerful reason why it might not be: The determination necessary to launch a successful business involves not caring too much what others think and what others have been doing. If we believe that our own project is especially compelling and unique, we aren't going to worry too much about other people's anxieties and mistakes.

Admittedly, these Western, middle-class, middle-aged women—who could be considered to represent an already well-studied group in social science research—had the privilege of sufficient cultural, social and economic capital to possess such self-assurance. Certainly, not everyone does. Yet their stories offer clues to broad truths that meet everyone who, for whatever reason, chooses to make something. Chief among them: The role of creative affordances, which claim perception and action as capital, in conferring creative identity.

Affordance theory does not explain creativity on its own but becomes invaluable when understood as part of a broader framework that includes identity and agency, and is expressed in creative action. It is in the struggle with and against a set of affordances that both a creative enterprise and a creative identity are forged. The unavoidable *doing* part of creativity and creative entrepreneurship means that the success—or otherwise—of creative ideas is made visible, sometimes painfully so. But this also means that the triumphs are hard-won and fully felt.

This signals an interesting relationship with Gidden's theory of structuration, in which things gradually change through the *doing* of them (for instance, when the norms for gender roles change over a few decades because a growing number of people have enacted them differently, leading to change in the norms themselves). Similarly, it is through *doing* things with and against affordances that the meanings—and actual results—of creative action are produced. By looking at affordances through the prism of creative identities and actions, we have seen how these women were able to turn a pastime into a project, and a project into a business.

NOTES

1. Holly's name is a pseudonym, as are the names of all the participants mentioned in this chapter.
2. Alessandro Biraglia and Vita Kadile, "The Role of Entrepreneurial Passion and Creativity in Developing Entrepreneurial Intentions: Insights from American Home Brewers," *Journal of Small Business Management* 55, no. 1 (2017): 170–88.
3. Alison McNicol, *Craft Business Heroes: 30 Creative Entrepreneurs Share the Secrets of Their Success* (London: Kyle Craig, 2012), 198–202.

4. Brian Moeran, *The Business of Creativity: Toward an Anthropology of Worth* (Walnut Creek, CA: Left Coast Press, 2014), 35–58.

5. Vlad-Petre Glăveanu, *Thinking through Creativity and Culture: Toward an Integrated Model* (Abingdon: Routledge, 2017), 213–28.

6. Mary Kay Culpepper, "'Yeah, That's What I Am Now': Affordances, Action, and Creative Identity," in *The Palgrave Handbook of Creativity at Work*, eds. Lee Martin and Nick Wilson. (Cham: Palgrave Macmillan, 2018), 107–24.

7. Ibid., 107–24.

8. David Gauntlett, *Making Is Connecting: The Social Power of Creativity, from Craft and Knitting to Digital Everything*, 2nd ed. (Cambridge, MA: Polity Press, 2018), 270–76.

9. Albert Bandura, *Social Foundations of Thought and Action: A Social Cognitive Theory* (Upper Saddle River, NJ: Prentice-Hall, 1968), 390–453.

10. Anthony Giddens, *Modernity and Self-Identity: Self and Society in Late Modern Age* (Stanford: Stanford University Press, 1991), 209–31.

11. Kimberly S. Jaussi, Amy E. Randel, and Shelley D. Dionne, "I Am, I Think I Can, and I Do: The Role of Personal Identity, Self-Efficacy, and Cross-Application of Experiences in Creativity at Work," *Creativity Research Journal* 19, no. 2–3 (2007): 247–58.

12. Vlad-Petre Glăveanu and Lene Tanggaard, "Creativity, Identity, and Representation: Towards a Socio-Cultural Theory of Creative Identity," *New Ideas in Psychology* 34 (2014).

12–21.

13. Bandura, *Social Foundations*, 391.

14. Giddens, *Modernity*, 32–34.

15. Ibid., 112.

16. Steven M. Framer and Pamela Tierney, "Considering Creative Self-Efficacy: Its Current State and Ideas for Future Inquiry," in *The Creative Self: Effect of Beliefs, Self-efficacy, Mindset, and Identity*, eds. Maciej Karwowski and James C. Kaufman (San Diego, CA: Academic Press, 2017), 23–47.

17. Maciej Karwowski and James C. Kaufman, eds. *The Creative Self: Effect of Beliefs, Self-efficacy, Mindset, and Identity.* (San Diego, CA: Academic Press, 2017) xvii–xxiii.

18. Hao Zhao, Scott E. Seibert, and Gerald E. Hills, "The Mediating Role of Self-Efficacy in the Development of Entrepreneurial Intentions," *Journal of Applied Psychology* 90, no. 6 (2005): 1265–72.

19. Brigalia and Kadile, "Entrepreneurial Passion," 173.

20. Giddens, *Modernity*, 54 (emphasis in original).

21. Glăveanu and Tanggard, "Creativity," 15.

22. Ibid, 15.

23. Culpepper, "That's What," 118–19.

24. David Gauntlett, *Creative Explorations: New Approaches to Identity and Audiences* (Abingdon: Routledge, 2007), 92–157.

25. Richard Ryan and Edward L. Deci, *Self-Determination Theory: Basic Psychological Needs in Motivation, Development, and Wellness* (New York: Guilford Press, 2017), 125–29.

26. Teresa M. Amabile, "Motivation and Creativity: Effects of Motivational Orientation on Creative Writers," *Journal of Psychology* 48, no. 2 (1985): 393–99.

27. James J. Gibson, "The Theory of Affordances," in *Perceiving, Acting, and Knowing*, eds. Robert Shaw and John Bransford (Hillsdale, NJ: Lawrence Erlbaum, 1977), 67–82.

28. James J. Gibson, *The Ecological Approach to Visual Perception* (Boston: Houghton Mifflin, 1979), 56.

29. Gibson, "The Theory of Affordances," 77.

30. Glăveanu, *Thinking through Creativity*, 275–80.

31. Moeran, *Business of Creativity*, 269–83.

32. Ibid., 35–59.

33. Glăveanu, *Thinking through Creativity*, 213–28.

34. Moeran, *Business of Creativity*, 60–245.

35. Ibid., 217.

36. Glăveanu, *Thinking through Creativity*, 387.

37. Peter Korn, *Why We Make Things and Why It Matters: The Education of a Craftsman* (London: Vintage, 2017), 102.

38. Ryan and Deci, *Self-Determination Theory*, 387.

39. Ibid., 387.

40. Mateja Drnovšek, Joakim Wincent, and Melissa S. Cardon, "Entrepreneurial Self-efficacy and Business Start-up: Developing a Multi-dimensional Definition," *International Journal of Entrepreneurial Behavior and Research* 16, no. 4 (2010): 329–48.

41. Danny Miller, "A Downside to the Entrepreneurial Personality?" *Entrepreneurship Theory and Practice* 39, no. 1 (January 2015): 1–8.

42. Raymond Williams, *Marxism and Literature* (Oxford: Oxford University Press, 1972), 212.

BIBLIOGRAPHY

Amabile, Teresa M. "Motivation and Creativity: Effects of Motivational Orientation on Creative Writers." *Journal of Personality and Social Psychology* 48, no. 2 (1985): 393–99.

Bandura, Albert. *Social Foundations of Thought and Action: A Social Cognitive Theory.* Upper Saddle River, NJ: Prentice-Hall, 1968.

Biraglia, Alessandro, and Vita Kadile. "The Role of Entrepreneurial Passion and Creativity in Developing Entrepreneurial Intentions: Insights from American Home Brewers." *Journal of Small Business Management* 55, no. 1 (2017): 170–88.

Culpepper, Mary Kay. "'Yeah, That's What I Am Now': Affordances, Action, and Creative Identity." In *The Palgrave Handbook of Creativity at Work*, edited by Lee Martin and Nick Wilson, 107–204. Cham: Palgrave Macmillan, 2018.

Drnovšek, Mateja, Joakim Wincent, and Melissa S. Cardon. "Entrepreneurial Self-Efficacy and Business Start-up: Developing a Multi-Dimensional Definition." In *International Journal of Entrepreneurial Behavior and Research* 16, no. 4 (2010): 329–48.

Framer, Steven M., and Pamela Tierney. "Considering Creative Self-Efficacy: Its Current State and Ideas for Future Inquiry." In *The Creative Self: Effect of Beliefs, Self-Efficacy, Mindset, and Identity*, edited by Maciej Karwowski and James C. Kaufman, 23–47. San Diego, CA: Academic Press, 2017.

Gauntlett, David. *Creative Explorations: New Approaches to Identity and Audiences*. Abingdon: Routledge, 2007.

———. *Making Is Connecting: The Social Power of Creativity, from Craft and Knitting to Digital Everything*, 2nd ed. Cambridge: Polity Press, 2018.

Gibson, James J. *The Ecological Approach to Visual Perception*. Boston: Houghton Mifflin, 1979.

———. "The Theory of Affordances." In *Perceiving, Acting, and Knowing*, edited by Robert Shaw and John Bransford, 67–82. Hillsdale, NJ: Lawrence Erlbaum, 1977.

Giddens, Anthony. *Modernity and Self-Identity: Self and Society in Late Modern Age*. Stanford, CA: Stanford University Press, 1991.

Glăveanu, Vlad-Petre. *Thinking through Creativity and Culture: Toward an Integrated Model* Abingdon: Routledge, 2017.

Glăveanu, Vlad-Petre, and Lene Tanggaard. "Creativity, Identity, and Representation: Towards a Socio-Cultural Theory of Creative Identity." *New Ideas in Psychology* 34 (2014): 12–21.

Jaussi, Kimberly S., Amy E. Randel, and Shelley D. Dionne. "I Am, I Think I Can, and I Do: The Role of Personal Identity, Self-efficacy, and Cross-Application of Experiences in Creativity at Work." *Creativity Research Journal* 19, no. 2–3 (2007): 247–58.

Karwowski, Maciej, and James C. Kaufman, eds. *The Creative Self: Effect of Beliefs, Self-efficacy, Mindset, and Identity*. San Diego, CA: Academic Press, 2017.

McNicol, Alison. *Craft Business Heroes: 30 Creative Entrepreneurs Share the Secrets of Their Success*. London: Kyle Craig, 2012.

Miller, Danny. "A Downside to the Entrepreneurial Personality?" *Entrepreneurship Theory and Practice* 39, no. 1 (2015): 1–8.

Moeran, Brian. *The Business of Creativity: Toward an Anthropology of Worth*. Walnut Creek, CA: Left Coast Press, 2014.

Ryan, Richard M., and Edward L. Deci. *Self-Determination Theory: Basic Psychological Needs in Motivation, Development, and Wellness*. New York: Guilford Press, 2017.

Williams, Raymond. *Marxism and Literature*. Oxford: Oxford University Press, 1972.

Zhao, H., Scott E. Seibert, and Gerald E. Hills. "The Mediating Role of Self-Efficacy in the Development of Entrepreneurial Intentions." *Journal of Applied Psychology* 90, no. 6 (2005): 1265–72.

Chapter Ten

Becoming a Craft Entrepreneur

Vishalakshi Roy

Oh gosh, it's very difficult to introduce yourself, because I have done so many things. It's not like I've just gone to university, done an art course and then started a business. So, I'm at the stage where I'm not quite sure how to introduce myself.

The craft sector in the UK comprises of a disproportionate number of micro companies, some of which are made up of a solitary maker who is also the business owner. This chapter illustrates the identity journey these individuals take from being a hobbyist to a creative entrepreneur, turning their interest and passion for a craft into their primary source of income. Using the empirical case of a female craftsperson, their identity work, "a set of active processes which serve to construct a sense of identity,"[1] is investigated. These processes manifest in how she navigates a series of career changes to harness her passion for knitting and start her own craft venture.

The contemporary view of identity in entrepreneurship accepts its dynamic nature and its multidimensional structure. Scholars have illustrated how tensions may stimulate identity work in different settings,[2] but they do not offer a satisfactory understanding of how multiple identities of an entrepreneur interact to promote identity work. One setting where identity work is prolific is in the founding stages of the venture when individuals transition into entrepreneurship. However, detailed accounts of the identity processes of the entrepreneur in this stage have not found favour in the entrepreneurship or craft literature. Therefore, the question at the heart of this chapter is: *How does a craft entrepreneur engage in identity work in response to identity demands caused by multiple identities in the founding stage?*

The reasons for investigating identity work of a craft entrepreneur stem from the observation that such individuals exhibit multiple identities that co-exist.[3] The craft sector is characterised by large numbers of small micro-businesses and sole traders with a relatively small number of larger organisations. While it is not possible to estimate the actual size and scale of crafts as a creative industry, its popularity due to the beneficial outcomes for individuals engaging in craft activity is well established.[4] Self-employment, entrepreneurship and business start-ups are significant career choices for many working in the sector. Similarly, many develop portfolio careers, juggling several part-time roles along with freelance work. Due to these factors, entrepreneurs that work in this sector display multiple (vocational) identities that occur concurrently.[5] While I acknowledge that entrepreneurs operating in other settings also hold multiple identities, the presence of these identities (as well as tension between them) is readily observable among entrepreneurs in the creative industries such as the craft sector.

Through this chapter I aim to provide readers with an appreciation of identity processes of a craftperson founding a craft business. Compiled through in-depth interviews with a female craftsperson, the findings of the two-year longitudinal research are presented in the form of a case study. The case study is written with a specific aim of highlighting the complexities of identity processes on one hand while outlining how simple events and incidents can be identity-forming for a craft entrepreneur. The story also highlights the importance of specific events, networks, and training in navigating identity demands. Through the chapter I aim to provide insights into the identity work of a craft entrepreneur during their founding journey. I believe that there is something in this story that will chime with anyone who has gone through changes in their career to start a business in the craft sector.

The chapter starts with a discussion of the theoretical background of the study, which comprises of a review of the literature on identity work in entrepreneurship and the craft sector. This is followed by a discussion of the method and then the findings in the form of a case study. The chapter concludes with a discussion of the case and identification of areas for future exploration.

This chapter relates to two strands of literature in entrepreneurship: that concerning entrepreneurship and identity, and second, identity work processes resulting from multiple identities. Where relevant, I also highlight studies into the identity of craftpersons and makers relevant to this chapter.

ENTREPRENEURSHIP AND IDENTITY

The term *entrepreneurial identity* is typically used to refer to a composite identity made up of components which may exhibit features, such as innovation, control, risk propensity and wealth creation.[6] On the other hand, *identity of an entrepreneur* refers to an individual's identity, which may or may not be entrepreneurial. Thus, an entrepreneurial identity refers to a type of identity whereas the identity of an entrepreneur relates to an individual (the entrepreneur). This chapter focuses on the identity of the entrepreneur and the related literature draws on the intellectual heritage of both strands of identity theory—that is, identity theory as proposed by Stets and Burke[7] and social identity theory as proposed by Turner and Tajfel.[8]

To understand the identity of entrepreneurs in more detail and respond to the research question, two key features of identity need further exploration: *multiplicity* and *stability*. Psychologists and sociologists have argued for the multiple nature of an individual's identity, stating that a response to the question "Who am I?" rarely yields a single answer. Scholars believe that there is a "parliament of identities within the same individual."[9] Consequently, entrepreneurship scholars have recognised that the identity of an entrepreneur is a composite of various sub-identities.[10] Research relating to identity in entrepreneurship has moved away from the idea of identity being monolithic to one that is multiple and composite.[11] The presence of multiple sub-identities may also force the individual to contend with competing priorities and tensions. When discussing how identities are developed, Wenger[12] proposed that identities are "pluralistic accomplishments that develop through a process of negotiating the meanings of our experience of membership in social communities." A core theme across social psychological theories of identity is that all people have multiple identities because they inhabit multiple roles and identify with multiple social groups.[13]

Moving on to stability, scholars continue to debate whether identities are stable, fixed and secure, or evolutionarily adaptive and fluid.[14] Historically, there is recognition among scholars that individuals need a relatively secure and stable sense of who they are within a given situation to function effectively.[15] This argument may be extended to state that the identity of the entrepreneur remains stable over the period of the venture and through the various stages.[16] Conversely, Neilsen and Lassen[17] argue that the identity of an entrepreneur is developed and modified as the venture unfolds. The idea of changing identities of entrepreneurs has also been highlighted in relation to the specific conditions and challenges associated with the founding stage of a venture.[18] Summarising these arguments, I find that while self-concepts may exhibit continuity over a period of time, there is need for flexibility provided by a suppler "working self-concept,"[19] which permits dynamic responses to changeable situations.

THE PROCESS OF IDENTITY WORK

Examining the two features of identity—multiplicity and stability—presents an interesting argument. If multiple identities exist in an entrepreneur and identities are changeable and unstable, it is fruitful to chart the interactions between these two features to further understand how identity evolves through the founding stage. I find that the overall self is constructed from a relatively stable set of meanings which change only gradually, such as during role or career transition.[20] Within these periods of large transitions, there are temporary instabilities which lead to identity work. During such periods of instability multiple sub-identities can be "acquired, lost, switched or modified much more quickly, and perhaps instantaneously as contexts and preferences alter" through a process of identity work.[21] This gradualist view of identity work states that identities adjust and evolve at times of disequilibrium "only to find and maintain an optimum balance or equilibrium position."[22]

As a concept, identity work is a significant metaphor in the analysis of how identities are constructed. The term was coined by social psychologists Snow and Anderson[23] in their seminal work analysing the change in self-concept of the homeless. In management literature, Sveningsson and Alvesson[24] define identity work as "a formal conceptualization of the ways in which human beings are continuously engaged in forming, repairing, maintaining, strengthening or revising the constructions that are productive of a sense of coherence and distinctiveness." Identity work builds on and brings together concepts that thus far appeared in academic literature under various phrases such as identity construction, identity management, identity achievement, identity manufacture and identity project.

A key motivator for undertaking identity work is the need to align work demands with self-identity so that work identity integrity is achieved.[25] A review of the literature shows that identity work is usually observed over time and during significant change or stimulus. A key outcome of identity work is to achieve coherence or a state of balance between identities which is also true in the case of the craftsperson discussed in this chapter.

The desire for identity coherence as defined by Sveningsson and Alvesson[26] is heightened when an individual is faced with the need to bring together competing priorities and related identities. The scholars illustrated how multiple identities of an individual are negotiated for the construction of managerial identities and proposed that identity work leads to integration and fragmentation of the multiple identities of the individual. Some scholars have also looked at more multidimensional strategies, such as Pratt and Foreman[27] drawing on individual-level theories to demonstrate strategies for identity work such as "deletion, aggregation, compartmentalization and integration."

In addition to some of the strategies proposed for negotiating multiple identities, a key motivator for undertaking identity construction is the need to align work demands with self identity, so that work identity integrity and coherence is achieved.[28] Additionally, identity work can also help resolve identity struggles, tensions and conflicts. Although the context of the literature varies greatly, scholars agree on the need for understanding how and why identity work occurs in response to identity conflict and tensions between multiple identities. Identity work is undertaken for coherence, or individuals' sense of their "own continuity over time, clarity in awareness of the connections between their multiple identities, a sense of completeness or wholeness."[29] Therefore, there is a need to appreciate how identity conflict stemming from multiple identities is negotiated and highlight the processes sought by individuals that feel this conflict.

IDENTITY OF CRAFT WORKERS

Within the craft literature, identity of craftpersons, workers and entrepreneurs has received some interest in relation to how the identity of the maker is constituted through their craft discourses.[30] Additionally, in relation to the activities of creating and marketing craft, the identity of the maker as "aesthetic labour" has been investigated by scholars.[31] Various aspects of the identity of a craftsperson (artisan and makers) and how it is interlinked to a place-based role such as their interaction with a specific regional or national identity have also been examined by scholars such as Bose[32] and Toraldo et al.[33] These studies primarily present ethnographic accounts of the life and work of these individuals. Another contemporary strand of research into identity of craft entrepreneurs which holds relevance to this chapter relates to female craft entrepreneurs. Here scholars examine areas such as how home-based making impacts on the professional identity of makers[34] and how female (crochet) makers network and develop their identities online.[35] The gradual identity construction of a maker in the process of developing their practice and venture, and how their multiple identities interact and contribute to this process, is yet to receive attention in the craft literature.

Having reviewed the literature that forms the theoretical background of the research, I illustrate the methods used, followed by the case study of a craftsperson in the founding stage of her craft venture. Through the case study I follow Sarah on her founding journey and underline the identity work undertaken by her in response to the demands and challenges presented by her venture. I note how she achieves a state of identity coherence at the end of the founding stage (i.e., two years from inception).

EMPIRICAL METHOD AND ANALYTICAL STRATEGY

To develop this chapter, I interviewed a craftsperson[36] about her evolving identity and venture journey over a twenty-two-month period. To understand identity work and processes during the founding phase, I created the follow-ing target profile: (a) she had started a new venture less than six months ago (start point was self-defined), (b) she trained and/or was a practicing artist, and (c) her artistic practice and business was primarily based in the craft sec-tor in the UK.

Data was collected primarily through three rounds of semi-structured inter-views. The first interview took the form of a life story where I requested infor-mation about her childhood, education and work history. This helped identify the sequence of events in historical order, thus reducing the likelihood of gener-ating retrospective rationalisations that might occur if she told me what she had done and then created a narrative to explain why. I maintained a careful tone of supportive neutrality throughout the data collection process in an attempt to minimise any social desirability bias in what Sarah reported. The chance of ret-rospective rationalisation was also minimised by the design of the study, which reduced my reliance on gathering data about past events but instead allowed me to focus on events that I could explore as they unfolded.

Later interviews were more structured as I explored emerging theoretical themes. For example, I asked about about specific occurrences that had an impact on how Sarah felt about herself and the progress of her venture. In most cases, as part of telling the stories of the venture, Sarah provided extensive biographical data, extending well before the founding stage. The life history data allowed me to place the identities I analysed in this chapter as important elements of Sarah's sense of self before founding. I supplemented data from the interviews with field notes after each interview and collected observational data and information published offline and online about the venture including marketing and social media-based feedback received from customers. Al-though I only use quotes from Sarah as illustrative evidence, the supplemen-tary data helped me make sense of the data to develop the case study.

The case study gives the reader an opportunity to observe the identity work unfold in a setting characterised by multiple identities. Where possible the identity work processes have been identified using the definition proposed by Sveningsson and Alvesson.[37]

HOW AND WHY SARAH STARTED THIS JOURNEY

At the inception of the data collection Sarah was embarking on her third career change—from scientist to secondary school teacher and now to crafts-person. With a doctorate in a scientific discipline, Sarah had worked in very structured and process driven roles in her initial career. Her first change of career was into teaching where she retrained as a secondary school teacher and worked in schools for thirteen years. Throughout these careers she still felt the need to "do something crafty," a passion that she had since she was a child. A craft that she was interested in but had never mastered was knitting, and Sarah decided to teach herself to knit. Sarah's decision to change her career away from teaching was also prompted by a diagnosis of a degenerative disease which made having a full-time career in teaching unsustainable.

Sarah placed great importance on being active and involved in a related network to learn and practice her newly developed skills. Interestingly, some of the initial identity work noted in Sarah relates to her reactions to the commercialisation of creative output. This is reflected in how she saw other, more experienced knitters' social identities.

> About 12 years ago I became one of the founding members of a local knitting group. I learnt an awful lot from them. I met a big group of ladies who have knitted for decades. They're all older, they have knitted for years. Some of them bred rabbits for angora to spin their own yarn, others spun, dyed yarn, wove, they did masses of stuff at a very high level and yet people would say—oh they're just amateurs because they didn't make a living from it.

One of the ways in which Sarah prompted a move away from the "amateur" label was by engaging in formal training. In all instances related to her career changes, I noted the importance Sarah placed on formal training and practice to embody and "strengthen"[38] her new identity—as a scientist, a teacher and a maker. Before she started her craft venture, having a qualification in that field was important to her. Doing an MA in Textile Design specialising in knitting gave her a sense of achievement and legitimacy as a professional craftsperson. The course also helped her experiment with different materials and tools and to try her hand at designing objects of various scales. This is the point at which Sarah started to think more clearly about her future as a crafts entrepreneur and inhabiting that identity, in addition to that of a maker.

> I just thought this is really what I want to do, I'd love to be able to make and sell.

MAKING IDENTITY AND VENTURE DECISIONS

In starting her venture, Sarah regularly faced negativity from people around her that questioned this change of career. This included her partner and some close friends. In "forming"[39] her new identity as a crafts entrepreneur, I found Sarah took a structured approach to defining her venture and researching how others have approached new ventures in this field. She extensively researched related businesses online in spite of some seeing this activity as "wasting time." Research into other ventures and craft entrepreneurs helped her refine her offer and provided meaningful comparisons to model herself and her venture.

While the venture and identity started to form, Sarah was still grappling with the practicalities of making a living from her new business. On one hand this was an issue of scale of operation, but on the other, there was an issue around quality. According to Luckman and Thomas,[40] the entrepreneurial principle of selling one's work conflicts with a craftsperson's commitment to make objects to a satisfactory level of aesthetic and technical skill. For further ideas on how the quality and aesthetics of a maker's work connects to the development of their creative identity, (see England's chapter in this volume). Sarah's commercial and creative aspirations appeared to be in conflict, which hindered the pace at which the venture developed. This also made Sarah worry about the future earning capacity of the venture, including grappling with questions such as, "Could you ever make a living out of it?"

Some of the questions Sarah was working through at the founding stage were not just about what the business was, but also who she was. This was compounded by the fact that her role as a craftperson and entrepreneur was her second career transition. Sarah found that while some people believed in her abilities and talents as a craftsperson, affirming their support for her new venture, others thought "it's a joke." At this stage Sarah chose to highlight different identities in defining herself, including "an artist, a designer, a tutor who specialises in knit." Her multiple sub-identities are evident in her self-definition and what her venture was about at this stage.

> I'd probably say I design knitted art, I make knitted garments, I sell patterns, I teach knitting.

In addition to designing, knitting and training, Sarah quickly found herself taking on many other roles. Learning new skills relating to all activities of running her venture and having control of the different aspects were important to Sarah and in the initial stages she taught herself a wide range of skills in order to set up the business. This included web design, photography, blogging and accounting. Sarah took a business start-up course which she found useful in planning how to market her work. On a personal level, as her business plan presentation was very well received by the course cohort, it gave her confidence in her approach to the venture. While Sarah was the only person making work and generating leads for the business, she was still somewhat uncomfortable with pricing and approaching people to sell her designs. Looking professional and delivering a quality product and service was very important to her. She found that the biggest challenge for her was holding her nerve while no money came in at the founding stage.

One of the main sources of revenue for the business was the sale of knitting patterns online through a website she created herself. Some of the feedback she received made her examine and, in some cases, "strengthen" and "revise"[41] her identity as a craft entrepreneur.

> Someone did say are you going to offer free patterns? I said well no because of the amount of time it takes (to make them). Most patterns you get free aren't actually very good. They only come in one size and no one's test knitted them. So yeah, I feel quite justified in charging for the patterns because I think that mine look quite good.

Through her website she found a voice and acceptance from her peers which demonstrated identity processes such as "revising" and "strengthening" her sense of self as a craftsperson and entrepreneur. She demonstrated a growing confidence and excitement in her new venture and career choice due to the feedback from and interaction with the community of makers and knitters online. The blog had views from individuals in twelve different counties, which was a source of joy for Sarah.

> Someone from Taiwan read my blog, why I don't know, but someone from Ukraine or Malaysia or, you know, places you just don't think have got anything to do with knitting and my business.

The online presence also helped Sarah generate leads for workshops and got her noticed by new individuals and organisations (e.g., craft magazines), providing a boost to Sarah's identity as a crafts entrepreneur. Sarah was invited to contribute her patterns to well-known knitting magazines and, although this did not generate income, she was hopeful that the exposure would lead to her name becoming more recognised, more people looking at her website, resulting in more sales.

By year two, Sarah appeared more comfortable in her role as a craft entrepreneur. She was busier and appeared more settled in the venture. She felt that she had worked hard in the first year and relied on herself to undertake the different functions needed to run the venture. Her growing confidence in her venture and identity saw her taking more risks in relation to the venture. However, she was finding it hard to analyse the viability of those risks as the venture was still in the founding stages. She outlines instances where taking certain decisions relating to booking spaces for workshops led to her losing money (and sleep!) but quickly highlighted how this was a learning experience. Although there were still many challenges, Sarah was feeling tougher and more resolved in her identity as a craft entrepreneur. Describing her current identity as a composite of the various roles, she highlighted a growing sense of coherence in her identity, primarily as a tutor, which was the main revenue earning part of the business. She is still keen to highlight the other more creative elements of her identity (e.g., artist, designer, maker) but feels that these are well "hidden" at this point in her venture. The addition of roles was initially difficult, but Sarah found a source of joy and contentment in the different roles she was now fulfiling. The fact that "no two days were the same" assisted the intense identity work undertaken by Sarah in this phase as she had the opportunity to explore a variety of situations and challenges on a daily basis. She evidences this by her growing confidence as a craft entrepreneur.

> I'm probably more confident (now), because despite having done some really good things and achieved some things in my life, confidence is not something I have a lot of before.

IT'S COMING ALONG NICELY NOW

At the end of year two Sarah was still worried about money and meeting the demands of the venture. She had learned a lot, felt more confident and happy, and had more visibility and exposure as a craftsperson or venture owner. The coherence in her identity as a craft entrepreneur is evident in her narrative. Reflecting on the identity work,[42] Sarah undertook processes of "forming, strengthening and revising" her identity as a craft entrepreneur.

By the final interview (at the end of year two) Sarah appeared comfortable in her various roles within the venture. She was surprised yet encouraged by the acceptance of her new identity as an entrepreneur by her peers and customers. She saw her new identity as a composite of a "designer, teacher, a marketer, a bookkeeper, a knitter and an artist." By year two Sarah had done more workshops, had more magazines featuring her work and sold more products than she expected in the initial stage of her venture. She was happier to promote herself and her products than when she first started. Overall, she appeared contented and was now focused on building a reputation for herself in the craft sector. In terms of her plans for the venture over the next six months, she was on track with most of her business goals. Sarah remarked how she is finally enjoying the "new routine" and fulfilling her role as a craft entrepreneur "in a more sensible way."

> You feel you have actually got a practice, rather than running directionless all over the place. I think there's a lot less of that going on now.

At this stage the identity work process includes "repairing, maintaining and strengthening."[43] Sarah believed that she had learned a lot in the founding phase, taken risks and "come out tougher and on top," much more than she had expected at this point her venture.

> Toughening up happens gradually doesn't it? I mean it's not that you set out to toughen up.

Sarah started life drawing art lessons, which she felt was feeding her creative energies and also exhibited some of her designs with a few other makers from her masters course. She felt that all her roles together enhanced her life and focused her time and efforts on her venture. At this stage Sarah reflected on the difference between a creative and an entrepreneurial identity and how they co-exist.

> I guess if you are creative, you're wanting to work in a particular medium or have a particular way of working, whereas the entrepreneur isn't bothered about how things are done, they just want to make the business successful. From that point of view, I'm probably more of a creative than an entrepreneur. But I am quite realistic, so I do realise I have to do the business stuff and probably having worked in a science background, I'm not a sort of creative who is totally disorganised and all over the place. I am actually a very organised person, which really helps.

CONCLUSION

The chapter and Sarah's case study highlight how identity work manifests in a craft entrepreneur in the founding stage when responding to identity demands. The chapter also illustrates how multiple roles and identities are negotiated to work towards identity coherence. The gradualist view of identity work accepts that identities adjust and evolve at times of disequilibrium "only to find and maintain an optimum balance or equilibrium position."[44] Such identity work is undertaken to move from fragmentation to coherence. While scholars acknowledge the existence of multiple identities within a single individual,[45] relatively few frameworks exist to explain "why multiple identities are harmful and when they are beneficial."[46] Some of the earlier work in this area reported that individuals that have few identities do not have the requisite strategies to respond to complex situations, while individuals with many identities have to deal with enhanced conflicts.[47] Disrupted identities and an imbalance in the identity structure can be "emotionally draining and take precious cognitive resources away from performing effectively."[48] Some of this disruption is evident in Sarah's case study towards the start when she was torn between her commercial and artistic priorities. Additionally, a level of disequilibrium in Sarah's identity due to the multiple roles in the initial stages had a negative impact on her confidence and well-being. This is evidenced through how she defined her identity at this stage. Scholars believe that understanding the dynamics of identity coherence can lead to greater esteem, self-worth, efficiencies and overall well-being.[49]

Strategies of identity work described by scholars suggest varying identity tactics, however at their core most recognise the dimensions of multiplicity and balance or "identity plurality" and "identity synergy."[50] Sarah's changing self-definitions were evident in the first interview where she highlighted the multiple roles she was undertaking and a level of disequilibrium on their relative importance. The evolution of her identity primarily as a craftsperson or artist and an entrepreneur is marked by changes in her venture.

Pratt and Foreman[51] label identity tactics as: aggregation (finding links between identities), integration (combining identities to build a new one), compartmentalisation (separating identities) and deletion (removing an identity completely). In Sarah's case, her identity at the end of the case study period demonstrated some level of aggregation (in how she merged her various business-related roles) and compartmentalisation (in her separation of business roles from those that fed her artistic energies). This type of separation of roles is a key identity work tactic proposed by scholars of identity work[52] for dealing with competing or conflicting identities.

Within craft literature, scholars have acknowledged that makers derive a sense of self from their craft and emphasise the connection of their practice with their personal stories.[53] The case study also illustrates a sense of self in the process—that is, how a craftsperson carves out a venture. Through Sarah's founding journey she used different aspects of her identity, her core skills and her capabilities, which supports Luckman and Andrew's[54] view that it takes a lot more than creative skill to carve out a successful craft business, and, by extension, a successful coherent identity as a craft entrepreneur.

The case study illustrates Sarah's struggles and worries about deriving a living from and commercialising the products and services of her venture. Luckman[55] illustrates this conflict stemming from the ultimate desire of a craftsperson "for defending their commitment to a certain level of craft skill." I argue that this commitment can at times hinder the development of a craft venture. Through the chapter I suggest that this conflict and resulting negotiations between the commercial and quality priorities leads to intense identity work.

Luckman[56] finds that presenting a craft venture online "provides reality and legitimacy to a makers' professional identity." Sarah's story illustrates that some of the activities online helped her build confidence as a craft entrepreneur. This included setting up a new website, writing a blog, getting new readers for her blog, putting her first knitting pattern up for sale online, receiving a request from her peers for free patterns and receiving an invitation to contribute her pattens to an online magazine. So, while her activities online were crucial in the founding stages to establish herself and her venture, the case study also illustrates the importance of other activities that triggered identity work, such as attending life drawing classes and organising an exhibition with her peers. Although some of these were not directly relevant to her venture, they contributed to her positive well-being and to her feeling more contented and secure in her venture. This emphasises the need for examining the overall life story of a craftsperson to understand their venture journey rather than focusing on research activities relating solely to the venture.

For this longitudinal study into the identity work of a craft entrepreneur to be deemed valid, I made the following assumption at its inception. First, as scholars have outlined, multiple identities are and can be managed by individuals. Additionally, these multiple identities involve multiple conceptions of that individual and their priorities—that is, what is important to them. Some of these identities may contradict or compete, as is the case with commercial and creative identities of creative entrepreneurs.[57] As the venture progresses through the founding stage, experience in the venture is gained. There are other external influences such as competitive success and innovation that also have an impact on identity work. Some of these external triggers and their impact on identity work in the founding stages have not been dealt with in this research and present avenues for future academic exploration.

This research was based on an in-depth study of a single craftsperson based in the UK. While I have conducted an inductive analysis of the data in a manner that supports theoretical generalisability,[58] any direct empirical generalisability of the findings is not possible. I believe that further research into staged approaches to identity work in other phases of craft ventures—that is, the growth or decline phase—are worthy areas for exploration. This will develop a more detailed understanding of identity changes of a craft entrepreneur over the life of the venture and address the gap in entrepreneurship and craft literatures relating to the relatively static perspective taken on entrepreneurs' identity. That said, Sarah's founding journey and identity work as a craft entrepreneur following a series of career transitions, including her final one as a craftsperson, illustrate that there is no one route to becoming a craft entrepreneur.

NOTES

1. Stefan Sveningsson and Mats Alvesson, "Managing Managerial Identities: Organizational Fragmentation, Discourse and Identity Struggle," *Human Relations* 56, no. 10 (2003): 1165.

2. Erin E. Powell and Ted Baker, "It's What You Make of It: Founder Identity and Enacting Strategic Responses to Adversity," *Academy of Management Journal* 57, no. 5 (2014): 1406.

3. Sophia Maalsen and Sung-Yueh Perng, "Crafting Code," in *Craft Economies*, eds. Susan Luckman and Nicola Thomas (London: Bloomsbury, 2018), 227.

4. Susan Luckman, *Craft and the Creative Economy* (New York: Palgrave Macmillan, 2015), 61.

5. Susan Luckman and Jane Andrew, "Establishing the Crafting Self in the Contemporary Creative Economy," in *Craft Economies*, eds. Susan Luckman and Nicola Thomas (London: Bloomsbury, 2018), 126.

6. Anisya S. Thomas and Stephen L. Mueller, "A Case for Comparative Entrepreneurship: Assessing the Relevance of Culture," *Journal of International Business Studies* 31, no. 2 (2000): 287.

7. Jan E. Stets and Peter J. Burke, "Identity Theory and Social Identity Theory," *Social Psychology Quarterly* (2000): 224.

8. John C.Turner and Henri Tajfel, "The Social Identity Theory of Intergroup Behavior," *Psychology of Intergroup Relations* 5 (1986): 7–24.

9. Michael G. Pratt and Peter O. Foreman, "Classifying Managerial Responses to Multiple Organizational Identities," *Academy of Management Review* 25, no. 1 (2000): 18.

10. Emmanuelle Fauchart and Marc Gruber, "Darwinians, Communitarians, and Missionaries: The Role of Founder Identity in Entrepreneurship," *Academy of Management Journal* 54, no. 5 (2011): 935.

11. Ha Hoang and Javier Gimeno, "Becoming a Founder: How Founder Role Identity Affects Entrepreneurial Transitions and Persistence in Founding." *Journal of Business Venturing* 25, no. 1 (2010): 45.

12. Etienne Wenger, *Communities of Practice: Learning, Meaning, and Identity* (Cambridge University Press, 1999:145.

13. Powell and Baker, "It's What You Make of It," 1410.

14. Andrew D. Brown, "Identities and Identity Work in Organizations," *International Journal of Management Reviews* 17, no. 1 (2015): 25.

15. Christopher P. Earley, *Culture, Self-Identity, and Work* (Cambridge: Oxford University Press, 1993), 23–55.

16. Herminia Ibarra, "Provisional Selves: Experimenting with Image and Identity in Professional Adaptation," *Administrative Science Quarterly* 44, no. 4 (1999): 770.

17. Suna Løwe Nielsen and Astrid Heidemann Lassen, "Identity in Entrepreneurship Effectuation Theory: A Supplementary Framework," *International Entrepreneurship and Management Journal* 8, no. 3 (2012): 385.

18. Fauchart and Gruber, "Darwinians," 436.

19. Hazel Markus and Paula Nurius, "Possible Selves," *American Psychologist* 41, no. 9 (1986): 954.

20. Ibarra, "Provisional Selves," 764–69.

21. Brown, "Identities," 27.

22. Brown, "Identities," 27.

23. David A. Snow and Leon Anderson, "Identity Work among the Homeless: The Verbal Construction and Avowal of Personal Identities." *American Journal of Sociology* 92, no. 6 (1987): 1336.

24. Svenningsson and Alvesson, "Managing," 1165.

25. Michael G. Pratt et al., "Constructing Professional Identity: The Role of Work and Identity Learning Cycles in the Customization of Identity among Medical Residents." *Academy of Management Journal* 49, no. 2 (2006): 235.

26. Svenningsson and Alvesson, "Managing," 1165.

27. Pratt and Foreman, "Classifying Managerial Responses," 20.

28. Pratt et al., "Constructing Professional Identity," 235.

29. Brown, "Identities," 27.

30. Emma Bell et al., eds. *The Organization of Craft Work: Identities, Meanings, and Materiality* (London: Routledge, 2018), 16.

31. Bell et al., *Organization of Craft Work*, 11.

32. Chandan Bose, *Perspectives on Work, Home, and Identity from Artisans in Telangana: Conversations Around Craft* (New York: Springer, 2019), 7.

33. Maria Laura Toraldo, Gianluigi Mangia, and Stefano Consiglio. "Crafting Social Memory for International Recognition: The Role of Place and Tradition in an Italian Silk-tie Maker." *The Organization of Craft Work.* (London: Routledge, 2018), 118–25.

34. Susan Luckman and Jane Andrew. "Organising the Home as Making Space: Crafting Scale, Identity, and Boundary Contestation." *The Organization of Craft Work.* (London: Routledge, 2018), 79–85.

35. Alison Mayne, "Feeling Lonely, Feeling Connected: Amateur Knit and Crochet Makers Online," *Craft Research* 7, no. 1 (2016): 11–20.

36. Names of individuals, locations, and companies have been changed throughout to maintain the anonymity of the participant of this study.

37. Svenningsson and Alvesson, "Managing," 1165.

38. Svenningsson and Alvesson, "Managing," 1165.

39. Svenningsson and Alvesson, "Managing,"1165.

40. Susan Luckman and Nicola Thomas, eds. *Craft Economies* (London: Bloomsbury, 2018), 21.

41. Svenningsson and Alvesson, "Managing," 1190.

42. Svenningsson and Alvesson, "Managing," 1188.

43. Svenningsson and Alvesson, "Managing," 1188.

44. Brown, "Identities," 27.

45. Dean Shepherd and J. Michael Haynie, "Family Business, Identity Conflict, and an Expedited Entrepreneurial Process: A Process of Resolving Identity Conflict," *Entrepreneurship Theory and Practice* 33, no. 6 (2009): 1245.

46. Pratt and Foreman, "Classifying Managerial Responses," 26.

47. Jon W. Hoetler, "A Structural Theory of Personal Consistency," *Social Psychology Quarterly* (1985): 118–25.

48. Glen E. Kreiner et al., "Where Is the "Me" among the "We"? Identity Work and the Search for Optimal Balance," *Academy of Management Journal* 49, no. 5 (2006): 1033.

49. Verena C. Hahn et al., "Happy and Proactive? The Role of Hedonic and Eudaimonic Well-Being in Business Owners' Personal Initiative," *Entrepreneurship Theory and Practice* 36, no. 1 (2012): 97.

50. Pratt and Foreman, "Classifying Managerial Responses," 38.

51. Pratt and Foreman, "Classifying Managerial Responses," 38.

52. Kreiner et al., "Where Is the Me," 1033.

53. Luckman, "Craft and the Creative Economy" 106.

54. Luckman and Andrew, "Craft Economies," 10.

55. Luckman, "Craft," 21.

56. Luckman, "Craft,"115.

57. Ann Markusen, "How Cities Can Nurture Cultural Entrepreneurs," 2013. Accessed December 3, 2019, http://dx.doi.org/10.2139/ssrn.2357724.

58. Kathleen M. Eisenhardt, "Building Theories from Case Study Research," *Academy of Management Review* 14, no. 4 (1989): 532–40.

BIBLIOGRAHY

Bell, Emma, Mangia Gianluigi, Scott Taylor, and Maria Laura Toraldo, eds. *The Organization of Craft Work: Identities, Meanings, and Materiality*. London: Routledge, 2018.

Bose, Chandan. *Perspectives on Work, Home, and Identity from Artisans in Telangana: Conversations Around Craft*. New York: Springer, 2019.

Brown, Andrew D. "Identities and Identity Work in Organizations." *International Journal of Management Reviews* 17, no. 1 (2015): 20–40.

Earley, P. Christopher. *Culture, Self-Identity, and Work*. New York: Oxford University Press, 1993.

Eisenhardt, Kathleen M. "Building Theories from Case Study Research." *Academy of Management Review* 14, no. 4 (1989): 532–50.

Fauchart, Emmanuelle, and Marc Gruber. "Darwinians, Communitarians, and Missionaries: The Role of Founder Identity in Entrepreneurship." *Academy of Management Journal* 54, no. 5 (2011): 935–57.

Hahn, Verena C., Michael Frese, Carmen Binnewies, and Antje Schmitt. "Happy and Proactive? The Role of Hedonic and Eudaimonic Well-Being in Business Owners' Personal Initiative." *Entrepreneurship Theory and Practice* 36, no. 1 (2012): 97–114.

Hoang, Ha, and Javier Gimeno. "Becoming a Founder: How Founder Role Identity Affects Entrepreneurial Transitions and Persistence in Founding." *Journal of Business Venturing* 25, no. 1 (2010): 41–53.

Hoelter, Jon W. "A Structural Theory of Personal Consistency." *Social Psychology Quarterly* (1985): 118–29.

Ibarra, Herminia. "Provisional Selves: Experimenting with Image and Identity in Professional Adaptation." *Administrative Science Quarterly* 44, no. 4 (1999): 764–91.

Kreiner, Glen E., Elaine C. Hollensbe, and Mathew L. Sheep. "Where Is the "Me" among the "We"? Identity Work and the Search for Optimal Balance." *Academy of Management Journal* 49, no. 5 (2006): 1031–57.

Luckman, Susan. *Craft and the Creative Economy*. New York: Palgrave Macmillan, 2015.

Luckman, Susan, and Jane Andrew. "Establishing the Crafting Self in the Contemporary Creative Economy." In *Craft Economies*, edited by Susan Luckman and Nicola Thomas, 119–28. London: Bloomsbury, 2018.

Luckman, Susan, and Jane Andrew. "Organising the Home as Making Space: Crafting Scale, Identity, and Boundary Contestation." In *The Organization of Craft Work*, edited by Emma Bell, Gianluigi Mangia, and Scott Taylor, 79–97. London: Routledge, 2018.

Luckman, Susan, and Nicola Thomas, eds. *Craft Economies*. London: Bloomsbury, 2018.

Maalsen, Sophia, and Sung-Yueh Perng. "Crafting Code." In *Craft Economies*, edited by Susan Luckman and Nicola Thomas, 223–49. London: Bloomsbury, 2018.

Markus, Hazel, and Paula Nurius. "Possible Selves." *American Psychologist* 41, no. 9 (1986): 954–69.

Markusen, Ann. "How Cities Can Nurture Cultural Entrepreneurs," 2013. Accessed December 3, 2019, http://dx.doi.org/10.2139/ssrn.2357724.

Mayne, Alison. "Feeling Lonely, Feeling Connected: Amateur Knit and Crochet Makers Online." *Craft Research* 7, no. 1 (2016): 11–29.

Nielsen, Suna Løwe, and Astrid Heidemann Lassen. "Identity in Entrepreneurship Effectuation Theory: A Supplementary Framework." *International Entrepreneurship and Management Journal* 8, no. 3 (2012): 373–89.

Powell, E. Erin, and Ted Baker. "It's What You Make of It: Founder Identity and Enacting Strategic Responses to Adversity." *Academy of Management Journal* 57, no. 5 (2014): 1406–33.

Pratt, Michael G., and Peter O. Foreman. "Classifying Managerial Responses to Multiple Organizational Identities." *Academy of Management Review* 25, no. 1 (2000): 18–42.

Pratt, Michael G., Kevin W. Rockmann, and Jeffrey B. Kaufmann. "Constructing Professional Identity: The Role of Work and Identity Learning Cycles in the Customization of Identity among Medical Residents." *Academy of Management Journal* 49, no. 2 (2006): 235–62.

Shepherd, Dean, and J. Michael Haynie. "Family Business, Identity Conflict, and an Expedited Entrepreneurial Process: A Process of Resolving Identity Conflict." *Entrepreneurship Theory and Practice* 33, no. 6 (2009): 1245–64.

Snow, David A., and Leon Anderson. "Identity Work among the Homeless: The Verbal Construction and Avowal of Personal Identities." *American Journal of Sociology* 92, no. 6 (1987): 1336–71.

Stets, Jan E., and Peter J. Burke. "Identity Theory and Social Identity Theory." *Social Psychology Quarterly* (2000): 224–37.

Sveningsson, Stefan, and Mats Alvesson. "Managing Managerial Identities: Organizational Fragmentation, Discourse and Identity Struggle." *Human Relations* 56, no. 10 (2003): 1163–93.

Thomas, Anisya S., and Stephen L. Mueller. "A Case for Comparative Entrepreneurship: Assessing the Relevance of Culture." *Journal of International Business Studies* 31, no. 2 (2000): 287–301.

Toraldo, Maria Laura, Gianluigi Mangia, and Stefano Consiglio. "Crafting Social Memory for International Recognition: The Role of Place and Tradition in an Italian Silk-tie Maker." In *The Organization of Craft Work*, edited by Emma Bell, Gianluigi Mangia, Scott Taylor, 118–33. London: Routledge, 2018.

Turner, John C., and Henri Tajfel. "The Social Identity Theory of Intergroup Behavior." *Psychology of Intergroup Relations* 5 (1986): 7–24.

Wenger, Etienne. *Communities of Practice: Learning, Meaning, and Identity*. Cambridge: Cambridge University Press, 1999.

Chapter Eleven

Craftswomen and Entrepreneurship

Annette Naudin

In this chapter, I explore the entrepreneurial careers of four relatively well-established craftswomen, with a focus on their gendered experiences. It is now recognised that working in the cultural and creative industries (CCI), of which craft is a small sub-sector, is fraught with difficulties including the precarious working conditions associated with self-employment and a lack of stability. In this study of craftswomen whose careers extend over a significant period (between twelve and twenty-five years), my intention is to examine the nature of craftswomen's careers: how they manage entrepreneurial modes of work, their aspirations as expert craft makers, and their perception of the position of crafts within the cultural sector. What does precariousness entail when craftswomen reflect on their careers and achievements? How are entre-preneurial careers in the craft sector managed over a period of time?

The individuals in this study demonstrate mixed sentiments about their careers as craftswomen. They reveal high levels of expertise as craft practitioners, developed through a passion for their craft or art form, and a commitment to developing their aesthetic and technical skills. Despite their relative modesty in terms of their entrepreneurial know-how, they are all adept at managing networks, seeking new opportunities, communicating about their work and managing their finances. They are undoubtedly proud of their abilities as craft makers but as they look back at their careers, they do not recognise their entre-preneurial competencies. In trying to explore these issues, I am concerned with the potential disparity between individual creative aspirations and women's experience of being a craft worker, specifically in relation to being self-employed and the idea of entrepreneurship. As women craft entrepreneurs, their experience is filtered through dominant perspectives associated with craft work but also by stereotypes associated with the entrepreneur. Furthermore, they them-selves understand and manage their work from gendered positions: as women entrepreneurs, as working women and as women working in crafts. All four participants have achieved significant milestones and accomplishments relating to their craft practice, such as significant exhibitions or commissions, but their successes seem tinged by disillusionment.

WHO IS A PROFESSIONAL CRAFT MAKER?

Defining professional craft makers is difficult but for the purposes of this chapter, I am discussing individuals who aim to earn a living by selling their craft products and by engaging in related activities such as running workshops and teaching, working either full time or part time. As such, they are broadly understood as being part of the creative economy despite crafts being often side-lined by more contemporary practices. As Gill and Pratt[1] explain, the CCIs have become dominated by media practices which are characterised as having positions of power and influence over cultural tastes and production processes. As a sub-sector of the CCIs, crafts are unlikely to be perceived as influential, given the comparatively small economic contribution they make. Yet, in other ways, the craft sector has experienced increased attention through maker movements and an interest in crafts as an alternative to capitalism[2] which in turn encourages a "do it yourself" approach.[3] Testifying to this is the rise of micro-celebrities sharing craft skills and products on various social media platforms, particularly Instagram (see @thecraftedlife or @abeautifulmess). While this has raised the profile of crafts in general, perhaps bridging a gap between digital media practices and craft, popular craft workers on platforms such as Instagram embody a very different set of qualities and skills. Craftspeople driving their practice predominantly through the use of online platforms could be described as promoting amateur crafts for the home or as gifts, demonstrating a set of skills for making handmade objects to inspire their online followers. The craftswomen which are the focus of this study are highly trained professional craftspeople and experts in their field, be it jewellery, textiles or in using innovative making techniques they have developed and perfected over many years.

In sectors such as crafts, the blurred lines between amateur and professional work draws our attention away from careers and working practices, thereby decreasing the value of craft work and increasing the value of the making process for its own sake. This also merges with contemporary romantic ideas associated with crafting and making with your hands as presenting a relaxing pursuit sometimes connected to fashionable ideas such as mindfulness.[4] In this study, my focus is those who identify as professional and who are engaged in work which equates to some financial remuneration and a sense of career for themselves. As self-employment in the sector is very common, particularly among women, this raises questions about craftswomen's experience of entrepreneurship and their status as professional craft workers. I find contradictions in women's experience of craft entrepreneurship, characterised as a tension between: emancipation and marginalisation; proud of their expertise and yet disheartened by a lack of recognition; flexible and skilled in adapting their practice but jaded as they discuss their future.

THE PROBLEM WITH "ENTREPRENEURS"

One of the concerns is the prevalence of the term entrepreneur, what it means to be an entrepreneur and the impact this has on craftswomen whose self-employed status defines them as craft entrepreneurs.[5] Feminist scholars who have explored gender and entrepreneurship from different contexts suggest that rather than studying the figure of the lone hero entrepreneur, a deeper understanding might be gained from investigating diverse forms of entrepreneurship. By contesting dominant personality-based theories, new narratives challenge the idea that being a woman is in conflict with the idea of being an entrepreneur.[6] An analysis of gendered stereotypes in which women are constructed as "deviant from the (male) norm"[7] reveals inequalities, both in research and in entrepreneurial practices. The language of entrepreneurship and published material on the subject favours dominant norms, restricting opportunities for non-conventional perspectives.[8] As a result, scholars exploring gender and entrepreneurship studies[9] have sought to highlight different role models and characteristics, celebrating female entrepreneurship through a feminist lens,[10] and attempting to connect female entrepreneurship with ideas of emancipation in the workplace. While this resonates with scholars who seek to break down barriers in entrepreneurship studies, popular stereotypes dominate and within the CCIs there are mixed feelings about being identified as an entrepreneur.[11]

Nevertheless, entrepreneurial modes of work tend to chime with creative autonomy and a bohemian lifestyle which, as Eikhof and Haunschild[12] suggest, fits an identity associated with CCI work. Seeking to identify with CCI work helps to manage the challenges of self-employment, including the rationale for what is often a low income, justified by the possibility of creative and personal fulfilment.[13] As many craft workers tend to be based at home or in a home studio, craft entrepreneurship appears to offer flexibility and the potential for a better work-life balance. As scholars have argued, this can disguise inequalities in the CCIs, particularly when we pay attention to everyday working conditions including paid and unpaid work.[14] Rather than emancipatory, critical feminist scholars argue that entrepreneurship presents a neoliberal version of work which relies on one's ability to self-regulate, to present a liberated woman in control of her career but with little evidence of the challenges associated with entrepreneurial work.[15] The process heightens the burden of individual responsibility to achieve success, encouraging a notion of choice and agency[16] which often does not match with the realities of self-employment in the CCIs.

For instance, although the "mumpreneur" presents a welcome unconventional version of the entrepreneur such as the hope of emancipation by combining motherhood with work, this mode of work also represents the drawbacks of entrepreneurship for women.[17] There are concerns with the question of women's work going back to a domestic space and of potentially leaving women out from competing within broader society for pay recognition and social status.[18] While it is understandable that women are looking for an entrepreneurial identity to contrast the heroic masculine entrepreneur, this opportunity is not available to all women and in reality, the lived experience is often less than idealistic.[19] Instead of emancipation, entrepreneurship can contribute to the potential for self-exploitation and normalised patterns of flexibility often associated with the way women have always had to work.[20] Optimistic and over-enthusiastic discourses found in entrepreneurship can lead to a level of performativity which acts as a shield for the realities of self-employment, a step backwards rather than freedom from traditional roles.[21] Adkins argues that through individualisation the blurred lines between private/public, family/labour has led to a flexibility which creates a muddled sense of what constitutes as employment. Some of this work is described as women's family work including gendered activities which help to construct shared identities and a sense of belonging.

> Individualization in terms of the labour market—becoming an individualized worker—may therefore be said to be a gendered process which relies on, or is founded upon the appropriation of women's labour in the private sphere.[22]

In the case of craft entrepreneurship for women, the assumption that individualisation offers freedom from traditional categories is in question—if instead of liberating women from traditional roles, new modes of work may re-socialise traditional gendered roles and relationships.[23] Following this argument, craftswomen's entrepreneurial work becomes entangled with their professional identities and their personal life.

HOPEFUL WORK

Yet, it is difficult not to see the attraction and the opportunities offered by self-employment, not to mention that self-employment for craftspeople and artists has long been an accepted way of working. Contemporary depictions of those working in crafts offer the potential for community building, on-line and offline, through craft fairs, knitting groups, activism in crafts and a shared passion for making. For a nuanced understanding, there is a need to understand the specificity of craft and other forms of creative work from a gendered perspective by investigating everyday experiences as a means of exploring these contradictions.[24]

> What consistently emerges here and across all levels of professionalism and suc-cess (or otherwise) in the contemporary craft economy, one of the few sectors of the cultural economy where women predominate, is precisely the centrality of having to negotiate working lives around the care of children.[25]

Home working, caring responsibilities and seeking to pursue one's passion for making are all legitimate reasons for attempting to establish a career as a craft entrepreneur.[26] And although critical scholars have done much to highlight the challenges of cultural work generally,[27] gendered dimensions contribute to the debate by illustrating the specificity of negotiating "good work"[28] in this sub-sector of the creative industries.

We know that despite evidence of self-exploitation, low pay, inequalities in the sector and the precarious nature of self-employment, many people still aspire to engage with CCI work. The need to construct a creative identity can be significant for those aspiring to have a career in the sector.[29] The potential for creative expression is equally meaningful,[30] as is the pull towards more sustainable ways of life associated with artisanal and craft work. But in the medium to long term, do other factors sustain a career as a woman craft entrepreneur? To explore this I draw on Alacovska's[31] work on hope as a significant factor in managing precariousness by of-fering the potential of future prospects and connecting work to a broader sense of purpose. This is explained as the notion that unpaid opportunities, or speculative work, are carried out because the CCI worker imagines and constructs a future for themselves which is hopeful. Alacovska considers hopeful endurance and hopeful moments in everyday practices as a means of sustaining oneself in the hope that eventually, a better paid opportunity will appear. This is hope as a practice rather than a passive attitude—a way of life and a way of imagining a way of life which finds purpose, even in difficult circumstances.

For craft entrepreneurs, hope might offset the disappointments of not being selected for a commission, the lack of sales at a craft fair or the insecurities of a career as a craft professional. As Alacovska argues, hope offers a "method of engagement with the world" and a way of adjusting one's expectations to man-age uncertainty.[32] This also leads to an acceptance of the realities of certain modes of work, offering a rationale beyond one's individual entrepreneurial work, but combining a mode of work with other responsibilities towards, for instance, family or extended community.

> These socially engaged practices signify a shift from artistic goals towards social goals, caring and mutual aid. Creative work-cum-art-for-social-change enshrines active hope that a better world is possible and that creative careers are nonetheless viable in circumstances of total despair.[33]

Instead of understanding work primarily in relation to one's own practice or entrepreneurial endeavours, the idea of hope embodies a socially engaged practice rooted in one's position within a social context, strengthening an individual worker's sense of their professional life. In that sense, a critical analysis of craftswomen's entrepreneurship should take note of how women situate their practice; how women navigate the complex relationship between being a craft worker, their gendered position and entrepreneurial modes of work.

METHODOLOGY

The research was carried out in the UK in the West Midlands, taking a case study approach. It is significant that the research focuses on an area outside of London, as capital cities provide particular kinds of contexts for cultural work, attracting international organisations and thereby setting them apart from regional environments. The rationale was a desire to capture the experiences of working in the craft sector outside of the potentially privileged surroundings of London, in terms of connections to markets and key institutions.

This case study draws attention to the careers of four women in their late forties and early fifties who are at a point where they have substantial experience, having achieved certain milestones as professional craft entrepreneurs. Although I present the women as craft "entrepreneurs," their status as professional and established workers was not defined by commercial success or entrepreneurial prowess. Longevity and persistence in developing their craft practice was an important factor, alongside some level of peer recognition through a substantial achievement such as taking part in a major exhibition. As with many of the craft workers discussed in this book, they are described as "entrepreneurs" as a means of expressing their self-employed status but also to question the promise of entrepreneurial modes of work in contrast with the reality. The myth of the entrepreneur is accentuated when we explore a sector whose workforce, according to the UK Crafts Council, had a mean income of £8,120 in 2015.[34]

The four women work in the areas of jewellery, textiles and mixed media craft practices, which do not fit neatly into a category but are on the boundaries between craft and other visual arts. Some of the women were known to me before and others were found through the major showcase for midlands crafts, the Made in the Middle exhibition, organised and curated by Craftspace, a West Midlands–based craft organisation. The research process involved semi-structured interviews and a textual analysis of the interview transcripts to extract themes in relation to the literature and new concepts revealed in the craft workers' narrative. Three of the four women had a university degree but only two of them had a degree in a craft or related field. Two of the women have children and have undertaken their work alongside caring for children, but all of them had some responsibilities towards caring for extended family members. I did not draw on any established sociological method for defining social class but two of the participants defined themselves as from a working-class background, based on their parent's background and being the first in their family to go to university. One of the women is British born and of Indian heritage while the remaining three describe themselves as white British. This small sample cannot be described as representative, but I would like to suggest that aspects of their experiences resonate with many craftswomen and with cultural entrepreneurs who have developed their careers over the last twelve to twenty-five years, particularly those outside of capital cities. In the next section, I present their experiences through three themes: first, in relation to entrepreneurship; second, how perceptions of craft work impacts on the women's sense of a professional identity; and finally, the idea of hopeful work to sustain a career in craft.

ENTREPRENEURIAL WORK

The craftswomen in this study do not completely reject the idea of being described as a "craft entrepreneur" but they are somewhat dismissive about it, describing their practice in entirely different terms. Although all participants demonstrate high levels of skills in entrepreneurship such as marketing, networking, selling their work and understanding and adapting to changes in the marketplace, they do not recognise these attributes in themselves.

> I don't really know what it means. I suppose, if I was to think about it . . . I'm very much wanting to be in the studio making artwork. I think that I see an entrepreneur as being much more clever and successful. . . . In the other things that you need to be successful, so marketing, successfully building a business in terms of finances, networking, seeing where there are gaps for certain things in the market and going with it regardless of whether that's your thing or not. Being quite clever and following trends. I'm probably not that. (Elizabeth)

Instead, they prefer to identify with terms which are descriptive of their creative practice, as artists, arts workers or project workers, or more specifically in ways that describe their current work which might be associated with a particular tradition or skills. At a time when there is some fluidity across different work in the CCIs, an emphasis on their expertise and a detailed means of describing their practice is important to my participants. For instance, one of the participants pinpoints her practice to "stitch" rather than embroidery, textiles or crafts, and others make connections to other forms of visual arts such as combining illustration and painting with jewellery-type techniques. Throughout the interviews, the participants articulate a professional confidence when discussing expertise in making: in their technical skills, artistic, design and aesthetic know-how. However, they rarely draw on competences associated with running an enterprise or promoting themselves. Yet, for those seeking to establish themselves as professional craftspeople, a significant element is the entrepreneurial aspect of their work: earning a living and developing a reputation.

> I can remember being at a conference. It has got to be early '90s, and somebody used the phrase that artists are like enterprising scavengers. At the time I was like, you cheeky f****r, you know! I didn't spend six years of college to be . . . but, actually, that's bang on the money. (Claire)

Claire acknowledges the entrepreneurial aspects of her practice reluctantly. Reflecting on this, Claire admits that there is a contrast between her expertise as a maker, having studied her craft for six years, and the ways in which she has to work, "scavenging" for opportunities and to earn a living. The pressure to make money is perceived as diverting attention from their core craft practice, as Elizabeth explains:

> For me, I've dipped in and out quite a lot. There's been the pressure of needing to survive which has been a real pressure. For instance, I might not have done some things but I've done them because of the financial income. We're all in that boat. (Elizabeth)

As with many other craftspeople, the participants in this study are involved in a range of potentially complimentary activities such as running workshops, teaching, curating, design work, acting as technician and managing creative projects. While all of them talked about the benefits of such work, as their careers have progressed, they all revealed a degree of resentment toward having to undertake so much work which was not directly making or creating craft objects. After a number of years of engaging in participatory activities and teaching, there was an expectation that by now, they should have more time to focus on their work. Whether that is realistic or not, it is clear that the participants in this study feel that this should be possible and perhaps that it is for some of their peers.

> Last year, in the run up to the show, it was eight months of solidly my own work, which is the only time in the last 22 years that's been the case. At the moment, it's all participatory work or teaching. (Elizabeth)

This sentiment does not appear to come from a position of entitlement, but rather a sense that after years of perfecting one's craft and establishing a relatively good profile nationally and in some cases internationally, they feel slightly aggrieved to find themselves in this situation. It is not what they imagined as they have developed their career, taking on all sorts of paid and unpaid "opportunities" as they came up. Hannah begins to explain how she has managed her career but part way through, we pause the interview as she finds it too upsetting.

> I've never focused on, "I must make X amount of money," but I've never made a loss. It just balanced out that I can keep going, but I am getting to an age where I'm working three times as hard and I'm earning probably three times less and I know that. I think I've been through a lot personally, which has really affected how I feel about my work and . . . [tears]. (Hannah)

Despite a willingness to embrace diverse opportunities, entrepreneurship in the craft sector is marred with compromises that have left the participants in this study with mixed feelings about the nature of their work. As a single mother balancing family and work, Hannah describes the early years of her craft practice as an ideal, flexible way of managing her responsibilities as mother and breadwinner. But this has not been without challenges.

> I literally felt like I gave birth and was on my jewellery bench, just literally, like, not sleeping, but it was good, I knew I could do it, and it was exciting. (Hannah)

For Alacovska,[35] the hope associated with this kind of flexibility leads to an acceptance of the realities of entrepreneurial modes of work, offering a rationale beyond one's individual work by combining a mode of work with other responsibilities. Similarly, Jackie was working full time at a leading furniture and fabric design retailer with opportunities for promotion, but having a family forced her to rethink her position as a means of managing motherhood and work.

> Because with my children, having children it changed my life, obviously. I needed to find a career that I could fit in working with them. . . . When I had my

two, I had no choice. I couldn't afford to pay for full-time childcare so I had to look at all sorts of different alternatives. So, I went to work in a school. It was just purely as an Art and Design Technician because the hours were great for me. . . . I worked at the school three days—working part-time hours. It was beneficial for me then to be able to do the talks and workshops around that. (Jackie)

Although Jackie suggests that her ability to balance earning a living as a school technician, developing her craft work and having a family is a positive outcome, her position is highly precarious and it relies on sacrifices at every level: as a mother, as a craftswoman and as someone with the potential to have a full-time job. The concept of hope helps us understand how Jackie justifies her predicament, enabling her to see the positive in her situation and to have a sense that her actions have led to a beneficial outcome for her and her family. Jackie is proactive in how she seeks to balance her life and her hopeful approach is to try to do the right thing for everyone. But hope also disguises a loss of job security and the challenges of balancing different priorities and, as Adkins would argue, this reinstates women in traditional gender roles.

PERCEPTIONS OF CRAFT WORK

In this section I discuss the position of crafts: how craft is perceived by both a wider public but also by policymakers and professionals in the CCIs. As I have argued, although running workshop activities and teaching can be fulfilling, after a number of years this can be draining and there are few opportunities for craftswomen to progress. This is experienced in different ways by my participants but all of them suggested that in general, the women in this study sense that crafts as a sector has been neglected and is taken less seriously than other CCIs, such as media industries.

I'm, in many ways, I think, I suppose what I'm trying to say is I think the world of art quilting is hugely neglected by the sector, by the wider arts industry. So, at Festival of Quilts they have 30,000 people through those doors, okay, over 4 days. Now, it must be said, there are some bloody awful things there, you know . . . [but] that whole sector is, I feel, hugely ignored and I think part of that is because it's done by, on the whole, nice, middle class, white, older women. (Claire)

The association of quilt making as a female pursuit, the fact that prices are skewed as there are so many amateurs and the lack of interest from the broader CCI sector create obstacles for makers such as Claire attempting to operate as craft professionals. For Jackie, people's perception of crafts can be a starting point for challenging their assumptions through her work: through scale, subject matter and the aesthetic qualities of her textile pieces she engages in challenging her audience.

> As soon as you start working, particularly in embroidery, people do tend to put you in a craft box. I suppose, in a way, I'm a bit of an anarchist really because I want to work beyond what people's perceptions are. (Jackie)

An eagerness to challenge perceptions is not unusual in cultural production, but in craft practice it feels noteworthy as it draws attention to the difficulties of being taken seriously, particularly in the light of attempting to sustain a long-standing career as a craft entrepreneur. Jackie sits between craft and fine art as her large scale textile work appears closer to a piece for a gallery in terms of the conceptual ideas behind the work and in the uses of her work. She experiences a snobbery between craft skills, textiles work which is predominantly perceived as a gendered practice, and the more "serious" art world, but Jackie describes that as an opportunity for a challenge, to be "a bit of an anarchist." As a British-born woman of colour, Hannah is frustrated with how her expertise is perceived and diminished by others, despite her years of experience and high level of skills in teaching, making and project management.

> If you say you're a jeweller, they have a different perception of what you might do. So, often, people might think I make [ethnic] jewelleries, is what they usually ask me if I say I'm a jeweller. (Hannah)

The assumptions about her and her work are immediately downgraded because she is a woman of colour producing jewellery. This perception is frustrating for Hannah who is highly trained and whose work is otherwise sold at major jewellery trade fairs, through galleries and individual commissions. These prejudices devalue craft work,[36] contributing to a sense that it has less worth than other cultural forms and adding further complexities to maintaining a craft career.

HOPEFUL WORK

For craft entrepreneurs, hopeful moments in their everyday practices are a means of sustaining themselves, in the hope that eventually, a better paid opportunity will appear. This is hope as a practice rather than a passive attitude, encouraging and supporting career decisions which without hope might be different. For instance, Elizabeth expresses her enjoyment of running workshops, working with different groups and the personal rewards she gains from this.

> Working for a refugee organisation, I learned a lot from that experience. Since then, right up until the present day, I've always tried to find projects working with people that are excluded or on the edge. Some of those themes, actually, I explore in my own work now. I really enjoy working with those groups. (Elizabeth)

Although in our interview, Elizabeth is clear that she would much rather be entirely focused on her practice, if she does have to undertake paid workshop activities, this kind of work seems to be fulfilling for her. Elizabeth's experience describes a socially engaged practice, rooted in her position within a social context, strengthening her as an individual worker and in her professional life.

Despite the rewards from making, from being creative and contributing to wider society through socially engaged activities, low financial rewards present considerable problems for craft entrepreneurs. For instance, none of my participants come from well-off backgrounds or have circumstances where their partners can completely support them. In some cases, it is the craftswoman being interviewed who is supporting her partner and family. As a result, the craftswomen in this study are finding that the hope that may have sustained them at the start of their careers has started to wear thin. Elizabeth talks about doing "participatory projects since 1994" and she adds:

> I think what I'm looking to do now is not necessarily rely on it to make me an income, so I do lots of other work because I got quite tired of doing the products to sell at craft fairs. I don't really enjoy craft fairs. I have to have my bread and butter money from other means. (Elizabeth)

Over the year this has led to many compromises and a tension between making the work that enables them to express their craft skills and creativity, for which they earn respect as experts, with undertaking other kinds of paid work. This is in contrast to more privileged or fortunate craft workers who don't have the same pressures to earn a living. As Claire explains, given the crossover with amateur practice, there are complications in costing one's time and pricing work to reflect actual hours of work.

> They don't need to earn a living doing it. So, I know people who do amazing work, absolutely amazing work, that I look at and I think, "I will never ever be that good," and some have had an art education, they've been to art school. You look at the work and it's beautifully done and it's conceptually sound, but they don't need to do it to pay the mortgage. (Claire)

At the beginning of a career, these discrepancies might be dismissed by craft workers as they forge a career, but after years of trying to establish a sustainable enterprise, this uneven playing field becomes a source of frustration. The issue of financial security has become critical for all my participants at different times of their careers but, significantly, usually in relation to their family or to major changes in their personal life. Despite working for many years, the participants in this study expressed the degree to which it is exhausting and demoralising to continue working like this, particularly alongside managing personal issues such as concerns with health, family and caring responsibilities.

> What I'm worried about is the amount of insecurity that, essentially, the financial insecurity and that the amount of chasing I'm having to do for very small amounts of money, that's what I'm getting tired of because it's becoming quite thankless, and there's not much evidence that it's going to get any better. (Claire)

All the participants have had some level of trauma in their personal life and while that might be the case for many people in middle age, managing the insecurities of entrepreneurial work alongside significant personal or family issues has been very difficult. But the paradox is that often, during challenging times, it is the craft work which sustains them. The result is that, as Jackie describes next, making and accepting the struggle of craft work is better than giving up her craft.

> I think I made choices in terms of health. I think I would rather have less money and enjoy my life and have better wellbeing. I shop second hand. You make choices. I buy all my clothes from charity shops. It depends where you want to put your money. I'd rather my money gave me time to do the things that I want to do. (Jackie)

Despite the uncertainties brought about by the kind of "choices" described, Alacovska's idea of hope as practice helps us to understand the rationale in Jackie's "choices." An alternative could be to opt for salaried work, but Jackie states that the lack of flexibility is unsuitable for her family life and for her personal well-being. Besides, as Hannah explains, despite her expertise and high levels of education, securing a salaried position is problematic after a career as a self-employed craftswoman.

> Every few weeks I'll look for a job and I always think, "It's not inspiring." I never find something that I think . . . what is this dream job that I'm looking for? I don't know. (Hannah)

Managing entrepreneurial modes of work for most of their working lives has left my participants feeling they are unemployable or that they do not know how to go about changing their careers. In the early stages of a career, entrepreneurial work might be manageable but as craftspeople develop their skills and begin to position themselves in a competitive market place, craft entrepreneurship becomes a struggle.

CONCLUSION

As some celebrate a revival of crafts and a renewed interest in making, those who have attempted to make a career as professional craftswomen find themselves in a situation where their expertise is not valued to the extent they had anticipated. The craft entrepreneurs in this study identify so completely with their abilities as makers and artists that their entrepreneurial skill or capacity to undertake a range of other activities is insignificant in comparison with the importance of making craftwork. This is not to suggest that as craftswomen, they have been reproducing the same kind of work—far from it. All participants have developed their practice and gained new skills as well as perfecting skills, embracing technology and adapting to new and different markets, but this has not led to a sustainable craft career.

Although these are familiar issues for working women, the difficulties in negotiating a craft career include additional complexities. In looking back at their careers, the women in this small study have faced a full range of life challenges from very serious illnesses in themselves and in their families and deaths of close family members through to managing distressing home environments. As Luckman[37] describes, images of women presenting "the good life" through platforms such as Etsy and Pinterest permeate our understanding of what it means to be a craft worker, but for many, this is in sharp contrast with reality. After years of developing a career, the hope imbued in their craft expertise, in their ability to tackle perceptions of crafts and in embracing entrepreneurial approaches, is wearing very thin. Despite that, it is their craft and making which sustains the women in this study; creating an impossible dilemma.

There is no doubt that some of these difficulties apply to both men and women working in the sector and this study does not attempt to make a comparison, but there are distinctive issues pertinent to women craft entrepreneurs. First, there is a disproportionately high level of women in the sector who struggle to earn a living through their craft practice. The experiences of the women in this study need to be understood within that context, particularly as the participants in this research have all focused on establishing a professional career from their craft. In exploring their experiences, the notion of hopeful work is a powerful element in pushing forward a craft enterprise and this is connected to a desire to make a contribution beyond their own creative expression. It is a driving force, as the women balance other commitments and make decisions to engage in related activities, make a social contribution and manage their own well-being. The idea of hope encompasses much of the women's practice and career until it seems they begin to run out of hope. Their expert skills in making and in being creative continue to offer fulfilment, but there is little appeal in continuing an entrepreneurial career as a craftswoman. Yet over the years, their professional and personal identities have become entangled with their expertise as craft makers, both in terms of how they are perceived by others but also their sense of who they are. As the women in this study look back at their careers, they present contradictory feelings demonstrating pride in their achievements and a continued passion for their craft work, but this is combined with a disappointment in their current situation.

NOTES

1. Rosalind Gill and Andy Pratt, "In the Social Factory? Immaterial Labour, Precariousness and Cultural Work," *Theory, Culture and Society* 25, no. 7–8 (2008): 1–30.

2. Susan Luckman, *Craft and the Creative Economy* (London: Springer, 2015).

3. Anna Mignosa and Priyatej Kotipalli, eds., *A Cultural Economic Analysis of Craft* (Rotterdam: Palgrave Macmillan, 2019).

4. Sandra Owen, "How to Practice Mindfulness through Craft," accessed August 17, 2019, https://blog.hobbycraft.co.uk/how-to-practice-mindfulness-through-craft/.

5. Kate Oakley, "Good Work? Rethinking Cultural Entrepreneurship," in *Handbook of Management and Creativity*, eds. Chris Bilton and Stephen Cummings (Cheltenham: Edward Elgar, 2014), 145–59.

6. Helen Ahl and Susan Marlow, "Exploring the Dynamics of Gender, Feminism and Entrepreneurship: Advancing Debate to Escape a Dead End?" *Organisation* 19, no. 5 (2012): 543–62.

7. Deirdre Tedmanson et al., "Critical Perspectives in Entrepreneurship Research," *Organization* 19, no. 5 (2012): 531–60.

8. Kathryn Campbell, "Rekindling the Entrepreneurial Potential of Family Business—A Radical (Old-Fashioned) Feminist Proposal," in *The Politics and Aesthetics of Entrepreneurship*, eds. D. Hjorth and C. Steyaert (Cheltnenham: Edward Elgar, 2009), 113–30.

9. G. Candida Brush, Anne De Bruin, and Friederike Welter, "A Gender-Aware Framework for Women's Entrepreneurship," *International Journal of Gender and Entrepreneurship* 1, no. 1 (2009): 8–24.

10. Laura Galloway, Isla Kapaso, and Katherine Sang, "Entrepreneurship, Leadership, and the Value of Feminist Approaches to Understanding Them," *Journal of Small Business* 53, no. 3 (2015): 683–92.

11. Annette Naudin, *Cultural Entrepreneurship: The Cultural Worker's Experience of Entrepreneurship* (London: Routledge, 2018).

12. Doris Eikhof and Axel Haunschild, "Lifestyle Meets Market: Bohemian Entrepreneurs in Creative Industries," *Creativity and Innovation Management* 15, no. 3 (2006): 234–41.

13. Bridget Conor, Rosalind Gill, and Stephanie Taylor, "Gender and Creative Labour," *Sociological Review* 63, no. 1 (2015): 1–22.

14. Conor, Gill, and Taylor, "Gender and Creative Labour," 1–22.

15. Nancy Fraser, "Feminism, Capitalism and the Cunning of History," 2009, *The New Left Review*, accessed February 9, 2016, http://newleftreview.org/II/56/nancy-fraser-feminism-capitalism-and-the-cunning-of-history.

16. Rosalind Gill, "Critical Respect: The Difficulties and Dilemmas of Agency and 'Choice' for Feminism," *European Journal of Women's Studies* 14, no. 1 (2007): 69–80.

17. Patricia Lewis, "'Mumpreneurs': Revealing the Post-Feminist Entrepreneur," in *Revealing and Concealing Gender*, eds. Patricia Lewis and Ruth Simpson (London: Palgrave Macmillan, 2010), 124–38.

18. Stephanie Taylor, "A New Mystique? Working for Yourself in the Neoliberal Economy," *Sociological Review* 63 (2015): 174–87.

19. Luckman, *Craft and the Creative Economy*.

20. Lisa Adkins, "Community and Economy: A Retraditionalization of Gender?" *Theory, Culture and Society* 16, no. 1 (2009): 116–39.

21. Annette Naudin and Annette Patel, "Entangled Expertise: Women's Use of Social Media in Entrepreneurial Work," *European Journal of Cultural Studies* 22(5–6) (2019): 511–27.

22. Adkins, "Community and Economy," 128.

23. Adkins, "Community and Economy," 116.

24. Luckman, *Craft and the Creative Economy*.

25. Luckman, *Craft and the Creative Economy*, 7.

26. Luckman, *Craft and the Creative Economy*.

27. David Hesmondhalgh and Sarah Baker, *Creative Labour*.

28. Luckman, *Craft and the Creative Economy*.

29. Stephanie Taylor and Karen Littleton, "Art Work or Money: Conflicts in the Construction of a Creative Identity," *Sociology Review* 56, no. 2 (2008): 275–92.

30. Hesmondhalgh and Baker, *Creative Labour: Media Work in Three Cultural Industries* (London: Routledge, 2011).

31. Ana Alacovska, "'Keep Hoping, Keep Going': Towards a Hopeful Sociology of Creative Work," *Sociology Review* 67, no. 5 (2019): 1118–36.

32. Alacovska, "'Keep Hoping, Keep Going'," 1118–36.

33. Alacovska, "'Keep Hoping, Keep Going'," 1130.

34. Craft Council, 2019, accessed February 17, 2020, https://www.craftscouncil.org.uk/what-we-do/research-and-policy-brief-january-2019/.

35. Alacovska, "'Keep Hoping, Keep Going'," 1118–36.

36. Karen Patel, "Diversity Initiatives and Addressing Inequalities in Craft," in *Pathways into Creative Working Lives*, edited by Stephanie Taylor and Susan Luckman (Basingstoke: Palgrave Macmillan, 2020).

37. Luckman, *Craft and the Creative Economy*.

BIBLIOGRAPHY

Adkins, Lisa. "Community and Economy: A Retraditionalization of Gender?" *Theory, Culture & Society* 16, no.1 (2009): 116–39.

Ahl, Helen, and Susan Marlow. "Exploring the Dynamics of Gender, Feminism and Entrepreneurship: Advancing Debate to Escape a Dead End?" *Organisation* 19, no. 5 (2012): 543–62.

Alacovska, Ana. "'Keep Hoping, Keep Going': Towards a Hopeful Sociology of Creative Work," *Sociology Review* 67, no. 5 (2019): 1118–36.

Banks, Mark. "Moral Economy and Cultural Work." *Sociology* 40, no. 3 (2006): 455–72.

———. *The Politics of Cultural Work*. Basingstoke: Palgrave Macmillan, 2007.

Brush, G. Candida, Anne De Bruin, and Friederike Welter. "A Gender-Aware Framework for Women's Entrepreneurship." *International Journal of Gender and Entrepreneurship* 1, no. 1 (2009): 8–24.

Campbell, Kathryn. "Rekindling the Entrepreneurial Potential of Family Business— A Radical (Old-Fashioned) Feminist Proposal." In *The Politics and Aesthetics of Entrepreneurship*, edited by Daniel Hjorth and Chris Steyaert, 113–30. Cheltenham: Edward Elgar, 2009.

Conor, Bridget, Rosaline Gill, and Stephanie Taylor. "Gender and Creative Labour." *Sociological Review* 63, no. 1 (2015): 1–22.

Eikhof, Doris, and Axel Haunschild. "Lifestyle Meets Market: Bohemian Entrepreneurs in Creative industries," *Creativity and Innovation Management* 15, no. 3 (2006): 234–41.

Fraser, Nancy. "Feminism, Capitalism and the Cunning of History," *The New Left Review*, 2009. Accessed February 6, 2016. http://newleftreview.org/II/56/nancy-fraser-feminism-capitalism-and-the-cunning-of-history.

Galloway, Laura, Isla Kapaso, and Katherine Sang. "Entrepreneurship, Leadership, and the Value of Feminist Approaches to Understanding Them." *Journal of Small Business* 53, no. 3 (2015): 683–92.

Gill, Rosalind. "Critical Respect: The Difficulties and Dilemmas of Agency and 'Choice' for Feminism." *European Journal of Women's Studies* 14, no. 1 (2007): 69–80.

———. "Cool, Creative and Egalitarian? Exploring Gender in Project-Based New Media Work in Euro." *Information, Communication and Society* 5, no. 1 (2002): 70–89.

———. "Unspeakable Inequalities: Post Feminism, Entrepreneurial Subjectivity, and the Reputation of Sexism among Cultural Workers." *Social Politics: International Studies in Gender, State and Society* 21, no. 4 (2014): 509–28.

Gill, Rosalind, and Andy Pratt. "In the Social Factory? Immaterial Labour, Precariousness and Cultural Work." *Theory, Culture and Society* 25, no. 7–8 (2008): 1–30.

Hesmondhalgh, David, and Sarah Baker. *Creative Labour: Media Work in Three Cultural Industries.* London: Routledge, 2011.

Hesmondhalgh, David, and Sarah Baker. "Sex, Gender and Work Segregation in the Cultural Industries." *Sociology Review* 63, no. 1 (2015): 23–36. https://journals.sagepub.com/doi/10.1111/1467-954X.12238.

Lewis, Patricia. "'Mumpreneurs': Revealing the Post-Feminist Entrepreneur." In *Revealing and Concealing Gender*, edited by Patricia Lewis and Ruth Simpson, 124–38. London: Palgrave Macmillan, 2010.

Loacker, Bernadette, "Becoming 'Culturpreneur': How the 'Neoliberal Regime of Truth' Affects and Redefines Artistic Positions." *Culture and Organization* 19, no. 2 (2013): 124–45.

Luckman, Susan. *Craft and the Creative Economy.* London: Springer, 2015.

———. *The Politics and Poetics of Rural, Regional and Remote Creativity.* Basingstoke: Palgrave Macmillan, 2012.

McRobbie, Angela. "Notes on the Perfect: Competitive Femininity in Neoliberal Times." *Australian Feminist Studies* 30, no. 83 (2015): 3–20.

Mignosa, Anna, and Priyatej Kotipalli, eds. *A Cultural Economic Analysis of Craft.* Rotterdam: Palgrave Macmillan, 2019.

Naudin, Annette. *Cultural Entrepreneurship: The Cultural Worker's Experience of Entrepreneurship.* London: Routledge, 2018.

Naudin, Annette, and Karen Patel. "Entangled Expertise: Women's Use of Social Media in Entrepreneurial Work." *European Journal of Cultural Studies* 22, no. 5–6 (2019): 511–27.

Oakley, Kate. "Good Work? Rethinking Cultural Entrepreneurship." In *Handbook of Management and Creativity*, edited by Chris Bilton and Stephen Cummings, 145–59. Cheltenham: Edward Elgar, 2014.

Owen, Sandra. "How to Practice Mindfulness through Craft." Accessed August 17, 2019. https://blog.hobbycraft.co.uk/how-to-practice-mindfulness-through-craft/.

Patel, Karen. "Diversity Initiatives and Addressing Inequalities in Craft." In *Pathways into Creative Working Lives*, edited by Stephanie Taylor and Susan Luckman. Basingstoke: Palgrave Macmillan, 2020, 175–191.

———. *The Politics of Expertise in Cultural Labour: Arts, Work and Inequalities.* London: Rowman & Littlefield International, 2020.

———. "Supporting Diversity in Craft Practice through Digital Technology Skills Development." Crafts Council UK, February 2019. Accessed July 11, 2019. https://www.craftscouncil.org.uk/content/files/19-03-19_Supporting_Diversity_in_Craft_Practice_report_FINAL.pdf.

Taylor, Stephanie. "A New Mystique? Working for Yourself in the Neoliberal Economy." *Sociological Review* 63 (2015): 174–87.

Taylor, Stephanie, and Karen Littleton. "Art Work or Money: Conflicts in the Construction of a Creative Identity." *Sociology Review* 56, no. 2 (2008): 275–92.

Taylor, S., and K. Littleton. "Negotiating a Contemporary Creative Identity." In *Cultural Work and Higher Education*, edited by Daniel Ashton and Catriona Noonan, 154–71. Basingstoke: Palgrave Macmillan 2013.

Tedmanson, Deirdre, Karen Verduijn, Caroline Essers, and William B. Gartner. "Critical Perspectives in Entrepreneurship Research." *Organization* 19, no. 5 (2012): 531–60.

Chapter Twelve

Making Makerspaces Work

How Feminist Makers Reconcile with the Logics of Entrepreneurialism and "Passionate Work" within Canadian Makerspaces

Jess Ring

Maker culture is premised on the simple notion that people should make things themselves rather than they buy them. This do-it-yourself (DIY) making ideology is rooted in previous craft-inspired activist histories like the arts and crafts movement, 1960s hippie environmentalism, 1970s DIY punk anarchism and open source/open hardware movements. Makerspaces are touted as the cornerstone of maker culture.[1] These creative spaces are collective offline community spaces where makers meet up to create, collaborate, learn and share. Following the ethics of maker culture, the primary intention behind creating these spaces is to simultaneously foster a sense of community for local makers, as well as develop a loose maker network with global reach. The number of makerspaces has grown exponentially around the world. According to user-generated data compiled by Nicole Lou and Katie Peek, as of 2016, there are approximately 1393 active or planned makerspaces worldwide, most of which are in Europe and North America.[2] Curious about Canada's numbers, in 2018 I created a simple list of Canadian makerspaces using data from the user-generated wiki hackerspaces.org and results from a basic internet query using "hackerspace," "makerspace," and "Canada." After removing duplicates, I found 103 active or planned Canadian makerspaces. However, while there are numerous resources available outlining how to correctly establish a makerspace—including "tool lists," floor plan layouts, and product recommendations[3]—there is very little guidance available that focuses on best practices for building a healthy maker *community*.[4] As such, when problems arise within makerspaces—such as needing more funds or managing poor behaviour—members often find themselves at a loss.

As such, investigating makerspaces uncovers a major flaw in maker culture ideology: democratising technology and technical knowledge/skills cannot (and will not) fix everything. In this chapter, I argue that this flaw can be further understood as stemming from two overlapping logics—neoliberal entrepreneurialism and "passionate work." And while I demonstrate that each of these logics contain their own sets of assumptions about people's choices and motivations, I conclude that they come together under the banner of maker culture to solidify "creative work" as a neoliberal enterprise. However, based on the conversations I held with Canadian feminist makers, I also maintain that these logics are not easily accepted. Instead, by including considerations of gender, empowerment and work, I contend that feminist makers are adapting these logics as a means for their own ends.

METHOD

To analyse the gendered impacts of entrepreneurialism and "passionate work" within makerspaces, this research focuses on feminist women/femme's[5] experiences of participating in Canadian makerspaces. Between 2017 and 2019 I visited seven Canadian makerspaces located in either Ottawa, Toronto or Montréal. In selecting spaces to visit, I intentionally selected sites that demonstrated the breadth of makerspace organization and design. For example, one space was a tiny collective with fifteen close-knit members, while another had "at least" sixty active members.[6] One makerspace was an explicitly feminist studio, another housed "maker businesses" and described itself as an "entrepreneurial hub," while a third had no permanent space at all and described themselves as "mobile."

From these site visits, I held eleven in-person conversations with self-identified feminist makers. One of my participants was not available for an in-person conversation but provided detailed typed answers to questions I provided her.[7] Two-thirds of my sample self-identified as women/female, and a quarter of my sample identified as non-binary/queer or only specified their pronouns. Three-quarters of the participants identified as white (50 percent)[8] or Francophone/Québécoise (25 percent), and all held a postsecondary degree (university-level) or diploma (college-level).[9] To protect their anonymity, all participants have been provided with a pseudonym.

The conversations I held with these feminist makers were audio recorded and lasted anywhere between forty-seven minutes to over two hours. Although a semi-structured question guide was created prior to the meetings, these conversations were free flowing and less transactional than typical interviews. Using the transcripts from these conversations, I applied a grounded theory approach to analyse common themes found across all the transcripts. Concerns of empowerment and care work/emotional labour, as well as maker identities, politics, boundaries and feminist praxis appeared often across all these conversations.[10]

ENTREPRENEURSHIP AS EMPOWERMENT

The concept of entrepreneurialism has expanded well beyond its original realm of business. Today, entrepreneurialism logics appear in countless contexts, from boardrooms to classrooms, and even the artist's studio. As Marnie Holborow states, "*Entrepreneur* is an ill-defined concept but an instantly recognizable one. . . . It incapsulates a social imaginary in which individuals are centre stage, wealth is understood in individual terms and wealth-seeking individuals are the role models. *Entrepreneurs* are the social icons of our neoliberal age."[11] Driving this neoliberal social imaginary is the fundamental belief that individuals are responsible for shaping their own destiny. As such, often entrepreneurialism appears as a necessary strategy for people to adopt in order to meet the demands of dynamic economic structures.[12] In this context, entrepreneurialism is typically packaged into a set of individual traits, such as creativity, self-reliance, self-empowerment, perseverance and a "can-do" positive attitude.[13] As such, entrepreneurialism is not just relegated to the realms of business and economics but is more broadly applied as a source for individual inspiration. Or, in the words of Holborow, the entrepreneur is "now seen as the benign improver of society and the kind of person we could all aspire to being."[14]

Philip A. Woods also points to the expanding reach of entrepreneurialism by examining its influence within public education. Using public policy from the UK, Canada, Australia, New Zealand and the US, Woods argues that education leaders are pressured to promote the notion of the "enterprising self" and to foster "an entrepreneurial, innovation-generating culture."[15] This push to entrepreneurialism appears both explicitly, such as through core curriculum development, and implicitly through the development of the "entrepreneurial mindset"[16] in all students. This entrepreneurial mindset is composed of generic skills and inclinations such as: "creativity, attacking problems with a solutions-oriented attitude, being prepared to take risks, working in teams . . . [and seizing] opportunities."[17] Furthermore, Woods states that the entrepreneurial mindset is not just about attaining certain skills or attributes, but also includes fostering a worldview that sees entrepreneurialism as the solution to fixing all the world's problems.

There is a strong overlap between these entrepreneurial logics and those that describe maker culture. Perhaps most obvious is that maker culture is often described as entrepreneurial, and its makers are seen as creating new small-scale products, businesses and practices that are revitalising global economies.[18] For example, Mark Hatch, a key figure in maker culture, stated that maker culture is imperative because it is "[l]owering the bar to entrepreneurialism [which] is the most liberating, democratizing, and just thing that can be done for those who are creative, bold, and daring enough to trust their talents and try."[19] Echoing Hatch's exultation of maker culture, other key figures like Chris Anderson, John Baichtal and Dale Dougherty claim that making things with your hands allows for individuals to develop essential skills relevant to successful entrepreneurship, such as innovative thinking, creativity and problem solving.

However, maker culture also fosters a strong maker identity that views DIY making as a way of life. As such, like entrepreneurialism, maker culture shapes individuals' identities and practices. For example, both entrepreneurialism and maker culture emphasise the need to foster a specific mindset. Woods described the "entrepreneurial mindset" with traits such as creativity, problem-solving, risk-taking and collaboration. Lisa Regalla lists similar traits when explaining the "maker mindset," including creativity, self-awareness, self-management, a collaborative disposition and resilience.[20] Sarah R. Davies states that these maker traits are also associated with the "ideal citizen: a politically thoughtful, proactive, and responsible person."[21] Therefore, it is perhaps of no surprise that "maker education" and makerspaces are at the forefront of public policy.[22]

Empowerment is another concept that is shared by entrepreneurialism and maker culture. Agency by Design, a maker education project from the Harvard Graduate School of Education, defines maker empowerment as "a sensitivity to the designed dimensions of objects and systems, along with the inclination and capacity to shape one's world through building, tinkering, re/designing, or hacking."[23] Within this framework, empowerment is understood as emerging from three key factors: personal motivation, knowledge/skill development and opportunities to innovate. Janette Hughes further explains that DIY making is always future-oriented and emphasises its emancipatory potential to create positive change.[24] Mark Hatch claims that DIY making is revolutionary because of its ability to "De Oppressor Liber"[25]—liberate the oppressed. Therefore, maker culture is described as liberating, empowering or emancipatory because it fosters a specific mindset and motivation that transforms everyday people from passive users and consumers of products into innovators and problem-solvers. Furthermore, because maker culture is premised on openness and collaboration ideals, this empowerment potential is also connected to democratisation and equality frameworks, which (theoretically) allow anyone to join in and make change. Similar logics of empowerment and change are also found within entrepreneurialism. Woods describes this narrative as the "entrepreneurial promise,"[26] and Holborow refers to it as "the entrepreneurial cure."[27] Both maintain that under this framework, increasing access to entrepreneurialism is viewed as the only viable pathway to creating new, effective and sustainable solutions to world problems. Therefore, in many ways maker culture is understood as imperative because it encapsulates and exaggerates these same promises and cures that are enmeshed in entrepreneurialism.

Empowerment is also a fundamental concept in feminism. In this context, empowerment is about redistributing power so that people who are left outside of decision-making processes and institutions are brought into the fold.[28] Throughout my conversations with feminist makers, the logics of empowerment often appeared as a justification for joining or establishing their makerspace. For instance, Jehanne, an organizer of a feminist makerspace in Montréal, told me that her group is a "bilingual feminist media arts centre that [is] an alternative to traditional institutions and that encourage[s] more women to take part in emerging forms of creative expression."[29] She continued to explain:

> In a context where only a few women used new technologies, [my space's] founders wanted to establish a support system for feminist engagement in the burgeoning world of 'cyberspace' and in the emerging field of media arts. [Our space] encouraged women to become 'creators' rather than 'spectators' by supporting active participation in the production of art and knowledge.[30]

In the realm of technology, the logics of empowerment are usually deployed as a mechanism to recruit marginalized people—like women, people of colour, First Nations, trans, and queer folks—into science, technology, engineering and mathematics (STEM) classrooms and industries. But, as Luce pointed out in our conversation, these learning environments are not really "emancipatory" because they are premised on false neoliberal promises of successful employment, rather than being sites for radical activism or social justice. Luce's scepticism here is similar to Holborow's critique of "the entrepreneurial cure," which forwards economic solutionism as the only viable pathway for social justice. To disrupt this entrepreneurial approach to empowerment, Luce explained to me that her workshops are about disrupting a "mental paradigm"[31] that constantly tells people that "women and technology just don't go together. That we're scared of technology. That we're unengaged. And it's *not* true. We engage constantly, but differently!"[32] So, for Luce, feminist workshops—especially those focused around technology—must start "from an emancipatory point of view"[33] in order to "change the narrative about what hacking is, or what engaging with technology is."[34] During our conversation, Luce proudly stated: "*every time, every single person* in the workshop is able to make the encryption work. *Every single time.* And, there's this like, emancipatory moment when it works and you see the joy in people's faces. Like, after 3 or 4 hours, and then suddenly it works and you feel *so proud* of yourself."[35]

Therefore, many of the feminist makers I met with echoed some of the log-ics of neoliberalism and entrepreneurialism that underlie the ethos of maker culture—such as democratisation and empowerment. Furthermore, for some of my participants, empowering women/femme folks through STEM skill development and knowledge-building was demonstrative of successful social change. For example, Samira, who works for a feminist makerspace, told me:

> Yeah, there is this ideology of 'change', like as a concept. But the way you make that happen is by planting seeds in people and for them to develop their own skills and take the initiative. Because [our space] can only do so much. Like, you know, it's like a space of five people so there's limitations. So, it's about empowering people and, yeah, have them do whatever they want to do.[36]

Yet, remembering Luce's point, empowerment within the logics of neo-liberalism and entrepreneurialism is short-sighted solutionism. While this empowerment logic may increase *some* women's presence in these systems, it is unlikely that their mere presence will foster more radical social change. Therefore, a conundrum emerges for feminist makers: while their politics seek to defunct oppressive power structures and institutions, economic reali-ties require them to remain beholden to those same structures.

This tension also appeared in Woods's work on entrepreneurialism in education. In his chapter Woods demonstrates that the overreach of entrepre-neurialism can be resisted through "adaptive strategies."[37] He explains that these adaptive strategies "acknowledge the co-existence of instrumental and values-based logics, and the tensions between them, and create possibilities for deeper educational values to be achieved by working sometimes with, sometimes against, the instrumental logic."[38] One of Woods's four adaptive strategies is amplification, where the generic traits and purposes of entrepre-neurialism are imbued with "deeper sensibilities,"[39] in order to displace its economic and technical solutionism. In other words, while these educators are still required to foster an "entrepreneurial mindset" in their students, they are also incorporating critical-thinking exercises. Similarly, most of the feminist makers I met with told me that they incorporate more holistic ap-proaches in their workshops that require participants to think more critically about technology. For example, Luce told me that while her workshops are focused on learning encryption, she also includes debates about the material-ity of digital technology, incorporating information about resource extraction, exploitative labour practices, and the Anthropocene.[40] Gabriela also told me that she loved attending feminist workshops because they prioritise critical reflection while learning, saying: "[a]nd, it's nice. It kinda keeps you sharp and makes you more focused on what *really* matters."[41]

However, whereas empowerment within entrepreneurialism and maker culture discourses tends to only focus on the self, feminist makers told me that empowerment requires a supportive community. For example, in my conversation with Gabriela she emphasised the importance of safe environments in fostering feminist empowerment: "I think a beautiful part of feminism and the people who are trying to create these spaces is that they are *trying* to make these moments happen where we can *breathe*, and feel at *ease*, and like, feel *heard* and feel *welcomed*."[42] Jo also talked about the role of comfort in fostering feminist empowerment:

> I think it's really valuable to, you know, see people like you, to be able to ask people like you questions, in order to be comfortable in showing up in all spaces. . . . Because, even if it's like, totally in my head to feel this way, I just feel like if I have a stupid question I feel like [some dudes] are, like, rolling their eyes at me and my question. And, maybe it's entirely internalized, but I just feel more comfortable asking femme people questions.[43]

Samira also echoed both Gabriela and Jo's experience, saying: "[a]nd, I know that, like myself, I would feel more comfortable doing a tech heavy workshop in a space like [this feminist makerspace] rather than other sites. . . . I know that coming here and the type of people that are going to be here that we'll have some understanding. . . . Whereas if I go to a 'bro-heavy' workshop I will not feel comfortable asking questions."[44] This emphasis on needing to establish comfort within their makerspace suggests that the democratising rhetoric—expressed as "openness," "freedom" and "equality"—that is engrained in maker culture and makerspaces is somehow missing the mark for feminist makers. And this connects to public statements made by other feminist makers who have reported that makerspaces tend to be uninviting and at times even hostile towards women, queer folks and people of colour.[45] Underlying these accounts is the assertion that makerspaces tend to be dominated by white men who espouse a particular "dudecore"[46] culture. According to Jo, many of these problems stem from ignoring the power of privilege:

> One thing that I think I've seen a lot and struggled with a lot in maker culture is that it is *really* white and it's *really* male. And people don't necessarily see that as a problem because, well, anyone is welcome. But I think seeing people like you around has a lot to do with whether or not you want to stick around. . . . And, I think there's this on-going assumption in maker culture that everyone's welcome so why aren't you showing up?[47]

Davies argues that one of the biggest ironies of maker culture is that despite its noble goals of empowering the oppressed, those who engage in makerspaces tend to be white, educated, affluent men who are already well-established in STEM industries.[48]

While each makerspace community has its own individual flair, I contend that if we conceptualise makerspaces as a loose and informal network, we can see that makerspaces are the physical manifestations of maker culture's entrepreneurial logics. As such, traits such as democratisation, self-empowerment, resilience and innovation formulate the community standard within makerspaces. These logics are often espoused through informal community expectations, such as having "open-door policies" where anyone can join a makerspace and strong sharing, collaboration and innovation ethics. However, this informal makerspace network highlights another logic that is widespread in creative industries—the notion of "passionate work." In the next section, I examine how the logic of passionate work circulates within craft work and makerspace discourses and argue that this focus on passion obscures the difficult realities of working in makerspaces.

MAKING MAKERSPACES WORK

In her book *Be Creative*, Angela McRobbie argues that the creative industries are touted as sites to engage in "passionate work"[49]—precarious and uncertain working environments where the primary reward is not traditional economic security and compensation, but rather the "personal reward of 'being creative.'"[50] Tim Christiaens argues that while creative industries are becoming increasingly more precarious, impoverished and exploitative, the fact that people choose to work in these industries contradicts the entrepreneurial motivators inherent to the neoliberal subject.[51] Christiaens explains that since working in the creative industries alone is unlikely to bring *most* people financial success, creative industry workers must employ a different cost/benefit system than the typical neoliberal entrepreneur. He maintains that fundamental to this revised cost/benefit system is the added value of joy, arguing that "the joys of creative work exceed the costs of permanent insecurity."[52] A similar logic underlies maker culture and makerspaces. Within maker culture discourses, makers are often described as passionate people who are "doing what they love." It is quite typical for this logic of passion to appear within the context of work. For example, Mitch Altman, the co-founder of the famous hackerspace Noisebridge, which was one of the first hackerspaces to open in the US, wrote that creating Noisebridge "was a lot of work, but since I loved it, it was way worth it."[53] Sarah R. Davies maintains that while maker culture touts noble ideals of revolution and emancipation, making things with your hands is also pleasurable. She writes that there is "something joyful" about overcoming the struggles associated with DIY making—whether that be working with challenging materials, having your solder not melt properly or stretching out that familiar stiffness in your hands from crocheting.[54]

However, rather than viewing passionate work as more freeing or less disciplinary to entrepreneurialism, neoliberal logics still govern creative workers' self-conduct.[55] McRobbie argues that in order for creative work to maintain its value as passionate work, creative industry leaders and individual creatives themselves self-monitor and self-regulate how they are viewed as workers, hiding or downplaying any aspects of passionate work that echo the nine to five daily grind of office or routine work.[56] Using Altman's quote as an example, we can see this tendency is also repeated by makers. While making is understood as "a lot of work," the actual details of the work required to make something (including a community) are often side-stepped by passionate work logics. But passionate work is not just about creating cultural objects, but also includes performing administrative duties, project management, human resources, event planning and so on.

In two chapters of her book,[57] Sarah R. Davies emphasises that while makers are passionate about making, creating makerspaces takes work, saying: "[t]hey don't just happen, but are initiated and managed, often in rather similar ways."[58] The bulk of this work involves maintaining these spaces, including chores like scheduling regular cleaning, collecting membership fees and fundraising.[59] However, at the same time makerspaces are often governed through non-hierarchical collective sensibilities, where all members are expected to take ownership of the space. As such, it is typical for makerspaces to have very few formal rules or clear divisions of responsibilities.[60] And while this type of organisation liberates members to do what they want when they want to, when difficult decisions or boring maintenance and administrative work needs to be done it is often difficult find members who will step up and help.[61] As one of Davies's research participants aptly points out: "[w]hen it's everyone's responsibility, sometimes it becomes no one's responsibility."[62] As such, Davies found that within makerspaces there is a general expectation that "someone" will take care of the space, resulting in the same few people constantly picking up the extra work required to keep a makerspace functional.[63]

Interestingly, Davies states that within makerspaces, there is an expectation that things will be "taken care of."[64] Arguably, many of the tasks that Davies lists, like taking out the garbage, cleaning the space and fundraising are tasks that also fall under the umbrella of "care work." As explained by Cecilia Benoit and Helga Kristín Hallgrímsdóttir, activities that commonly fall under the category of care work "are in some way or other connected with the social reproduction of human beings on a daily and generational basis."[65] However, they also maintain that care work has always been gendered and that these duties are more often carried out by women and girls in the private sphere (e.g., at home).[66] Furthermore, due to gender inequality and sexist oppression, Benoit and Hallgrímsdóttir maintain that "over time, caring activities became to be seen less and less as economic and more and more as if they were not work at all."[67] Additionally, while care work does encompass various physical tasks, such as cooking, cleaning and disciplining, care work also requires emotional labour. Referring to Arlie Hochschild's work on paid emotional labour,[68] Benoit and Hallgrímsdóttir explain that emotional labour requires care workers to "manage their own and others' emotions . . . to exaggerate positive feelings towards clients, while suppressing negative ones."[69]

While care work is more traditionally relegated to domesticity—such as childrearing—care work is also found within the public sphere. Benoit and Hallgrímsdóttir list health care, teaching, food and retail industries and social work as examples of care work as a career.[70] Although David Hesmondhalgh and Sarah Baker do not use the concept of care work, they echo Benoit and Hallgrímsdóttir and argue that creative work is also segregated by gender. For example, Hesmondhalgh and Baker report that men often work as "the creatives"—writers, composers, playwrights, directors—or work in technical or craft jobs, such as camera operators, editors, technicians or road crews.[71] On the other hand, jobs that are more commonly held by women—administrators, managers, planners—are not often considered "creative" but rather supportive roles. As explained by Hesmondhalgh and Baker: "the core of these jobs is to organize and handle the creative outputs of others."[72] In viewing care work as connected to the social reproduction of human beings, it is clear that these "supportive roles" commonly held by women in the creative industries are also care work.

Care work can also be found within Canadian makerspaces. In my conversations with feminist makers, care work and emotional labour were terms that appeared often. However, where care work was viewed as a positive necessity to prevent burnout, emotional labour was a term used to describe the exhaustiveness of managing a makerspace, such as when dealing with in-fighting or poor behaviour. For example, Jo told me about a time in her old makerspace where the emotional toll of being a board member resulted in her resignation: "I stepped away from being on the board after there was a huge fight where the whole board yelled at each other and cried. It was really bad. . . . Yeah, there were a lot of weird emotions going on, strong personalities clashing, definitely a gender dynamic at play. It was all very bizarre and intense."[73] When I asked Jo to elaborate on what she meant by the "gender dynamic" being at play during these heated arguments, she explained that the board was comprised of three men and three femmes/women and at times there were clear sides taken on issues based on gender. She maintains that the emotional toll of dealing with these dynamics resulted in her stepping off the board and starting her own smaller makerspace.

Becky also mentioned that managing a large makerspace requires significant emotional labour: "it is an exhausting amount of emotional labour to, like, uphold a sort of steady inflow of people coming to be a part of something."[74] Becky later explained that for her, this emotional labour element is not unique to makerspaces themselves, but rather is something that happens once a group exceeds a certain number of people. She told me that as these groups grow, the ability to vet new members to ensure they align with the ethos of a community grows exceedingly difficult. The result is a clashing of personalities or politics that can make the surrounding makerspace environment tense and unpleasant to work in. Molly told me about a time where she actually had to evict a member from her makerspace, saying: "that was our *toughest* moment. . . . [He just had] a total complete disregard and largely because of that old-fashioned maker mentality of like, 'I do what I want when I want.'"[75] Molly told me of another instance where a disgruntled ex-organiser of the makerspace posted a public podcast that was a misogynist rant. What is interesting about both Becky and Molly's experiences is that this emotional labour stems from problems that arise from generic maker culture ideals that emphasise open doors and personal freedoms. Although honourable on paper, in practice the lack of clarity that draws the line in terms of acceptable behaviours means that some makerspaces are at risk of becoming welcoming "hang-outs" for sexists, racists and the like.

Another instance where emotional labour was mentioned was in describing the effort it took to create an *inviting* makerspace environment:

Jo: And like, you know, it is a lot of *work* to host people and to be welcoming. I can see why people don't necessarily do it. . . . [A friend of mine] is pretty dedicated to finding people . . . following up with them, contacting them, reaching out, asking them to come back. Like there is a lot of actual work that goes into that. And, a lot of friendships and relationships that exist very much due to their work of reaching out again and again.[76]

Luce: You know, for instance I entered the space . . . and no one welcomed me, and I was like deet-de-dee-dee [drumming fingers on table]. . . . [A]nd then there were a few guys that kind of pointed to the woman educator and me and were like "Go and talk to her." And so, that was a bit *awkward* because I didn't necessarily *want* to be "greeted" or "welcomed" by a woman just because I was one too. I was fine with being greeted by a man in that space.[77]

As pointed out by Jo, creating an inviting makerspace takes more than simply opening the door—it requires active engagement, follow-up and relationship building. However, many of my participants told me that this "welcoming work" was usually done by women/femme folk. Like Luce, feminist makers acknowledge that there is almost an expectation that women/femme folks will only want to socialise with other women/femme folks. As such, it is perhaps of no surprise that almost all my participants recounted a story of being recruited into their makerspace by a fellow woman/femme maker.

Whereas in-fighting, managing poor behaviour and welcome work highlight the emotional labour required to run a makerspace, feminist makers also pointed to care work as a strategy to prevent burnout. For example, Cam claims her makerspace has an unofficial '80/20 rule': "80 percent of the time in this space is *your* time. You work and you do whatever want. But, since this is a community, 20 percent of your time has to be given back in some way."[78] She goes on to explain that by creating this balance, *all* makers share in the responsibility of fostering the community, while also creating a clear division in makerspace responsibilities. Samira and Yvette told me that their makerspace had a rough period where staff members were burning out and leaving the organisation. To resolve this issue, Samira explained that the staff in her makerspace all employ informal care work strategies: "[e]veryone is kind of aware of checking in [and] being like: 'Okay, you have worked a lot today, you should finish up.'. . . Like, it's okay to not be 100 percent productive. And when I talk to other friends working in the cultural sector it's *definitely not* the same experience."[79] Yvette claims that to her, this attention to care work is integral to the feminist approach of her makerspace, saying that it makes the space accessible for staff and members who have families or other responsibilities.[80] Therefore, within this context care work is seen as a tool to foster a supportive feminist community. In acknowledging the role of both emotional labour and care work within Canadian makerspaces, feminist makers highlight the complex ways in which DIY making is both pleasurable—such as in its feminist community-building potential—and laborious. In recognising that making and makerspaces bring about both personal fulfilment and struggle, my aim here is to highlight the ways that creating a functional and healthy makerspace takes time, effort, planning and support. To become a sustainable movement, all makerspaces must implement care work strategies. Failure to do so not only lead to inequitable work structures, but an impossible standard that many cannot (and should not) meet.

CONCLUSION

Although the logics of entrepreneurialism and "passionate work" were analysed as separate sections of this chapter, maker culture brings them together in such a way that they mutually constitute each other. In many ways maker culture makers embody both the archetypical neoliberal entrepreneur and passionate creative worker, which I call "the passionate entrepreneur." These makers are simultaneously described as innovative, self-empowered, risk-taking "go getters" who are passionate about making and motivated by "doing what they love." The duality of these makers is perhaps most evident by the way they are heroised in maker culture. For example, throughout Mark Hatch's book he provides numerous examples of daring and passionate maker entrepreneurs who successfully turned making from a hobby to a multimillion dollar companies.[81] John Baichtal wrote a whole book called *Maker Pro*, which celebrated makers who quit their full-time jobs to pursue making as a profession. And while these stories are about real people, the way they are told involves constructing a careful linear progression story that resoundingly mimics Woods's "entrepreneurial promise" or Holborow's "entrepreneurial cure." Yet a prelude about the importance of finding one's passion always begins these success narratives.

Although maker culture focuses heavily on success, the stories I was told by Canadian feminist makers troubled this public image, focusing on its lack of diversity, its dismissal of privilege and its failure to create equitable work environments. And although this research focused on feminist women/femmes's experiences, additional studies exploring the experiences of other people who have been marginalised in maker culture, such as BIPOC[82] makers, gay/lesbian/queer makers, trans makers and poor makers, would allow for further consideration of the various intersecting issues creating barriers of entry into makerspaces. Although makerspace doors are open, until these barriers are addressed, only the privileged will be able to enter.

NOTES

1. Mark Hatch, *The Maker Movement Manifesto: Rules for Innovation in the New World of Crafters, Hackers, and Tinkerers* (New York: McGraw-Hill Education, 2014).

2. Nicole Lou and Katie Peek, "By The Numbers: The Rise of the Makerspace," *Popular Science*, February 23, 2016, https://www.popsci.com/rise-makerspace-by-numbers/.

3. An example of which being Hatch, *The Maker Movement Manifesto.*

4. One notable exception being Sarah Fox, Rachel Rose Ulgado, and Daniela Rosner, *Feminist Hackerspaces: Hacking Culture, Not Devices* (University of Washington: Human Centered Design and Engineering Department, 2015).

5. Individuals who participated in this research identified themselves using their own gender terms, including woman, female, she/her, and non-binary, but all were feminine presenting folks. Therefore, I use woman/femme to represent both cisgender participants and those who were femme presenting.

6. Membership numbers were approximated by my participants.

7. Furthermore, I did not collect this participant's demographic information. Also, some participants left this portion blank. As such, the demographic numbers to not add up to 100 percent.

8. This racial categorisation also includes one participant who identified as Jewish.

9. Three of my participants did not provide educational information on follow-up studies, so they were excluded from this statistic.

10. For further discussion on these other themes, see my forthcoming dissertation: *Re-Tooling the Sisterhood* (Doctoral Dissertation), Carleton University, Ottawa, Ontario, Canada.

11. Marnie Holborow, *Language and Neoliberalism* (New York: Routledge, 2015), 72; emphasis in original.

12. Philip A. Woods, "Sense of Purpose: Reconfiguring Entrepreneurialism in Public Education," in *Understanding the Principalship: An International Guide to Principal Preparation*, eds. Charles L. Slater and Sarah W. Nelson (West Yorkshire: Emerald Publishing, 2013).

13. Holborow, *Language and Neoliberalism*, 77.

14. Holborow, *Language and Neoliberalism*, 74.

15. Woods, "Sense of Purpose," 225.

16. Woods, "Sense of Purpose," 227.

17. Woods, "Sense of Purpose," 227.

18. Chris Anderson, *Makers: The New Industrial Revolution* (New York: Random House, 2012); Hatch, *The Maker Movement Manifesto*; John Baichtal, ed. *Maker Pro: Essays on Making a Living as a Maker* (Sebastopol: Maker Media, 2014); Dale Dougherty, *Free to Make: How the Maker Movement Is Changing Our Schools, Our Jobs, and Our Minds* (Berkeley, CA: North Atlantic Books, 2016).

19. Hatch, *The Maker Movement Manifesto*, 110.

20. Lisa Regalla, "Chapter 17: Developing a Maker Mindset," in *Makeology, Volume 1: Makerspaces as Learning Environments*, eds. Kylie Peppler, Erica Rosenfeld Halverson, and Yasmin B. Kafai (New York: Routledge, 2016).

21. Sarah R. Davies, *Hackerspaces: Making the Maker Movement* (Cambridge: Polity Press, 2017), 23.

22. Davies, *Hackerspaces*, 23.

23. Agency by Design, "Maker-Centered Learning and the Development of Self: Preliminary Findings of the Agency by Design Project," January 2015, www.agen cybydesign.org, 5.

24. Janette Hughes, "Meaningful Making: Establishing a Makerspace in Your School or Classroom," *What Works? Research into Practice*, April 2017, Research Monograph #68, http://www.edu.gov.on.ca/eng/literacynumeracy/inspire/research/ meaningful_making_en.pdf.

25. Hatch, *The Maker Movement Manifesto*, 9.

26. Woods, "Sense of Purpose," 225.

27. Holborow, *Language and Neoliberalism*, 74.

28. Aminur Rahman, "Women's Empowerment: Concept and Beyond," *Global Journal of Human Social Science, Sociology and Culture* 13, no. 6 (2013).

29. "Jehanne," written response collected by Jessi Ring, October 25, 2017, Montréal, Québec, Canada.

30. "Jehanne," written response.

31. "Luce," interviewed by Jessi Ring, October 10, 2017, audio, 80:10, Montréal, Québec, Canada

32. "Luce," interview.

33. "Luce," interview.

34. "Luce," interview.

35. "Luce," interview.

36. "Samira," interviewed by Jessi Ring, October 25, 2017, audio, 47:43, Montréal, Québec, Canada.

37. Woods, "Sense of Purpose," 234.

38. Woods, "Sense of Purpose," 234–35.

39. Woods, "Sense of Purpose," 235.

40. "Luce," interview.

41. "Gabriela," interviewed by Jessi Ring, October 25, 2017, audio, 84:36, Montréal, Québec, Canada.

42. "Gabriela," interview.

43. "Jo," interviewed by Jessi Ring, July 26, 2017, audio, 62:56, Toronto, Ontario, Canada.

44. "Samira," interview.

45. Sophie Toupin, "Feminist Hackerspaces as Safer Spaces?," *Feminist Journal of Art and Digital Culture* 27, 2013, http://dpi.studioxx.org/en/feminist -hackerspaces-safer-spaces#sthash.v6nd8Lz6.dpuf; Sophie Toupin, "Feminist Hackerspaces: The Synthesis of Feminist and Hacker Cultures," *Journal of Peer Production*, October 2014, http://peerproduction.net/issues/issue-5-shared-machine-shops /peer-reviewed-articles/feminist-hackerspaces-the-synthesis-of-feminist-and-hacker -cultures/; Liz Henry, "The Rise of Feminist Hackerspaces and How to Make Your Own," *Model View Culture*, February 3, 2014, https://modelviewculture.com/pieces /the-rise-of-feminist-hackerspaces-and-how-to-make-your-own; Rebecca Greenfield, "Why Silicon Valley Needs the Coder Grrrls of Double Union, the Feminist Hacker Space," *Fast Company*, July 14, 2014, http://www.fastcompany.com/3031944/most -creative-people/why-silicon-valley-needs-the-coder-grrrls-of-double-union-the -feminist.

46. Toupin, "Feminist Hackerspaces as Safer Spaces?"

47. "Jo," interview.

48. Davies, *Hackerspaces*, 106–7.

49. Angela McRobbie, *Be Creative: Making a Living in the New Culture Industries*. (Cambridge: Polity Press, 2016), 36.

50. McRobbie, *Be Creative*, 36.

51. Tim Christiaens, "The Entrepreneur of the Self Beyond Foucault's Neoliberal *homo oeconomicus*," *European Journal of Social Theory* (2019): 2.

52. Christiaens, "The Entrepreneur of the Self," 4.

53. Mitch Altman, "Making a Living Doing What You Love," in *Maker Pro: Essays on Making a Living as a Maker*, ed. John Baichtal (Sebastopol: Maker Media, 2014), chap. 11.

54. Davies, *Hackerspaces*, 25.

55. Christiaens, "The Entrepreneur of the Self," 14.

56. McRobbie, *Be Creative*, 38.

57. Chapters 4 and 6.
58. Davies, *Hackerspaces*, 44.
59. Davies, *Hackerspaces*, 48.
60. Davies, *Hackerspaces*, 55.
61. Davies, *Hackerspaces*, 86.
62. Davies, *Hackerspaces*, 88.
63. Davies, *Hackerspaces*, 88.
64. Davies, *Hackerspaces*, 88.
65. Cecilia Benoit and Helga Kristín Hallgrímsdóttir, *Valuing Care Work: Comparative Perspectives* (Toronto: University of Toronto Press, 2011), 3.
66. Benoit and Hallgrímsdóttir, *Valuing Care Work*, 3.
67. Benoit and Hallgrímsdóttir, *Valuing Care Work*, 3.
68. Arlie R. Hochschild, *The Managed Heart: Commercialization of Human Feelings* (Berkeley: University of California Press, 1983).
69. Benoit and Hallgrímsdóttir, *Valuing Care Work*, 4.
70. Benoit and Hallgrímsdóttir, *Valuing Care Work*, 4.
71. David Hesmondhalgh and Sarah Baker, "Sex, Gender and Work Segregation in the Cultural Industries," in *Gender and Creative Labour*, eds. Bridget Conor, Rosalind Gill and Stephanie Taylor (Chichester: Wiley Blackwell/The Sociological Review, 2015), 27–28.
72. Hesmondhalgh and Baker, "Sex, Gender and Work Segregation," 28.
73. "Jo," interview.
74. "Becky," interview.
75. "Molly," interviewed by Jessi Ring, October 26, 2017, audio, 82:41, Ottawa, Ontario, Canada.
76. "Jo," interview.
77. "Luce," interview.
78. "Cam," interview.
79. "Samira," interview.
80. "Yvette," interviewed by Jessi Ring, October 25, 2017, audio, 47:43, Montréal, Québec, Canada.
81. Hatch, *The Maker Movement Manifesto*.
82. Black, Indigenous and People of Colour.

BIBLIOGRAPHY

Agency by Design. "Maker-Centered Learning and the Development of Self: Preliminary Findings of the Agency By Design Project." January 2015. www.agencybydesign.org.
Altman, Mitch. "Making a Living Doing What You Love." In *Maker Pro: Essays on Making a Living as a Maker*, ed. John Baichtal. Sebastopol: Maker Media, 2014.
Anderson, Chris. *Makers: The New Industrial Revolution*. New York: Random House, 2012.

Baichtal, John, ed. *Maker Pro: Essays on Making a Living as a Maker.* Sebastopol: Maker Media, 2014.

"Becky." Interviewed by Jessi Ring, July 26, 2017, audio, 67:58, Toronto, Ontario, Canada.

Benoit, Cecilia and Helga Kristín Hallgrímsdóttir. *Valuing Care Work: Comparative Perspectives.* Toronto: University of Toronto Press, 2011.

"Cam." Interviewed by Jessi Ring, October 2, 2017, audio, 91:07, Ottawa, Ontario, Canada.

Christiaens, Tim. "The Entrepreneur of the Self Beyond Foucault's Neoliberal *homo oeconomicus.*" *European Journal of Social Theory* (2019): 1–19.

Davies, Sarah R. *Hackerspaces: Making the Maker Movement.* Cambridge: Polity Press, 2017.

Dougherty, Dale. *Free to Make: How the Maker Movement Is Changing Our Schools, Our Jobs, and Our Minds.* Berkeley, CA: North Atlantic Books, 2016.

Fox, Sarah, Rachel Rose Ulgado, and Daniela Rosner. *Feminist Hackerspaces: Hacking Culture, Not Devices.* University of Washington: Human Centered Design and Engineering Department, 2015.

"Gabriela." Interviewed by Jessi Ring, October 25, 2017, audio, 84:36, Montréal, Québec, Canada.

Greenfield, Rebecca. "Why Silicon Valley Needs the Coder Grrrls of Double Union, the Feminist Hacker Space." *Fast Company,* July 14, 2014. http://www.fast company.com/3031944/most-creative-people/why-silicon-valley-needs-the-coder -grrrls-of-double-union-the-feminist-.

Hatch, Mark. *The Maker Movement Manifesto: Rules for Innovation in the New World of Crafters, Hackers, and Tinkerers.* New York: McGraw-Hill Education, 2014.

Henry, Liz. "The Rise of Feminist Hackerspaces and How to Make Your Own." *Model View Culture,* February 3, 2014. https://modelviewculture.com/pieces/the -rise-of-feminist-hackerspaces-and-how-to-make-your-own.

Hesmondhalgh, David, and Sarah Baker. "Sex, Gender and Work Segregation in the Cultural Industries." In *Gender and Creative Labour,* edited by Bridget Conor, Rosalind Gill and Stephanie Taylor. Chichester: Wiley Blackwell/The Sociological Review, 2015.

Hochschild, Arlie R. *The Managed Heart: Commercialization of Human Feelings.* Berkeley: University of California Press, 1983.

Holborow, Marnie. *Language and Neoliberalism.* New York: Routledge, 2015.

Hughes, Janette. "Meaningful Making: Establishing a Makerspace in Your School or Classroom." *What Works? Research into Practice,* April 2017. Research Monograph #68, http://www.edu.gov.on.ca/eng/literacynumeracy/inspire/research/ meaningful_making_en.pdf.

"Jehanne." Written response collected by Jessi Ring, October 25, 2017, Montréal, Québec, Canada.

"Jo." Interviewed by Jessi Ring, July 26, 2017, audio, 62:56, Toronto, Ontario, Canada.

Lou, Nicole, and Katie Peek. "By The Numbers: The Rise of the Makerspace." *Popular Science*, February 23, 2016. https://www.popsci.com/rise-makerspace-by-numbers/.

"Luce." Interviewed by Jessi Ring, October 10, 2017, audio, 80:10, Montréal, Québec, Canada.

Martinez, Sylvia. "The Maker Movement: A Learning Revolution." *ISTE Blog*, February 11, 2019, https://www.iste.org/explore/In-the-classroom/The-maker-movement%3A-A-learning-revolution.

McRobbie, Angela. *Be Creative: Making a Living in the New Culture Industries.* Cambridge: Polity Press, 2016.

"Molly." Interviewed by Jessi Ring, October 26, 2017, audio, 82:41, Ottawa, Ontario, Canada.

Rahman, Aminur. "Women's Empowerment: Concept and Beyond." *Global Journal of Human Social Science, Sociology and Culture* 13, no. 6 (2013): 9–13.

Regalla, Lisa. "Chapter 17: Developing a Maker Mindset." In *Makeology, Volume 1: Makerspaces as Learning Environments*, edited by Kylie Peppler, Erica Rosenfeld Halverson, and Yasmin B. Kafai. New York: Routledge, 2016.

"Samira." Interviewed by Jessi Ring, October 25, 2017, audio, 47:43, Montréal, Québec, Canada.

Toupin, Sophie. "Feminist Hackerspaces as Safer Spaces?" *Feminist Journal of Art and Digital Culture* 27, 2013. http://dpi.studioxx.org/en/feminist-hackerspaces-safer-spaces#sthash.v6nd8Lz6.dpuf.

———. "Feminist Hackerspaces: The Synthesis of Feminist and Hacker Cultures." *Journal of Peer Production*, October 2014. http://peerproduction.net/issues/issue-5-shared-machine-shops/peer-reviewed-articles/feminist-hackerspaces-the-synthesis-of-feminist-and-hacker-cultures/.

Woods, Philip A. "Sense of Purpose: Reconfiguring Entrepreneurialism in Public Education." In *Understanding the Principalship: An International Guide to Principal Preparation*, edited by Charles L. Slater and Sarah W. Nelson, West Yorkshire: Emerald Publishing, 2013.

"Yvette." Interviewed by Jessi Ring, October 25, 2017, audio, 47:43, Montréal, Québec, Canada.

Index

About the Contributors

Julia Bennett is the Crafts Council's Head of Research and Policy. She writes about craft, develops policy and advocacy strategies and manages research, strengthening evidence to improve the conditions for craft. Julia has worked independently with small arts organisations, as well as for several national advocacy bodies.

Dr. Katherine Champion is lecturer in Media and Communication within the Division of Communications, Media and Culture at the University of Stirling. Her research interests include the role of place to the creative and cultural industries, creative economy policy and creative labour, and she has published widely in these areas.

Dr. Mary Kay Culpepper is postdoctoral fellow at the Creativity Everything lab in the Faculty of Communication and Design at Ryerson University in Toronto. Before undertaking academic studies in creativity, she was for several years editor-in-chief of *Cooking Light*, the top-selling US food magazine during her tenure.

Dr. Lauren England is Baxter Fellow in Creative Economies at the University of Dundee. Lauren has published research on the resilience of craft knowledge and skills in post-industrial regions, craft social enterprises and craft higher education. Her PhD was conducted in partnership with Crafts Council UK.

Professor David Gauntlett is Canada Research Chair in the Faculty of Communication and Design at Ryerson University, Toronto, where he founded the Creativity Everything lab. He has worked with organizations such as the

BBC, the British Library, S4C and Tate, and for more than a decade has collaborated with LEGO on projects incorporating creativity and play.

Dr. Hristina Mikić is Head of Research in the Institute for Creative Entrepreneurship and Innovation in Serbia. Her research interests include cultural and creative industries, female and ethnic creative entrepreneurship, interrelation of creative industries, cultural heritage, craft, tourism and public policies.

Dr. Annette Naudin is associate professor (Learning and Teaching) in the Birmingham Institute for Media and English, Birmingham City University, UK. Annette has had a leading role exploring enterprise education for the media and cultural entrepreneurship and for EU-funded projects at Birmingham City University.

Dr. Karen Patel is research fellow in the Birmingham Centre for Media and Cultural Research at Birmingham City University, UK. Her research interests centre on the politics of expertise in cultural work, inequalities in craft and cultural work and creative workers' use of social media.

Professor Andrea Peach is professor of Craft History and Theory at Konstfack University of Art, Craft and Design in Stockholm, Sweden. Her research interests focus mainly on craft as commodity and cultural industry, as well as the construction of national and cultural identity through the craft object.

Jess Ring is PhD candidate (ABD) in Communication and Media Studies at Carleton University, Ottawa, Canada. Her dissertation explores Canadian feminist engagements in maker culture and makerspaces. In addition to work/labour concerns, other key topics include understanding hegemonic and marginal boundary-work practices and aligning do-it-yourself practices with feminist praxis.

Dr. Vishalakshi Roy is fascinated by the tension between creative and entrepreneurial behaviour of individuals that manifests itself in developing and managing creative and cultural enterprises. She is assistant professor at the Centre for Cultural and Media Policy Studies, University of Warwick, and director of strategic consultancy at Earthen Lamp.

Dr. Guillaume Sirois is assistant professor in the Department of Sociology at the Université de Montréal. With a background in art history and communication studies, he conducts research on contemporary art and other visual practices, including design, architecture and fashion. His work has appeared in various journals and edited books.

www.ingramcontent.com/pod-product-compliance
Lightning Source LLC
Chambersburg PA
CBHW021814270326
41932CB00007B/187